P9-AEY-991

SUPERVISING POLICE PERSONNEL

The Fifteen Responsibilities

Sixth Edition

Paul M. Whisenand, Ph.D.

President, PMW Associates
Professor Emeritus, Department of Criminal Justice,
California State University, Long Beach

PEARSON

Prentice Hall

Upper Saddle River, New Jersey 07458

Library of Congress Cataloging-in-Publication Data

Whisenand, Paul M.
  Supervising police personnel: the fifteen responsibilities/Paul M. Whisenand—6th ed.
    p. cm.
  Includes index
  ISBN 0-13-172237-9
  1. Police—Supervision of.   2. Police—Supervision of—United States.   I. Title.

HV7936.S8W48 2006
363.20683—dc22

2005053524

Executive Editor: Frank Mortimer, Jr.
Assistant Editor: Mayda Bosco
Marketing Manager: Adam Kloza
Managing Editor: Mary Carnis
Production Liaison: Brian Hyland
Production Management: Janet Bolton
Director of Production and Manufacturing: Bruce Johnson
Manufacturing Manager: Ilene Sanford
Manufacturing Buyer: Cathleen Petersen
Design Director: Cheryl Asherman
Cover Image: Photo Disc
Cover Designer: Amy Rosen
Composition: Integra Software Services
Printing and Binding: R.R. Donnelley, Harrisonburg
Copy Editor: Judith Mara Riotto
Proofreader: Maine Proofreading Services

10 9 8 7 6 5 4 3 2 1
ISBN 0-13-172237-9

For my best friend, prized and deeply loved brother, John C. Whisenand, and in memory of an admired, longtime, trusted friend and coworker, Robert R. Beans, Sergeant (Retired), Los Angeles Police Department. These two guys have profoundly influenced and enriched my life and made it fun.

Contents

Preface

A couple of years ago, the acclaimed secular ethicist Michael Josephson wrote:

> I just attended a moving graduation ceremony marking the transition of 40 men and women from police academy cadets to sworn officers in the Long Beach Police Department (California).
>
> At the beginning, the officers were fully uniformed, but they had no badges, and without the badges their uniforms were undistinguished. Yet once their shields were affixed, the uniforms and the people in them were transformed.
>
> So I began to think about the badge not only as an official symbol of authority and responsibility, but also as a symbol of honor—a symbol we should look up to and they must live up to. Although the badges were highly polished, experience teaches us that it will take vigilance and integrity to keep them untarnished.
>
> Looking at the very serious faces of Class #77, one could see both determination and pride as they officially accepted the huge responsibilities of a hugely important job captured in the Code of Ethics printed on their program.
>
> "My fundamental duty," the Code begins, "is to serve mankind, to safeguard lives and property; to protect the innocent against deception, the weak against oppression or intimidation, and the peaceful against violence and disorder; and to respect the Constitutional Rights of all men to liberty, equality and justice." It concludes, "I recognize the badge of my office is a symbol of public faith, and I accept it as a public trust."
>
> Sure, most officers spend most of their time involved in important but unheroic activities like investigations, traffic regulation and crowd control, but they stand at the ready to put themselves in danger at a moment's notice and after the experience of September 11, I fear we don't appreciate them enough.

This book was written for those who are responsible for making this "code" a reality, as opposed to lofty, politically correct but shallow words.

The responsible person I'm referring to is the police supervisor. You will find that to fulfill this vital role, your *character* not merely counts—but counts big-time. You'll be asking yourself, "What do I, or should I, stand for as a supervisor—as a leader?" You'll also find that you are responsible for ensuring that you and those who work for you fulfill the fifteen responsibilities discussed in this book.

Being responsible (the "R" word) means exercising self-discipline and self-restraint. It means doing your very best and being self-reliant and accountable for the consequences of your decisions. The very nature of supervising resides in and depends on making decisions. If you're not willing to make, or comfortable with making, decisions about yourself and others, then it's best you not become a supervisor. The number one responsibility of a supervisor is making decisions!

Being a police supervisor is more than having more pay, more authority, more influence, more status, and the like. It is much more. It is a set of core responsibilities that you will soon encounter and consider in the chapters that follow.

Part 1 of this book, "Team Fundamentals," provides the infrastructure for contemporary police work: community-oriented policing. The chapters in this section deal with character and integrity of purpose—*values, ethics,* and *vision*—and with the allocation of the requisite time to communicate all three.

"Team Building," Part 2, starts with a supervisor's responsibility for serving as a *team leader.* This naturally encompasses *motivating, empowering,* and *training* one's staff while ensuring that everyone is mentally and physically *well.*

The final part, "Teamwork," covers *organizing for action, measuring performance, resolving conflicts,* and making certain that *community-oriented policing* works. I am convinced that it takes teamwork to make it work. Finally, the supervisor-as-leader is challenged to *anticipate* incoming demands or needs for change.

My warmest thanks to Frank Mortimer at Prentice Hall, who coached and inspired me during the writing of this edition, and also to Marilyn Whisenand, Pat David, and Rosie O'Shea, who expertly manicured and critically edited the manuscript. I would also like to thank Vincent Benincasa, Hesser College, Manchester, NH; Peter B. Thomas, ICM School of Business, Pittsburgh, PA; and Michael C. Walker, Passaic County Community College, Paterson, NJ for their review and comments of this edition.

Paul Whisenand, Ph.D.
San Clemente, California

About the Author

Paul M. Whisenand, Ph.D., is the founder and president of PMW Associates (www.pmwassociates.com), which for thirty-five years has been dedicated to police training, leadership consulting, and personnel selection for law enforcement agencies.

A professor emeritus at California State University at Long Beach, Dr. Whisenand gained his practical law enforcement experience as a police officer with the Los Angeles Police Department and as a reserve deputy sheriff with the Orange County Sheriff's Department.

Dr. Whisenand has lectured and trained in law enforcement agencies, police academies, and professional conferences worldwide and has authored or coauthored sixteen books, including the celebrated text *Managing Police Organizations* (Prentice Hall).

He received his doctorate in public administration from the University of Southern California. Now living in San Clemente, California, he enjoys international travel, running, surfing, and spending time with his wife, five children, and twelve grandchildren.

A Starting Point

The responsibility of a police supervisor is to lead other people in the performance of their jobs. Easily stated but not easily accomplished. Leading others—getting their followership—is a complex and challenging process. Why? You'll see.

Leading is an active verb. A true leader is a catalyst for action, and the proper measurement of leadership is change.

> The test of leadership is: What is different now because of you?

The police supervisor is the linchpin connecting the line employee with the management staff. The word *responsibility* best defines this role. A responsible supervisor must be an example of excellence and of ethics. He is a mentor and a motivator, responsible for conveying the values and vision of a department and of a community. A communicator and counselor, the responsible supervisor is an enthusiastic leader, one who combines the best attributes of command and control with an empowerment of those who work for and with him. There should be no doubt that to a police organization, or any other organization, the quality of the supervisory level is vital to the success of the entire team.

However, all supervisors are not leaders. The positions to which supervisors are promoted and appointed automatically enable them to use legitimate authority, the right to command. This power is granted by virtue of their position within a police organization. Leadership is an altogether different quality. It is dependent not on the position one holds within an organization or the number of stripes on a uniform or a badge that says "Sergeant." Rather, it has everything to do with the individual's skills, knowledge, competence, and character—and character is integrity.

> Supervision is the right to command. Leadership is the capacity to command.

If you want to be a police supervisor, you can become one. Work hard, study hard, maintain your professional and personal integrity, and look for opportunities to learn by observing other supervisors. Leadership skills, in particular, are best learned by the example of others whom you consider to be good leaders. Many prospective leaders/supervisors are identified, developed, and mentored by existing leaders.

1

CHARACTER AND COMPETENCE

Character and competence are the primal pillars of leadership and supervision. The deeper, the larger, the stronger these twin pillars, the greater the leader and the better the supervisor.

Successful leaders and supervisors motivate us. They ignite our passions and inspire the best in us. When we seek to explain why they are so effective, we frequently mention strategy, vision, or powerful ideas. The answer is actually much more fundamental. It is as much what they are doing as it is how they are doing it.

> Character is both what we stand for and how we stand for it. Competence is both what we perform and how we perform it.

Unfortunately, the "what we stand for" and the "what we perform" are often emphasized to the point where the "how" is ignored. You'll discover both the "what" and the "how" of your becoming a police supervisor and leader via our journey through this book. You'll learn how the supervisor uses authority to get results, how the leader uses teamwork to get quality results, and how the supervisor commands while the leader convinces.

A person of character seeks true happiness in living a life of purpose and meaning, placing a higher value on significance than success. In the workplace, character is devoted to acquiring and demonstrating professional values and a work ethic. Competence encompasses the requisite skills, knowledge, and abilities to perform the technical and technological aspects of the job of "overseeing" the work performance of line-level police employees. How supervisors accomplish this work is not the same as why it is necessary to do it. Whatever leaders set out to do—whether it is creating strategy or mobilizing teams into action—their success depends on how they do it.

Let's face it: It's not easy to become a person of character. First and foremost, you must have a purpose and a mission. Then add a good heart, the wisdom to know right from wrong, and the discipline to do the right thing even when it's costly, inconvenient, or unpopular. The number one value for a person of character is integrity. Without integrity, supervisors—no matter how astute, how powerful, how convincing—will be distrusted and avoided and will eventually fail.

> Even if they get everything else right, if leaders fail in the primal task of driving character in the right direction, nothing will work as well as it could or should.

Is one—character or competence—more preeminent than the other? I agree with Teddy Roosevelt, Warren Buffett, and Michael Josephson that it's character. President Roosevelt wrote, "To educate a person in the mind but not the morals is to educate a menace to society." Warren Buffett said, "When I select a manager, the first thing I look at is the person's character." And Michael Josephson has spent most of his life pointing out that "character counts."

Character and responsibility are linked. The more you get of one, the more you get of the other. Everything is your responsibility when you're the leader—but much more so when there's a problem than when there's a victory. You share the credit and take the blame.

THE "R" WORD

It is easy to dodge our responsibilities, but we cannot dodge the consequences of dodging our reponsibilities.

—Sir Joseph Stamp

There is a disturbing and unfortunate trend of people ducking responsibility while telling everyone else what to do. I'm not a part of this problem. It's all of those "other folks" who fail to stand and be accountable while simultaneously casting guilt on others. I'm kidding, of course. At times I am tempted to back off and seek protective cover and then point at the other guy as being responsible for the mess.

Have you noticed that those who shirk their responsibilities and refuse to be held accountable frequently attempt to lay blame for irresponsibility on someone or something else? This phenomenon is sucking us into behavioral and political absurdities, which erode our character. It can be observed in both private and government organizations. We see it happening in police agencies.

> Our nation's legal language on rights is highly developed, but the language of responsibility is meager. This situation has hamstrung self-reliance, inner autonomy, and risk taking. No society, organization, or police agency can operate if everyone has rights and no one has responsibilities.

The blame game is perpetuated by a low tolerance for mistakes. This is especially prevalent in police work. Many police managers are quick to boast, "In our agency, we want our employees to take risks!" After a while, some believe that taking a calculated risk for all the right reasons will be supported. Then some poor person takes a risk and fails, and all hell breaks loose. Ridicule, sanctions, ostracism, tainted career, and more come down on the risk taker. Is it any surprise that many police organizations have a culture of risk avoidance? "Risk taking—that's not my responsibility. Let some other fool try it."

An often-overlooked obligation of ethical supervision is to establish an atmosphere where police employees are truly expected and willing to accept responsibility for improving the quality of programs and services—even if it means challenging existing policies or management decisions.

BEING OUT IN FRONT

Think for a moment. What is the title of the boss of an orchestra? An orchestra manager, orchestra supervisor, or orchestra leader? "Leader" is the correct answer, but why is it correct? Because he or she is in front of (not on the side of or behind) the players. The orchestra members can actually see the leader in action. They're able to follow by visual example rather than by memo, e-mail, or prior training. Being in front of the team is a clear-cut demonstration of responsibility.

> The leader is responsible for leading by example. Being in front and being seen are the only way to do this.

Getting in front, and staying there, has always been difficult, but it is becoming even harder for police supervisors. It's a matter of time. Supervisors are frustrated by not having enough of it or more control of it. They realize that to lead, they have to be seen (and not just for fifteen minutes at roll call). They have to be with and in front of their team. But tons of paperwork (e.g., personnel investigations), expanding technology (e.g., e-mail messages), and advancing administrative trivia (e.g., new rules, new regulations, new details) checkmate their quest to lead. They find themselves exclusively forced into the role of supervisor—giving commands, spot-checking to see if they're followed, processing paper, and receiving and sending messages.

Effective supervisors, the ones who want to lead, are making being in front their number one priority, and they are managing their time accordingly. Tough to do, at times risky, but worth it! The team gets the leader it deserves, the police agency gets the quality of work it deserves, and the community is all the better for it. But there is no one best way to do this.

DIVERSITY

We have a lot in common as members of the human race. We have wants and needs, hopes and aspirations, likes and dislikes, successes and failures, and more. But we're also very different. My hopes may not be yours, we may not share the same problems, and our needs may be different. What motivates you may not motivate me. These differences are referred to as "human diversity."

Dealing with human diversity is a significant challenge to a supervisor's success. Diversity guarantees that there is no one best way to handle every individual and every situation. Some employees respond best to a polite push, while others require a strong shove. Some want to be empowered; others want to be instructed. Some want to be listened to; others want to be mute. Some want a lot of challenge; others want routine.

> The leader is responsible for leading a team of diverse police employees. Diversity is an asset and should be celebrated.

There is no Supervisor's Golden Rule or set of proven methods for supervising. That is probably bad news for you. Then again, if supervising the work of others were a simple process, everyone would want the job.

There is good news, however. There are fifteen job-related responsibilities that, if fulfilled, are likely to produce success. All fifteen deal with the basic challenge of a police supervisor: building and maintaining teamwork.

THERE IS NO *I* IN *TEAMWORK*

We are born into this world totally dependent on others for meeting our survival and social needs. From our earliest beginnings, we strive to kick aside our dependence and replace it with independence. We gradually gain dominance over our survival and social needs. We decide when and where we want to eat, when and where we want to sleep, what to buy and when to save, whom to pal around with and whom to eschew.

Independence is great. We prize it. But it causes problems when manifested in an organization, especially a police organization. Imagine for a moment a police agency consisting of sworn and civilian employees who think and, worse yet, act independently. I wouldn't feel secure in that type of working atmosphere. Would you?

Police leaders are trained to think independently, but the work for which they are accountable takes place in teams.

Most police personnel want to be recognized and accepted as individuals. Being yourself in a police agency is important, but being yourself in a team effort to provide much valued police services is more important.

> It is a police leader who is able to ensure one's individuality (independence) *and* develop one's teamwork (interdependence).

WHAT IT'S ALL ABOUT

This is a book about leading and supervising people within a police agency. It points out the differences between leadership and supervision. It is about being accountable for yourself and being responsible for the work of others. It is about character and competence. It acknowledges that the origin of our purpose and meaning lies in our character. It argues that to be a leader, one must have integrity, express it by example, and in doing so, build teams out of diverse employees. Leading and supervising people is not only a responsibility, but also an honor and a privilege.

> *The first step is to understand the rationale for the various privileges you may have acquired as a leader. Every privilege should assist in meeting organizational objectives—and it is the objective you should be committed to, not the privilege.*
>
> —Gandhi

The fifteen responsibilities that follow are leadership characteristics and competencies. The first is foundational and singular: the supervisor as a decision maker. The remaining fourteen responsibilities are divided into team fundamentals, team building, and teamwork. If you learn these responsibilities, observe them in others, and watch for opportunities to practice them yourself, you are on the right path to becoming a supervisor and leader.

> Every supervisor can become a leader! That is the goal of the chapters that follow.

RESPONSIBILITY | I

Decisions

The police supervisor is responsible for making decisions about the leadership of police personnel in the successful performance of their duties.

Responsibility I is to have the mental toughness to make decisions about problems and pressures without panic or surrender; to overcome negative emotions; and to rebound from disappointment, cascading change, rejection, or unhappiness without being overwhelmed or behaving in a dysfunctional manner.

Nothing is more difficult, and therefore more precious, than to be able to decide.

—Napoleon Bonaparte

Decision making is the major element of supervision. Indecision and inaction can cause as much harm, or more, as a poor decision. The most important measure of leadership is this: Will the person be decisive? A frequent complaint in police work concerns the frustration of waiting for a supervisor to make a decision. The only thing worse than a bad decision is the refusal to make one. Some would argue that not making a decision is, in fact, a decision. I agree with this premise. However, when in a position of leadership, a supervisor is responsible for taking action and being decisive.

The primary responsibility of a supervisor is making decisions.

FREEDOM TO CHOOSE

The history of free men is never written by chance, but by choice—their choice.

—Dwight D. Eisenhower

Many of us actually want to believe that we have to do something. "I've got to work." "I've got to diet." "I've got to read this book." This is a false paradigm, and I reject it. It is not only wrong but harmful to us. We are free to choose. Next to life itself, one's freedom of choice is our greatest gift.

The essence of being human is being able to direct our own lives. The essence of leadership is being able to influence the choices of others. Supervisors make choices based on their personal values and ethics. (Responsibilities 2 and 3, which follow, demonstrate this.)

The power of choice means that we are not merely a product of our genetic heredity or social acculturation. We are not an outcome of how others have treated us or defined us. While our past, our genes, and our experiences all influence our choices, they do not determine them.

> Through our choices, we exercise self-determination.

As a leader, the freedom and power to choose is affirming because it excites a sense of potential and achievement. It is also frightening because it requires an acknowledgment of responsibility. We become accountable. Perhaps we've taken shelter in explaining that our supervisory problems are due to past or present circumstances beyond our control. Suddenly, we have no excuses. Leaders know that they have both the freedom and the responsibility to make choices. This freedom and responsibility compose our "space."

> Between stimulus and response there is a space. In that space lies our freedom and power to choose our response. In that choice lie our professional growth and our individual happiness.

Supervisory Space

The receipt of a stimulus indicates the need for a response—a decision. Between a stimulus (a personnel problem, for example) and your decision as a leader is a space in which you must make a choice. How you use that space to evaluate the problem and make a decision determines the correctness of the decision. Marginal supervisors see their "choosing space" as limited. Superior supervisors see their choosing space as flexible and expandable. This attitude is one of the qualities that separates the marginal supervisor from the superior supervisor.

> If there is even a fraction of a second between stimulus and response, that space represents our power to choose the correct response to the situation.

Think long and hard about the gift of choice. Reflect on what kind of space you have developed and nurtured as a police supervisor. Is it small and rigid? Or is it large and expandable? Your space determines the quantity and quality of your supervisory decisions.

Much scientific evidence discounts this notion of space or free will. We are told that our decisions and actions are highly susceptible to outside influences. It is reported that our unconscious mind can override our conscious decision making with snap judgments. While I appreciate that there is empirical data to this effect and agree with it to some extent, the freedom we are given in our "space" to exercise our power to choose is a far more powerful tool. Our use of this space can be protected and enlarged until the very nature of our responses will begin to shape the stimuli, literally creating the world we wish to live in both at work and at home.

Choosing Our Emotions: Emotional Intelligence

A police leader's emotions are contagious! If the leader makes decisions with energy and positive enthusiasm, the organization thrives. If the leader spreads negativity and dissonance, the organization flounders. For too long, police supervisors have seen emotions at work as noise, distracting from rational decision making.

> No matter what you set out to do—whether it's deciding strategy or mobilizing work teams to action—your success depends on *how* you do it. Even if you get everything else just right but fail to drive your emotions in the right direction, nothing will work as well as it could or should.

Emotions have never been completely welcome in our work lives. Most of us have traditionally been conditioned to leave emotions "at home," believing that to be effective, we need to base all our team strategies and decisions only on cold, logical "intelligence." And yet, as we all know, emotions are a fundamental part of who we are and how we work with others. Emotions can't be left out of the picture. In fact, to do so often guarantees that suppressed emotions will flare, causing increased conflict and affecting climate and morale.

Let's view emotions in a different way altogether, as another kind of intelligence beyond reason and logic—an intelligence that, if we could learn to access it, could become nothing short of a touchstone to greater collaboration, a higher level of influence with others, more productivity, and increased effectiveness. The fact is, such an intelligence exists. It's called "emotional intelligence." Unheard of only a decade or so ago, emotional intelligence (EI) has become something remarkable in the past few years—the centerpiece of mainstream team training.

> As the pace of workplace change increases, and our workplaces make ever-greater demands on our cognitive, emotional, and physical resources, emotional intelligence will continue to emerge—not as something "nice" to have, but as an increasingly important set of "must-have" skills.

The good news is that unlike your IQ, EI is not fixed at birth. Emotional intelligence can be developed and raised to higher levels. Although we all must experience our emotions, we can choose to express or repress them. The goal is to express them intelligently for our advantage and for the benefit of others.

What Is EI?

EI is knowing how we and others feel, why we feel that way, and what can be done about it. EI is our ability to understand and use the power of our emotions wisely. It's learning the difference between "I think" and "I feel" and hearing the difference when others say it. Just as importantly, EI is learning to manage our emotions rather than letting them control us. The thing to remember is that emotions are not good or bad. Emotions are information. By listening to them, we can use our IQ more effectively because we reason better when our feelings are taken into account. They give us valuable information that we can't get anywhere else.

Police employees most often screw up because they can't (1) handle change, (2) build a team, or (3) cope with interpersonal relations. Those who really screw up believe and act as if feelings do not count. They believe and act on only what can be counted or quantified. Their thinking centers on "What're the numbers?" "What's your point?" and "Only facts matter."

> Eighty-five percent of a leader's abilities involve EI.

Leaders who cultivate a greater range and depth of emotional intelligence find that not only is their professional life more successful, but also that their heightened self-awareness, empathetic understanding, and self-mastery lead to more harmonious relationships in their personal life.

Understanding the powerful role played by emotions in decision making is what sets the best leaders apart from supervisors—not merely in such tangibles as fewer personnel complaints and greater retention of talent, but also in more difficult to quantify, but equally important, factors like higher morale, motivation, and commitment. In any group, the supervisor has the power to make choices that sway the emotions of the entire group.

Climate

Leaders drive the service climate and thus the predisposition of the police agency to satisfy citizens. Research findings confirm that, overall, climate—how people feel about working for an organization—accounts for 20 to 30 percent of performance. If climate drives performance, what drives climate? Between 50 and 70 percent of how employees perceive their organization can be linked to—guess who?—the leader.

> How well leaders manage their emotions and recognize their effect on the emotions of others is not just a private matter but a determining factor in how well a police organization will perform.

The glue that holds employees together within a team and commits them to an organization is the range of emotions they feel. Real leadership occurs when decisions of the heart and head—feeling and thought—meet. Without a healthy dose of heart, an aspiring "leader" may be only a supervisor who cannot lead.

Emotional intelligence consists of four capabilities. The capabilities can be learned, which means that you can choose to drive your emotions positively. This is a foundational step toward achieving congruity and leading others. The four capabilities are

- Self-awareness
- Self-management
- Social awareness
- Relationship management

Capability 1: Self-Awareness.

For a supervisor, emotional self-awareness means reading one's own emotions and recognizing their impact—using "gut sense" to guide decisions. It requires an accurate self-assessment—that is, knowing one's strengths and limits. It requires self-confidence, a sound sense of one's self-worth and capabilities. Self-awareness means having a deep understanding of one's

- Emotions
- Limitations
- Motives
- Strengths
- Values
- Goals
- Intuitions
- Dreams

Capability 2: Self-Management.

From self-awareness—understanding one's emotions and being clear about one's purposes—flows self-management. Self-management requires the police leader to make choices about the following:

- *Emotional self-control:* Keeping disruptive emotions and impulses under control.
- *Transparency:* Displaying honesty and integrity; trustworthiness.
- *Adaptability:* Flexibility in adapting to changing situations or overcoming obstacles.
- *Achievement:* The drive to improve performance to meet inner standards of excellence.
- *Initiative:* Readiness to act and seize opportunities.
- *Optimism:* Seeing the upside in events.

The most important decision responsible leaders can make is to discipline their state of mind.

Capability 3: Social Awareness.   To be socially aware, a police leader must possess the following:

- *Empathy:* Sensing others' emotions, understanding their perspective, and taking an active interest in their concerns.
- *Organizational awareness:* Reading the currents, decision networks, and politics at the organizational level.
- *Service awareness:* Recognizing and meeting subordinates' and citizens' needs.

Social awareness and *empathy* are synonyms. They are decisions that attune our own biology to the dominant range of feelings of the other person so that our emotional states tend to converge. A second and equally important part of this capability is expressing one's emotions with conviction because those emotions are clearly authentic—that is, rooted in deeply held values.

Capability 4: Relationship Management.   The triad of self-awareness, self-management, and social awareness comes together in the final EI domain: relationship management. A police leader has six key tasks when managing relationships:

- Providing inspirational leadership
- Using influence
- Acting as a catalyst for change
- Managing conflict
- Building bonds
- Fostering teamwork and collaboration

The art of handling relationships well begins with decisions about authenticity and genuine feelings. Once you have identified your own values and vision, and tuned into the emotions of the group, then you can use your relationship management skills to interact with others in ways that create resonance.

It's not just a matter of friendliness. Rather, relationship management is a decision about friendliness with a purpose: moving people in the right direction, whether that's agreeing on a new computer system or being enthusiastic about a new team member.

PURPOSE-DRIVEN DECISIONS

Without a purpose, leading becomes motion without meaning, activity without vision, and results without significance. Leaders with high emotional awareness (emotional intelligence) know that without a purpose, their decisions are likely to be pointless.

Why must emotionally strong leaders have a clearly articulated purpose? There are five benefits of purpose-driven leadership. Together they promise increased emotional intelligence.

Knowing Your Purpose Gives More Meaning to Your Leadership

Without purpose, leadership lacks meaning. A purpose is as essential as air and water. Hope comes from having a purpose, and we need hope to cope. When leadership has meaning, you can bear tremendous burdens to achieve your purpose. Without meaning, these burdens can seem unbearable. Emotional intelligence seeks meaning and leads to meaningful decisions.

Knowing Your Purpose Makes Decision Making Easier

Your purpose as a supervisor defines what you will and will not do. It sets the standard you use to evaluate which tasks are essential and which are not. Without a clear purpose, there is no benchmark by which you can make decisions, allocate your time, and commit your resources. Leaders who do not know their purpose take on unnecessary projects that cause stress, fatigue, and hostility.

> Purpose-driven decisions are less ambivalent decisions that promote an organized work agenda. Keeping it simple is a key element of leadership and emotional awareness.

Knowing Your Purpose Focuses Your Leadership

For your leadership to have impact, you must focus it. With your purpose firmly in mind, you are able to concentrate your decisions and your energy on what is vital. Without a clear purpose, you tend to procrastinate and become easily distracted by minor issues, spinning at a frenetic pace but going nowhere.

Knowing Your Purpose Motivates You and Those You Lead

Purpose generates enthusiasm. Nothing captivates our emotions like a clear and valued purpose. Conversely, energy wanes when you lack purpose. "If I can't see it, why should I pursue it?" Meaningless work typically wears us down faster than hard work. The majority of police employees are ready to commit themselves—but only when they know why. As a police leader, if you project a clear picture of the purpose of your efforts, those you lead are likely to follow. Without an expressed purpose, the most you can expect is blind obedience with a ho-hum attitude. Explain the purpose of your mission, and motivation will follow.

Knowing Your Purpose Is Rewarding

Successful leaders and their followers share many attributes, one of which is a sense of fulfillment. If we don't know our purpose, how do we know if we have accomplished it? Where is the goal line? Did we achieve success or not? Emotionally mature leaders and followers want to experience the sensation of completion—goal fulfillment. Without an expressed and understood purpose, how can anyone feel rewarded? Without a purpose, there can be no reward. All emotionally aware employees want to be rewarded for a job well done and want to know what defines it. Purpose-driven decisions lead to clear purpose-driven expectations.

FIVE RULES FOR DECISION MAKING

Decision making is the major responsibility of the police supervisor. The other fourteen responsibilities discussed in this book depend on it. Simply put, supervisors are constantly required to make decisions—to assess two or more choices and to select the best approach. A leader's legacy is often determined by the long-term effect of his or her decisions.

> The most critical decisions made by supervisors are ethical decisions.

Consider these five general rules when making a decision.

Rule 1: Never Make a Decision That Should Be Delegated

Before making a decision, the supervisor must first ask, "Is this decision mine to make, or should one of my staff make it?"

> Unfortunately, some supervisors believe that since they have the authority to decide a certain issue, and the responsibility for the decision, they must personally make the decision.

Some supervisors fear that a subordinate may make a bad decision, so they make the decisions themselves that would be better left to others. They feel that because they are better trained, more experienced, more expert, and ultimately accountable, they must make all decisions. This type of thinking reveals that the supervisor is not ready to supervise and lead.

Why delegate? There are three compelling reasons to delegate decision making.

- *Empowerment.* When you empower others to do their job, you actually expand your own power base. Also, the decisions made by those you have empowered are apt to be more accurate and timely because the personnel closest to the situation are engaged in making the decisions. Through empowerment, you are building trust, morale, and expertise among your subordinates, resulting in a more coherent and stronger work team.

- *Time.* Making good decisions is difficult and time-consuming. No leader can make all of them. The sheer number of decisions confronting police supervisors forces them to delegate. The supervisor who will not delegate is destined to "crash and burn." As a supervisor, you must carefully reserve for yourself only those decisions that are clearly supervisory in nature and must cheerfully delegate the rest. In this manner, everyone benefits—the department, the supervisor, and the police officers.

- *Mentoring.* When you delegate, you help others mature professionally, and you enrich their job satisfaction. You can't expect your staff to grow in expertise and judgment unless you give them the opportunity to make real decisions that have real consequences for the department. Employees find it demeaning and demoralizing to be second-guessed and micromanaged by their supervisor. The result is turned-off and tuned-out employees who do not feel respected. True delegation—really letting go—is an inspiring, appreciated, and empowering experience for all involved.

> Delegation and leadership are inseparable.

Rule 2: Never Make a Decision Today That You Can Reasonably Delay

The operative word in this rule is *reasonably*. It doesn't mean that you should ignore critical incidents that demand an immediate decision. Nor does it mean that you should suspend thinking about them. However, most supervisory decisions (personnel issues, for example) do not require a quick judgment. It has been reported that President Harry Truman was constantly pressured for snap decisions. The first thing he would ask of his staff was, "How much time do I have?" In other words, is it essential that the decision be made now, in an hour, today, or next week? Truman recognized that all decisions are not equal in priority.

> The timing of a police supervisor's decision is as important as the decision itself.

This concept is not artful procrastination; rather, it is strategic timing that avoids the risk of rushing into a fast (and wrong) fix. The advantage of this rule is that it usually opens up many more choices for the leader. The downside is that by waiting too long, options may be foreclosed. Timing a decision is an art, not a science. Decisive timing is an act of courage because it involves risk taking. Surrendering a decision to fate amounts to cowardly procrastination.

Rule 3: Decide If the Decision Is Yours to Make

When required to make a decision immediately, ask yourself, "Do I have the authority and the responsibility to make this decision?" Perhaps the decision is beyond your purview. Some unfortunate supervisors get into trouble for overstepping the bounds of their authority. They make brilliant decisions on issues that lie outside of their jurisdiction and are then embarrassed and reproached.

If it is your decision to make, make it or delegate the making of it. If not, express an opinion if invited to do so, but beyond that—butt out!

Whenever possible, avoid engaging in a two-front battle when it comes to decision making—that is, arguing over who has the authority to make a particular decision as well as arguing over what the decision should be.

Rule 4: Take Extra Care with Important Decisions

Certain decisions are considered big-ticket items. These decisions involve the likelihood of extreme consequences for the decision maker as well as everyone else with a stake in the matter. In these cases, the leader must slow down, focus, and take extra care to think long-term.

A decision merits this special time and attention if the answer to any of the following questions is yes:

- Could the decision cause serious physical or emotional injury?
- Could the decision jeopardize important relationships?
- Could the decision undermine or damage reputations or credibility?
- Could the decision adversely affect the values and vision of the department?

Rule 5: Enforce the Rules

Leadership in any environment, from parenting to supervising a group of police officers, requires that the leader lay down the rules and evenhandedly enforce them. While it may seem counter to today's feel-good culture, fair but strong discipline administered by a leader with the proper respect for justice will give rise to a strong sense of security and teamwork among the staff.

I am not recommending that a supervisor punish all rule violators. Nor am I suggesting that a supervisor suspend compassion and forgiveness. I am simply pointing out that the failure of a leader to enforce the rules due to a desire to remain popular or to avoid negative emotions can quickly bring that leader to ruin.

DECISION MAKING

Once a police supervisor has chosen a particular decision to make, and knows the time frame within which he or she must make it, one question remains: How should he or she make the decision? With the input and advice of staff and peers, the boss, outside experts? Or, should the supervisor's decision be made based solely on his or her own judgment and experience? What about community members and other stakeholders outside of the organization? Should they be involved?

Process

Process counts! It is vital to carefully consider the needs and desires of those likely to be affected by the decision. Even more critical is having all those who will be affected by the decision participate in some way in the decision-making process. This does not mean that others make your decision. That remains your responsibility. However, allowing others to participate in the process gives them an opportunity to voice their ideas, concerns, opinions, and hopes. In this manner, they feel more a part of the process. Ultimately, even though others may not like the decision you make, they are more apt to understand it and support it if they were part of the process. (This subject is also covered in Responsibility 8, "Empowerment.")

> Abraham Lincoln once took a vote among his Cabinet on an issue that he favored. When he had counted the votes, Lincoln announced, "One aye and seven nays— the ayes have it!"

I've been appalled at how insensitive some police supervisors can be toward their own staff, their peers, and, incredibly enough, their own bosses. Time and again I've observed supervisors offend, humiliate, and anger their coworkers or miss a chance to build their leadership capacity. When this happens, the decision-making process is broken and must be repaired.

Probabilities

Every decision includes some element of risk or chance—probabilities. Decision making is a game of chance in which the leader is betting on success. Some supervisors become anxious about the sheer speculation inherent in a decision. All of us prefer to make a safe, 100% guaranteed accurate decision. However, only amateur decision makers would delude themselves by thinking that their decisions can be measured and calculated to ensure this level of certainty.

> Niccolò Machiavelli wrote that slightly more than half the outcome of any bold undertaking is due to luck.

Intuition

An important tool used in the making of a decision is personal judgment—intuition. Supervisors must select choices that are sometimes based as much on intuition (gut feelings) as on precise analysis and objective logic. The central part of supervisory decision making involves moving ahead with a choice based on informed intuition. Experienced supervisors know that in most decision-making situations, facts are incomplete and frequently inaccurate. They must rely instead on their own good sense and intuition, along with those of their advisers, to make the best choice.

Intuition frequently involves rapid cognition, or "thin slicing." This refers to the ability of our unconscious to find patterns in situations and behavior based on very narrow "slices" of experience. Thin slicing is part of what makes the unconscious, or intuition, so dazzling. But it's also what we find problematic about rapid cognition. How is it possible to collect the necessary information for a complex decision in such a short time? The answer is that when our unconscious engages in thin slicing, what we are making is an intuitive, automated, and accelerated decision.

Intuition is tricky and at times can be misleading. It emanates from the subconscious mind, which harbors unconscious attitudes that may be contrary to our stated conscious values. Nonetheless, supervisors continue to depend on intuitive decisions. We hope that these decisions are also based on facts and objective analysis.

Investment

Decisions made by a leader can only influence the future, not the past! What's done cannot be undone, and leaders must steel themselves to that fact and look forward. Even though there may be huge emotional or political pressures urging them to justify past decisions and commitments, they must have the courage to take a fresh look and disregard past mistakes. Poor purchasing or personnel decisions, for example, must not be allowed to define the future decisions or limit the future choices of the supervisor.

> The wrong decisions of the past, even those that involve reputation, time, and money, must be acknowledged as wrong to avoid repeating them and to be free to succeed in the future.

Conscience

As mentioned earlier, when making difficult decisions, leaders must listen carefully to those who will be affected. When making the really tough, gut-wrenching, soul-searching decisions, they must also carefully listen to their heart. The operative word here is *listen.* Unfortunately, when most of us consult our inner voice, we do all the talking. That's because some of us are afraid of what we might hear. However, if we are quiet and patient and listen carefully to our conscience, we will find that our "inner voice" can be a strong ally in making good decisions in difficult times.

> The hardest thing to do and the right thing to do are often the same thing!

SNAP DECISIONS

In his much celebrated book, *Blink,* Malcolm Gladwell argues that snap decisions (rapid cognition) are frequently as good as, or even better than, decisions made after lengthy deliberation. Deliberate decisions are useful in certain situations, but we actually use snap decisions more often.

> Truly successful decision making relies on a balance between deliberate and instinctive thinking.

Snap decisions are made when our brain reaches a conclusion before it informs our consciousness. The part of our brain that jumps to judgment is called the "adaptive unconsciousness," and the study of this kind of decision making is an important new field of psychology. The term *adaptive unconsciousness* does not refer to the unconscious described by Freud as a dark, murky place full of disturbing desires, fantasies, and memories, but rather a kind of giant computer that rapidly and quietly processes a lot of data that we need to function as human beings. It "thin slices" our experiences, searching for what is meaningful and discarding superfluous information that would impair our ability to solve problems or to know our own mind. At times, too much information can result in bad or poorly timed decisions.

Rapid cognition has incredible power for good as well as bad. Snap judgments are generated by our experiences and our environment. If we rely only on negative experiences, we will intuit wrong, stupid, or unethical decisions about events and people. Good news! We can alter the way we thin slice—by substituting new positive experiences for old negative information. This requires that we take active steps to manage and control what resides in our adaptive unconsciousness.

We need both analytic and intuitive decision making. Where we err is in using one or the other in inappropriate circumstances. For example, suppose you are in a situation involving a barricaded suspect with a hostage. Do you consult a strategic plan or the police chief for assistance in making your decision? Of course not! You experience rapid cognition—you thin slice your past experiences and information and quickly make a snap, and hopefully correct, decision.

> If you get caught up in the production of information in order to make a decision, you risk drowning in the data.

Deliberate thinking is a wonderful tool when we have the luxury of time, a computer, the Internet, and a clearly defined task. The results of that type of deliberative analysis can set the stage for accurate, rapid cognition and correct first impressions.

Our snap decisions come out of a locked room, and we cannot look inside that room. But with experience—in this case supervisory experience—we become expert at using our behaviors and our training to interpret and decode what lies behind our snap judgments and first impressions. Whenever we do something that we are good at—something we care about—that experience and passion fundamentally change the nature of our thin slicing. With self-discipline, experience, and care, we can be assured of making successful snap decisions as police supervisors.

THE CENTERPIECE OF LEADERSHIP

Decision making is the centerpiece of leadership. It integrates all of the responsibilities for which a supervisor is accountable. The leader's responsibility for making principled decisions is both the starting point and the focal point for the other fourteen supervisory responsibilities.

> *The great things a man does appear to be great only after they are done. When they're at hand, they are normal decisions and are done without knowledge of their greatness.*
>
> —General George S. Patton

KEY POINTS

- The primary responsibility of a supervisor is decision making.
- One of the greatest gifts to humankind is the freedom to choose.
- Between the stimulus for a decision and the decision is a space within which a choice exists.
- A leader's legacy is most often determined by the long-term effect of his or her decisions.
- We can choose our emotions.
- Our emotional intelligence (EI) consists of self-awareness, self-management, social awareness, and relationship management.
- Without a purpose in mind, leading lacks meaning, vision, and significance.
- Never make a decision that should be delegated.
- Never make a decision today that can be reasonably delayed.
- Decide first whether the decision is yours to make.
- Take extra care with major decisions.
- Enforce the rules (and follow them yourself).
- Making decisions involves process, probability, intuition, investment, and conscience.
- Our adaptive unconsciousness helps us make snap decisions.

EXTENDED LEARNING

1. Do you agree that decision making is the most important of all supervisory responsibilities? Explain.
2. What is meant by "supervisory space"? What can be done to increase or flex this space?
3. When should you delegate a decision to others? What are the benefits of doing so?
4. What is the difference between timing a decision and procrastinating about it?
5. What was the last major work-related decision that you made? How did you approach it? What did you do to make certain that the decision was a correct one?
6. Should the rules be enforced exactly the same for everyone? Should every violation be punished?
7. What is the difference between using your intuition and using your conscience to make a decision?

PART I

Team Fundamentals

RESPONSIBILITIES

RESPONSIBILITY 2

Values

> The police supervisor is responsible for developing consensus within the work team on its values and then ensuring that it behaves accordingly.

> Values provide the character, courage, and consciousness for determining where the work team is going and how it is going to get there.

*What lies behind us and what lies before us are tiny matters
compared to what lies within us.*

—Oliver Wendell Holmes

It's relatively easy for people to agree on the characteristics of an effective leader: He or she communicates well, has a clear and compelling vision, inspires trust, thinks strategically, and sets goals. But it is impossible to judge whether a leader is good or bad without considering his or her values. The "goodness" of a leader, as opposed to his or her effectiveness, depends on the degree to which the leader's decisions reflect his or her values.

*You can easily judge the character of a man by how he treats those who can
do nothing for him.*

—Goethe

Find a quiet place to read and think about the next few paragraphs. Make a conscious effort to project yourself into the following situation.

Picture yourself driving to a retirement dinner for a coworker who is also a close friend. You park your car and walk inside the restaurant. You locate the assigned ballroom and enter. As you wander in, you notice the banners and flags. You spot the smiling faces of your coworkers and their spouses. You sense gaiety and happiness in the room.

As you approach them, you look up at the head table and see your name card on it. You also see the name cards of your spouse and three children. Overhead on a banner, printed in large letters, is your name and "Congratulations for Twenty-Five Years of Service." Below that banner is another that reads, "A Happy Retirement to You." This is your retirement! And all of these people have come to honor you, to express feelings of appreciation for your work.

You're escorted to the head table, where your spouse and children join you. You're handed a program. There are five speakers. The first is your spouse. The second is one of your children. The third speaker is your closest friend. The fourth speaker is an employee. The final speaker is your boss. All of these people know you very well, but in different ways.

Now, think carefully. What would you expect each of these speakers to say about you and your life? What kind of spouse, parent, and friend would you like their words to reflect? What kind of supervisor? What kind of subordinate?

What values would you like them to have seen in you? What contributions and what achievements would you want them to remember? Look carefully at the people who have gathered to wish you well. What difference would you like to have made in their lives?

WHY VALUES?

> *The modern individual is assailed from every angle by divergent and contradictory value claims. It is no longer possible, as it was in the not-too-distant historical past, to settle comfortably into the value system of one's forebears or one's community and live out one's life without ever examining the nature and the assumptions of that system.*
>
> —Carl R. Rogers

Understanding human values—held individually and organizationally—serves four very critical purposes for police agencies, their employees, and especially police supervisors:

- Compass
- Communications
- Leadership
- Understanding

Compass

It is not enough to rely on supervisory authority to enforce moral or legal behavior. The compass of values has to be within a person and the department. Often one hears the contrary: that a police department should be an efficiency instrument, a bureaucratic machine that maximizes its output within rules set by the community; that departments that get distracted from this goal by community responsibilities become ineffective. My own belief is that just the opposite is true.

For one thing, no community can control a police institution as well as the institution itself can, and if a department places outcomes above core values, then that organization is vulnerable to violating community standards, no matter how stringently laws and codes are written. And those violations will demoralize the workforce, produce ill will in the community, and perhaps result in lawsuits that will have a long-term negative impact. Conversely, the police agency that orients itself toward serving its community will reap long-term rewards in the form of loyal citizens and positive community relations. The police supervisor must never lose sight of the purpose of the job, and the managers who run the agency should never compromise their values for the sake of expediency. Without purpose and values, both the police agency and the leaders who work for it are in danger of losing their direction, given the continually changing landscape they must negotiate.

Communications

The underpinning of effective communication within the workplace is the understanding of human values. I have to know myself first—my value system. Then, and only then, am I in a position to understand another's set of values. To understand and to be understood do not indicate agreement. We can understand someone else's values but not always concur with them. When we don't agree on our individually held values, at least—and most importantly—we understand why.

Once we understand one another's values, then we can really communicate. With this interaction arrives a basis for mutual trust. It is at this point the police supervisor has a perfect opportunity to gain the role of team leader.

Leadership

Because your staff is much more likely to do as you do than do as you say, it's important to think about the values you are conveying by your actions, especially when you think no one is looking. Your staff is keenly aware of how you cope with good news and bad news. They notice whether you are accountable or shift blame and make excuses, whether you make decisions or avoid making them. Everything you say and do sends a message. If you want to help your staff build the type of character you are proud of, always act as if they are watching you. And remember, they are!

Understanding

Human values are important to us because they are us. Simply stated, our past values have determined who we are and what we are pursuing in life, our present values are likewise shaping our life today, and our future primarily will be shaped according to the values that we possess at each coming point in time.

It is vital for the police supervisor to understand and appreciate human values because they serve as a destiny (an end or a goal) and a path (a means or a guide) to reach that destiny. In summary, then, each of us should understand our own values because they underpin our character, personality, and leadership style and performance. This chapter will assist you in clarifying your own value system so that you can eventually apply it in a way that will support, rather than detract from, your responsibility to be a "good" leader.

> All that we value becomes a part of us. And thus we are what we value, and we supervise others and ourselves according to our value systems.

Please reread and give a lot of thought to the above conviction. It is an assertion that you and I—in our daily lives—are value-driven. Further, it states that you and I consciously and unconsciously transmit our values to others. We do this as a parent, a friend, a brother or sister, and especially as a supervisor. What follows will substantiate the central place of values in our lives.

WHAT ARE VALUES?

The term *value* has a variety of uses. For example, one may value one's family, value one's leisure time, value one's reputation, value one's position as a police supervisor, or value jogging. Each of these five values is different in several respects. One is a goal-oriented value: one's reputation. Another value, jogging, is a means to another desired state: one's physical and mental health. Yet another value, one's position as a police supervisor, is temporal; that is, it is a temporary position. We have a tendency to forget that what some may value highly, others may not. (For example, you may place a high value on the promise of a promotion, while someone else, satisfied with his or her present job, may not.) In fact, people are alike or different due to the commonality or the incongruence of their professional, personal, and societal values.

> A value is an enduring belief that a specific goal and means of attaining that goal are very important.

Consider the definition above. Note that for a person to hold a value, it must be (1) an "enduring belief," not random or fleeting; (2) a "goal," or desired end state; and (3) a "means," or acted on. For example, do you value your job? If so, you would value it consistently (enduring) and not in a casual or haphazard way. Further, you would strive to do good work (goal). Finally, each day you would perform your tasks to the best of your ability (means).

Because each of us possesses more than a single value, it is essential that we think in terms of a *value system*, which is an enduring organization of beliefs concerning preferable modes of conduct of end states of existence in a "hierarchical ranking" of relative importance. Hierarchical ranking means that some values supersede others. For example, which is the more important value for you: family or job; spouse or friend; health or compassion?

There is not always a one-to-one connection between a means and a goal. One usually has approximately forty end-state values (goals) and seventy-plus modes-of-conduct values (means). For example, assume that one of your values is success. How many ways or means are there for you to achieve success?

VALUES-DRIVEN POLICE SUPERVISION

Values-driven supervision is based on the idea that the police supervisor has a responsibility to the staff and the community that makes such supervision necessary. Values-driven supervision seeks to maximize its impact by integrating prized values into as many day-to-day activities as possible. To do that, values must lead and be included in a department's mission statement, strategy, and operating plan.

By incorporating an agency's concern for the community into its strategic and operating plans, values-driven police supervisors can make everyday decisions that actualize the department's goals at the same time. Instead of choosing areas of activity based solely on the short term, the values-driven supervisor recognizes that by addressing community problems along with efficiency concerns, a department can earn a respected place in the community and a special place in the public's heart, too.

SOURCES OF OUR VALUES

The process of value creation may actually begin long before birth. Many experts suggest that some behavior patterns in our primitive ancestors might have been encoded in DNA, which in turn now guides our behavior patterns. Whatever the degree of genetic input, for our purposes it is enough to assume that genetics shape broad patterns of human behavior. Our concern is with behavior patterns that are learned from the moment of birth forward.

Our value-programming periods can be categorized as imprinting, modeling, and socialization.

Imprinting

During the first six to seven years of age, in addition to physical behavior development, a tremendous amount of mental and values development takes place. The popular analogy "As the twig is bent, so the tree shall grow" is perhaps so obviously simple that we frequently fail to apply it to children. The early years of childhood may be compared to the foundation and frame of a building. The foundation determines the quality and strength of the structure that goes on top. The completed structure depends on its base, even if additions are built. The foundation of a person is the child, as values are programmed in his or her early years. The key figures here are Mom and Dad and a few others. Even though real "formal" learning does not start in the preschool period, there are many important stages that determine how, how much, how well, and what the child will learn as she or he develops. The question that we must answer and comprehend is, By whom and how were children value-imprinted in their formative years?

Modeling

From about seven to fourteen years of age, the process of value identification—initially with the mother, then with the father and important "others" around the child—expands. The child shifts into intense modeling, relating to family, friends, and external "heroes" in the surrounding world. People the child would "like to be like" are carefully observed. As a result, our initial close models give way to more expanded contacts. Soon group membership begins to exert its influence. We identify not only with playgroups or gangs as a whole, but also with certain "important" individuals within them. New values and behavior patterns are combined with the ones we absorbed from our family. Once we are in school, the process of identifying extends to the heroes of history and fictional stories. Furthermore, our increasing involvement with media during this period will introduce characters from movies and television as additional heroes. We use these models to construct our internal value ideal, the person we would like to become.

The hero models in our lives are very critical people. They are the people we try to behave like, the people that we want to be like when we become adults. The modeling period is a critical period during which we absorb values from a diverse selection of models. Do you remember your own modeling activities? When you were ten years old, whom did you want to grow up to be like? Whom did you secretly look up to, try to imitate in the way you talked, the way you walked, the way you dressed, the way you wanted to be? What about your coworkers? Who were their value models when they were ten or eleven?

Socialization

From around thirteen to twenty years of age, our social life becomes structured primarily in terms of our friends. This intense socialization with peers results in people of common values grouping together for reinforcement. During the period of adolescence, we define and integrate the values, beliefs, and standards of our particular culture into our own personalities. It is during this period that we achieve full physical maturity and a dominant value system. This system determines our basic personality. During this period of socialization, we engage in experimentation, verification, and validation of our basic life plan. From about age twenty on, the value system programmed during childhood and adolescence locks in, and we repeatedly test it against the reality of the world.

People of like interests, behavior, and developing value systems associate intensely with one another and reinforce one another's development. Think back to your teen years. Who were your friends? What was your best friend like? What did you talk about? What were your views on sex? Were you a leader or a follower, a joiner or a loner? Did your friends have a nickname for you? What did you do together? How long have your friendships lasted? These questions should be asked about your coworkers.

CHANGING OUR VALUES

Our values, while enduring, can be changed. This transition can occur in one of two ways. The first is a traumatic or significant emotional event (SEE). The second revolves around major dissatisfaction.

Significant Emotional Events

The common denominator of SEEs is a challenge or disruption to our present behavior patterns and values. In job situations or family relationships, such challenges might be artificially created (e.g., being fired or promoted), but more likely, SEEs occur in an unplanned, undirected manner (e.g., being seriously injured or winning an athletic contest). We must be careful to distinguish between SEEs, which actually change our gut-level value system, and external events, which simply modify our behavior. For example, a departmental order imposed on us may demand that we pay attention to the needs of the employees. Our behavior may change accordingly, but our values remain the same. The closer SEEs occur to our early programming periods, the more likely it is that significant change will occur. The less dramatic the event is, the longer we hold our programmed values, and any change in values will occur more slowly, if at all. It is possible to "teach an old dog new tricks," but the learning is much more difficult than for the younger animal. SEEs are neither good nor bad. Their frequency, their type, and how we cope with them determine if they are positive or negative for us.

Profound Dissatisfaction

To be successful in this most difficult of transitions—psychological growth—requires a special combination of inner and, to a degree, outer circumstances.

A person must possess three attributes if he or she is to make a substantial psychological step forward:

- The individual must be deeply dissatisfied. Otherwise, why change?
- The individual must possess much psychological and physical energy. Few things are harder to break than old bonds, old views, old prejudices, old convictions, old loves.
- The individual must have or acquire the psychological insight to know what will slake the driving dissatisfaction. Without this, the effort to change will be directionless, ceaseless, and pointless.

Only when all three of these factors are present simultaneously will a person have the motivation to change, the drive to act on the motivation, and the foresight to know where to go and when he or she has arrived. See Figure 2–1, which graphically describes how values are formed and how they are changed.

WHAT DO VALUES DO TO AND FOR US?

In a general sense, values tell us much about who we are as individuals, as citizens, as consumers, as a nation, and as police supervisors. As you examine the remainder of this section, keep in mind the following:

- The total number of values that each person possesses is relatively small (thirty to sixty).
- Everyone everywhere has the same values, but to different degrees.
- Values are organized into value systems.
- The origin of human values can be traced to one's formative years, culture, institutions, society, and—to some limited extent, perhaps—to one's unique genetic makeup.

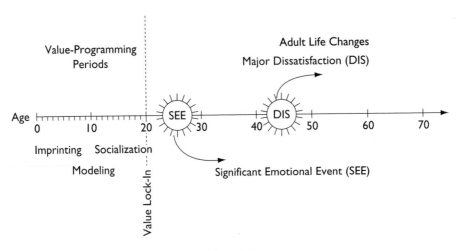

FIGURE 2–1   Value-programming periods and change.

- The consequences of one's values will be manifested in virtually all that one feels, thinks, and does.
- A large part of a police supervisor's effectiveness, or lack of it, is dependent on his or her value system.
- The success of a police leader is a direct result of knowing his or her values and the values of coworkers (bosses, other supervisors, and line employees).

Our values determine our attitudes and behavior, creating

- Paradigms
- Generation gaps
- Individual differences
- Standards
- Conflict resolvers
- Emotional triggers
- Thought provokers
- Motivators
- Attitudes
- Personality

Paradigms

Our values set up paradigms. They influence what we can or can't see, acting as physiological filters. What may be perfectly visible to me, you may have difficulty in seeing. What may be perfectly believable to you, I may find impossible to accept. We may see the same individual, and I will perceive him to be honest and you will see him as dishonest.

Consider the value of integrity. My paradigm of integrity is that if I commit an illegal or immoral act and no one knows about it, I'm still guilty. Is this a universal paradigm of integrity? No. Some people have a far different paradigm, believing that unless they are caught in an illegal or immoral act, there is no problem. What is your paradigm of justice, freedom, God, and so on? We may share the same values, but they are significantly shaped and altered in accordance with our personal paradigms.

Generation Gaps

In recent decades, the acceleration in the rate of change of technology, law, social behavior, education, and economic systems has created vastly diverse programming experiences between generations. The differences in these experiences have created a spectrum of widely varying value systems within our society. The "generation gap" is a popular phrase—but it is much more. In volumes of material, people have attempted to reconcile differences between generations that, in reality, are irreconcilable—perhaps understandable, but nonnegotiable. The fundamental value systems are, in fact, dramatically different between the generations that presently exist simultaneously in our society. Police organizations can have employees from four or more generations. Obviously, this can, and usually does, present a problem for the supervisor.

Individual Differences

Value programming is not simply a process of indoctrination. Nor is the behavior of people the result of a series of processes that simply overlay a particular culture on the biological core of individuals. Rather, society shapes a person's inherited temperament, but it does not transform that person into a complete opposite of his or her own basic nature. Each of us emerges with somewhat distinctive ways of behaving, despite the influences in our generation's programming. A wide range of inputs influences our basic physical and mental abilities. In broad categories, the major sources of programming experiences for all of us were (1) family, (2) formal education, (3) religion, (4) the media, (5) our friends, (6) where we grew up, and (7) our wealth.

Standards

A value system acts as a set of standards and thus guides our conduct. It causes us to take a position or to abandon one previously adopted, predisposes us to accept or reject certain ideas or activities, gives us a sense of being right or wrong, aids us in making comparisons, acts as a basis from which we attempt to influence others, and affords us an opportunity to justify or rationalize our actions. Thus our value system is, in effect, our individual "code of conduct."

Conflict Resolvers

We frequently find ourselves in conflict with another person because of individual value system disparities. In an intrapersonal way, however, value systems more often than not support us in making choices. "I prefer blue over brown" and "I choose to allocate my police personnel in a crime-prevention program rather than a crime-specific program" are illustrations of this. Briefly, one's value system assists in making decisions. Nonetheless, when individuals possess different values, they are apt to conflict with one another.

Emotional Triggers

Most people give the value of fairness a high rank. As a consequence, when we see or experience unfair personnel practices, our emotional threshold is normally breached, and we feel angry, depressed, threatened, or a combination of all three. If we were the perpetrator of the unjust act, then we probably feel guilt. The police supervisor who disciplines an errant employee with reasonable cause may feel some sadness because of his or her value for the family unit, feeling that the employee deserved being disciplined but also feeling sorry for the employee's spouse and children.

Thought Provokers

If we value being an effective police supervisor, does it not make sense that this value should provoke us into thinking about what means (e.g., enhancing one's job knowledge) would best achieve the desired outcome (success)? Fortunately, there are techniques for recording and exploring one's thoughts in a meaningful way so that we can put these thoughts to use. The techniques range from keeping a diary to following planned exercises. I will cover a number of such techniques later; in the meantime, remember that values generate thoughts as well as guide them.

Motivators

The terms *motivation* and *motive* denote desire or actual movement toward an identified end. A person's value system motivates him or her to choose one path (means) over others. Thus one can feel or see one's motivations by inspection of or introspection on one's behavior. What moves a person to act, or to want to act, in a particular manner stems from his or her own value system. In essence, one's values underpin and generate one's motives. As a result, if you value supervision, it is reasonable for you to be motivated to become a police supervisor. This sense of being motivated further serves as a motivation for acquiring the skills, knowledge, and abilities necessary for supervising a group of police officers.

Attitudes

Although our values influence our attitudes, they don't necessarily determine them. Attitudes can be chosen. Granted, you cannot choose your circumstances, and as an adult, you have already acquired a set of powerful values. However, you can still choose your attitudes if you really want to.

> The single most important decision you make on a daily basis is the choice of your attitude.

Most of us spend more time fretting over the things that can't be changed than we do giving attention to one of the things that can be changed, our attitude. As long as we believe we are creatures shaped solely by outside conditions, we will fail to exercise our free will and miss the chance to be masters of our own destiny.

An understanding of attitudes, attitude formation, and attitude change is important for four reasons:

- Attitudes can be found in every aspect of police work. We have attitudes about most things that happen to us, as well as about most people we meet. In view of the universality of attitudes, an understanding of their nature is essential for supervisors.
- Attitudes influence behavior. Much of how we behave at work is governed by how we feel about things. Therefore, an awareness of attitudes can assist supervisors in understanding human behavior at work. Changes in police employee behavior can be expected to the extent that supervisors can change or control employee attitudes.
- Bad attitudes on the job cause problems. Poor job attitudes can be reflected in subsequent poor performance, citizen complaints, equipment abuse, turnover, and absenteeism, all of which result in direct costs to the police agency.
- When an employee is expressing negative, carping, malcontented opinions, the typical response is "Officer X has a bad attitude," when, in effect, the officer is voicing a *value issue*.

Personality

Individuality and personality are not synonymous. Individuality is a natural covering for the protection of the personality or personal life. Individuality is reflected in our independence and self-assertiveness. Personality is a characteristic evidenced by our willingness to be a team member, by how we care for others, and by our self-discipline. Personality is you in relationship to others.

> Your value system determines how you relate to your family, what products you buy, and how you vote. It dictates your leisure-time activities, what information you absorb, and your religious convictions. Of significance here is that your values decide how well you perform your job as a police supervisor.

VALUE CLARIFICATION

What you are speaks so loudly I cannot hear what you say.

—Ralph Waldo Emerson

Select something that is important to you (e.g., your job, family, or health), and if you can answer each of the following questions with a "yes," you have identified and confirmed one of your values.

In terms of a particular value, are you

- Choosing freely?
- Choosing from options?
- Choosing after thoughtful consideration of the consequences of each option?
- Prizing being happy with the choice?
- Willing to make a public affirmation of the choice?
- Performing (doing something with the choice)?
- Using the choice in a pattern of life?

Choosing Freely

The values that you choose freely are those that you will internalize, cherish, and allow to guide your life. Society or your physical environment may impose a value, but it does not necessarily become your own.

Choosing from Options

It follows that if there are no options, then there is no freedom of choice. It would be hard to convince someone that he or she valued employment with a specific police department when in fact it is the only one that would hire him or her.

Choosing after Thoughtful Consideration

A value must be freely chosen after a careful review of the consequences of each option. In other words, the consequences must be known to whatever extent possible. After all, if we do not realize the consequences of a particular alternative, we do not know what is likely to occur and therefore cannot have freely chosen that alternative.

Prizing Being Happy

Briefly, a value is something that we cherish, respect, and show pride in.

Making a Public Affirmation

If you value a person, an object, or a concept, it seems only reasonable that you would profess it openly. Are you pleased and proud to tell others that you are a police supervisor?

Performing

Your behavior reflects your values. The importance of a particular value (such as acquiring a college education) can be assessed by how much time you spend on it (such as taking three units a semester rather than nine). There is an obvious difference between thinking about a value and acting on it. Thinking about a value (such as losing ten pounds) may be an early indication that you are forming a specific value, but it is in performing the value (actually losing weight) that you can attest to its being a full value.

Using the Choice in a Pattern of Life

Values, because we act on them, become a dominating influence in our life. They establish patterns in thought and deed. Consequently, they motivate us to attend church or not, to get married or not, to have children or not, and to supervise effectively or not. It is interesting that we frequently think that we possess a value that, in reality, we no longer hold. We assume that because we once held a particular value, we continue to hold it, and we may be shocked to find that it is no longer a value, or at least no longer an important one. There are two value clarification exercises in this chapter to assist you in analyzing your value system.

STRUCTURED EXERCISE 2–1

VALUE INDICATOR LIST

Take the next few minutes to explore some of your individually held values. The following two exercises can be accomplished either alone or in a group.

To begin with, complete the Value Indicator List by quickly writing down the ten things that you enjoy (value) in your professional, social, or personal life. In other words, of all the things in your life, list the ten that you enjoy the most. (They can range from the tangible [e.g., money, car, and family] to the intangible [e.g., love, respect, and freedom]). We are value-driven, and consequently it is critical for us to identify the values in our value system.

Value	Rank	Symbol
1.		
2.		
3.		
4.		
5.		
6.		
7.		
8.		

(continued)

STRUCTURED EXERCISE 2–1 *(continued)*

Value	Rank	Symbol
9. _____	_____	_____
10. _____	_____	_____

Now study your list, and rank your values in order of priority. Use 1 to indicate the most valued, 2 the next most valued, and so on. Next, where they apply, place the following symbols in the last column.

1. Put a "$" by any item that costs forty dollars or more each time you perform it. (Be certain to look for hidden costs.)
2. Put a "10" by any item that you would not have done ten years ago.
3. Put a "X" by any item that you would like to let others know you do.
4. Put a "T" by any item that you spend at least four hours a week doing.
5. Put a "M" by any item that you have actually done in the last month.
6. Put an "E" by any item that you spend time reading about, thinking about, worrying about, or planning for.
7. Put a "C" by any item you consciously choose over other possible activities.
8. Put a "G" by any item that you think helps you to grow as a police supervisor.
9. Put a "R" by any item that involves some risk. (The risk may be physical, intellectual, or emotional.)

Look at your list. The more symbols you have put next to an item, the more likely it is that the activity is a value for you. This list is not necessarily a compilation of your values; rather, it may be an indication of where your values lie. Count the number of symbols next to each value, and rank them—the value with the most marks being first, and so on. Now, compare your first ranking (left side) with your second ranking (right side), and note the following:

1. Do your rankings match?
2. Is your highest value in the first ranking the one that has the most symbols next to it?
3. Can you see any patterns in your list?
4. Have you discovered anything new about yourself as a result of this activity?
5. Is there anything you would like to change about your preferences as a result of this exercise?

If you are studying as a group, you may want to divide into subgroups of four or five members each and share what you have learned about your values. This was an awareness exercise and not a test. Hence your judgment—and not some outside criteria—measures its accuracy. Basically, if there are more symbols next to the values that you ranked the highest, then you've achieved "confirmation." Conversely, if the highest-ranked values have few symbols, then you're looking at "discovery." Finally, if the pattern is erratic, you're probably seeing some confirmation and some discovery.

The main thing is, you have identified your ten core values.

FAILING TO ACT ON OUR VALUES

We fail to act on our values when we

- Concentrate on short-term objectives that do not relate to our long-term goals.
- Relive past failures.
- Succumb to the "we can't change" syndrome.
- Substitute egocentrism for altruism.
- Allow conformity to overpower courage.
- Ignore our purpose in life, and in so doing, place the ladder of success against the wrong wall.

STRUCTURED EXERCISE 2–2

Let's take another approach that is more supervisor-oriented. Complete the following statements by assigning 1 to the highest priority, and then, in descending rank order, 2, 3, and 4.

If possible, form groups of four or five to discuss individual rankings and try to have them reach a consensus. Look for commonalities, trends, and surprises.

1. I think that the best police supervisor is one who:
   _____ tells you what should be done.
   _____ consults with you on important issues.
   _____ persuades you to live up to your ideals.
   _____ facilitates a consensus on important issues.
   _____ other: _____

2. For recreation, I prefer:
   _____ conversation in a small group.
   _____ doing something together in a group.
   _____ watching TV.
   _____ reading the newspaper.
   _____ other: _____

3. In my role as a police supervisor, I like to:
   _____ work by myself.
   _____ work with others.
   _____ delegate responsibility to others.
   _____ other: _____

(continued)

STRUCTURED EXERCISE 2–2 (*continued*)

4. I like to use my free time to:
   _____ be by myself.
   _____ visit my friends.
   _____ catch up on work.
   _____ other: _____

5. In my retirement, I would want to:
   _____ work on my hobbies.
   _____ travel.
   _____ take a part-time job.
   _____ other: _____

6. For my professional future, I should:
   _____ stay just as I am.
   _____ take on new interests.
   _____ renew present interests.
   _____ drop some of my present interests.
   _____ other: _____

7. With police supervisor colleagues, it is best to:
   _____ keep quiet about yourself and your work.
   _____ ask for help, advice, or consultation when you need it.
   _____ be friendly but not talk about personal or important business matters.
   _____ tell them about yourself and your work.
   _____ other: _____

8. Does this list leave out any important areas? If so, add other areas, including possible approaches to those areas, and then rank them as above.

FROM VALUES TO ETHICS

The capacity to care is the thing which gives life its deepest significance.

—Pablo Casals

As a preview to responsibility three, ethics:

- Our values serve as the birthplace of our ethics.
- Some values are ethical in quality, and all ethics are values.
- Our ethics become a part of us.
- We supervise and lead others and ourselves according to our ethics.

STRUCTURED EXERCISE 2–3

Return to the scenario at the beginning of this chapter. Answer in writing each of the questions posed. When finished, answer a final question: What did you learn about yourself?

The real meaning of our lives is defined by how we are remembered. If you want to know how to live your life, just think about what you want people to say about you after you die, and then live backward.

KEY POINTS

- The four main reasons for understanding human values are that they
  (1) Act as an individual compass.
  (2) Connect communications and mutual trust.
  (3) Convey leadership characteristics.
  (4) Increase self-awareness.
- We supervise and lead others and ourselves according to our value system.
- A value is an enduring belief that a means or a goal is vitally important.
- Values-driven police supervision attempts to fuse higher-ordered values into the police department.
- Our values stem from three periods in our life: imprinting, modeling, and socialization.
- Although enduring, our values can be modified by a significant emotional event or profound dissatisfaction.
- Our values play ten significant functions in our personal and professional lives:
  (1) paradigms
  (2) generation gaps
  (3) individual differences
  (4) standards
  (5) conflict resolvers
  (6) emotional triggers
  (7) thought provokers
  (8) motivators
  (9) attitudes
  (10) personality
- Our values can be clarified, and it is important that we do so.

EXTENDED LEARNING

1. How does the phrase "we are what we value" pertain to the police supervisor?
2. Identify the most significant input to your value system during each of the three value-programming periods.

3. Have you had an SEE lately? What did it do to your value system?

4. Identify a value like personal safety. Discuss how this value acts as a paradigm, reflects generation gaps, produces individual differences, creates standards, resolves conflicts, triggers emotions, provokes thoughts, and motivates you.

5. How does the right and the responsibility to choose your attitude affect your value system? Which is more powerful—your freedom of choice or your values?

6. What did you learn from Structured Exercise 2–3?

RESPONSIBILITY 3

Ethics

Earlier, we learned that we supervise ourselves and others according to our value system (Responsibility 2). Likewise, we also supervise ourselves and others according to our ethical standards. In the next chapter, we will see how important it is for the supervisor to constantly communicate and consistently reinforce both (Responsibility 4).

A responsibility of the police supervisor is to ensure that the employees understand and adhere to a professional code of ethics.

The time is right to do what is right.

—Martin Luther King Jr.

We can't deny it; moral and ethical issues are embedded in almost every aspect of leadership. All leaders discover that they must come to terms with their own moral beliefs and be held accountable in the end for the decisions they make based on those beliefs.

While most of us have a high self-image when it comes to ethics, being a good person and doing the right thing are easier said than done. For one thing, it's not always easy knowing what's right. Second, having the moral willpower to put ethical principles above self-interest and always do the right thing takes a lot of character, especially when no one else seems to be living up to such high standards.

The fact is that for most of us, trying to live a good life engages us in an ongoing conflict between what we want to do and what our duties tell us to do. The best police supervisors may fib occasionally, cut corners a little, and rationalize about responsibilities. It's human nature; none of us is perfect. However, it is also human nature to seek perfection and to care about our character. Basically, while we may have some faults, the majority of us want to improve our character.

ETHICS AND ETHOS

Certain types of values are ethical values. Values and ethical values are a branch of philosophy. Ethics are concerned with moral duties and how we should behave regarding both ends and means. Police work is an intrinsically practical service enterprise that judges its employees and acts only in terms of the effective use of power and the achievement of results.

Ethos is the distinguishing character, moral nature, or guiding beliefs of a person, group, or institution. What are your guiding beliefs, those of your work group, those of your department? Does your ethos support or conflict with your ethics? For example, the following are ethical values:

- Honesty
- Fairness
- Trustworthiness
- Integrity
- Respect for others
- Thoughtfulness
- Compassion
- Honor
- Law-abidingness
- Loyalty
- Accountability

Let us assume that you possess the preceding values. Now, does your ethos agree? Further, do your acts reflect these values? There are three vital steps to ethics:

- Knowing what is right
- Being totally committed to it
- Doing it

Here are some useful definitions that will assist us as we progress with this responsibility:

Ethics: A body of moral principles or values
Morals: Right conduct
Honesty: Intending to act morally and thus subscribing to ethical principles
Integrity: Behaving morally and thus manifesting ethical principles
Integral: Wholeness

THERE IS NO SUCH THING AS POLICE ETHICS

Think of the most ethical people you know. Do a lot of people come to mind or only a few? Now, if asked that question, how many people who know you well would name you? Almost all? About half? Just a few? And do you care?

STRUCTURED EXERCISE 3–1

Imagine that you are a police officer and that you're at roll call training. The newly assigned sergeant starts the training by introducing himself and then adds, "If you have any doubts about how I want you to treat our citizens, treat them exactly the way I treat you!"

Now imagine that you're a police sergeant and you've just introduced yourself to your newly assigned shift officers. One officer raises her hand and asks, "How do you expect us to treat the citizens?" What is your reply? On a sheet of paper or in the margin of this page, write down your response. Share this information with others in your group.

There are some people who would argue that there is a distinction between ethics and a legal obligation. Further, they would allege that police ethics and business ethics are different. I believe that a legal obligation is an ethical one—not a simple business decision. A legal obligation is also an ethical duty; it's a part of being trustworthy—having character. I also believe that there isn't any difference between police ethics and business ethics, or any other type of ethics (medical, sports, spiritual, etc.). Ethics are ethics!

The theory of "police ethics" flourishes because some police employees compartmentalize their lives into personal and police domains, assuming that each is governed by different standards of ethics. In police work, the argument goes, ethical principles like trustworthiness, respect, responsibility, fairness, caring, and good citizenship are simply factors to be taken into account. As a result, fundamentally good people who would never lie, cheat, or break a promise in their personal lives delude themselves into thinking that they can properly do so in police work. This rationale is fatally flawed.

Ethics are not concerned with descriptions of the way things are but prescriptions for the way they ought to be. Though we may face different sorts of ethical challenges at work, the standards do not change when we enter the workplace. There is no such thing as "police ethics." There is only ethics.

What is most puzzling about most instances of police wrongdoing is that they clearly contradict both the values that are held by most of us as individuals and the collective standards that we have established for appropriate professional behavior.

Here's a brief quiz. Do you

1. Consider yourself to be an ethical person?
2. Believe that it's important for police agencies to function in an ethical manner?
3. Believe that you know an ethical dilemma when you see it?
4. Believe there are clear answers to ethical problems?
5. Believe that you always know an ethical dilemma when it arises and always know how to resolve it?

Clearly, all of us feel strongly about ethics in the abstract. But at the same time, each of us is keenly aware of the struggle we face as ethical dilemmas arise. It is a common struggle between our own desire to be ethical and the competing pressures of police performance. Police supervisors struggle every day with how to create an organizational culture that promotes ethical behavior.

STRUCTURED EXERCISE 3–2

Some of the following comments are signposts of ethical wrongdoing. Have you heard them in your organization? Discuss this exercise as a group.

Denying or Trivializing Its Significance

- "Show me a victim."
- "It's not illegal."
- "You can't legislate morality."
- "It's just a technicality."

Invoking the Double Standard

- "Morality is a personal matter."
- "I don't mix business with my personal feelings."

Arguing Necessity

- "It's cutthroat out there."
- "If I don't do it, someone else will."
- "It's my job."
- "It will save some jobs."

Arguing Relativity

- "It's not illegal elsewhere."
- "In the United States, ideals are turned into laws."
- "No act is inherently illegal."
- "We are no worse or better than society at large."

Professing Ignorance

- "I wasn't told."
- "Ethics are a gray area."
- "The rules are inscrutable."

ETHICAL DILEMMAS: THREE APPROACHES

When examining the ethics programs of police departments, it is useful to bear in mind the three very different approaches to dealing with ethical dilemmas.

These are

- Neglect—or the absence of any formal ethical programs
- Compliance-based programs
- Values-oriented programs

Neglect

It is hard to imagine that any police agency could rationally ignore the importance of ethics or fail to develop management policies and programs, given the effect ethical breaches can have on performance, reputation, and community support. But some departments clearly don't get the message.

The departments that ignore ethics do so on the basis of assumptions that are false and never challenged. They seem to view ethics either as unimportant or as a costly and inconvenient luxury. They are wrong on both accounts.

Compliance-Based Programs

Compliance-based programs are most often designed by legal counsel. They are based on rules and regulations with the goal of preventing, detecting, and punishing legal violations. The centerpiece is a comprehensive collection of regulations that spells out a universal code of police ethics. The code lays out rules for hiring practices, travel expenses, compliance with local laws, improper payments, gifts, and potential conflicts of interest. It is a long and weighty list of do's and don'ts for people to follow.

This approach doesn't work well. First, rules beget rules; regulations beget regulations. The agency becomes buried in paperwork, and anytime it faces a unique ethical issue, another rule or regulation is born. Second, a compliance-based program sends a disturbing message to the employees: "We don't respect your intelligence or trust you!" Finally, one of the most compelling reasons for shedding this approach is that it doesn't keep police supervisors or employees from exercising poor judgment and making questionable decisions.

Values-Oriented Programs

The values-oriented approach relies on the identification of ethical principles. Each police agency must develop its own core ethical values. For now, we will use the six advocated by the Josephson Institute of Ethics. Together they are referred to as the Six Pillars of Character; they define for us our moral duties and virtues.

We examine ethical issues by first identifying which of these six ethical principles applies to the particular ethical decision. Then we determine which internal and which external stakeholders' ethical concerns should influence the decision. This principle-based approach balances the ethical concerns of the community with the values of the police organization. It is a process that extends trust to an individual's knowledge of the situation. It examines the complexity of issues that must be considered in each decision, and it defines the role each person's judgment plays in carrying out his or her responsibilities in an ethical manner. This integrates ethics with departmental culture, which includes diversity, open communications, empowerment, recognition, teamwork, and honesty into every aspect of police work—from personnel practices to relationships with the community. This integration is the adhesive of a seamless organization.

Six Pillars of Character

TRUSTWORTHINESS

Ethical persons are worthy of trust. Trustworthiness is an especially important ethical value because it encompasses four separate ethical values: honesty, integrity, promise-keeping, and loyalty.

RESPECT

The ethical value of respect is fundamental. It imposes a moral duty to treat all persons with respect. This means we recognize and honor each person's rights to autonomy and self-determination, privacy, and dignity.

RESPONSIBILITY

Ethical persons are responsible, an ethical concept that embodies three separate values: accountability, self-restraint, and pursuit of excellence.

FAIRNESS

Another fundamental ethical value is fairness. The concept embodies the values of justice, equity, due process, openness, and consistency. Fairness is one of the most elusive ethical values, since, in most cases, stakeholders with conflicting interests sharply disagree on what is fair.

CARING

At the core of many ethical values is concern for the interests of others. Persons who are totally self-centered tend to treat others simply as instruments of their own ends, and rarely do they feel an obligation to be honest, loyal, fair, or respectful.

CIVIC VIRTUE AND CITIZENSHIP

An ethical person acknowledges a civic duty that extends beyond his or her own self-interests, demonstrating social consciousness and recognizing his or her obligations to contribute to the overall public good. Responsible citizenship involves community service and doing one's share.

Source: Josephson Institute of Ethics—reprinted with permission. CHARACTER COUNTS and the Six Pillars of Character are service marks of the CHARACTER COUNTS Coalition, a project of the Josephson Institute of Ethics, www.charactercounts.org.

AN ETHICAL CULTURE

Suppose a traffic sergeant wants his unit to appear highly effective in the eyes of the chief. He knows he can order the administrative assistant to "cook" the numbers by adding a few citations here and there or slipping the decimal point to the left. Whether the sergeant will engage in this scheme and order his assistant to participate, and whether the assistant will actually do so, is not a matter of personal character alone, but also of departmental culture. The decisions of employees like the sergeant and his assistant will be strongly influenced by the department's own ethical paradigm, the integrity of the department as a whole, and its willingness to enforce the rules. The combination

STRUCTURED EXERCISE 3–3

As a member of a SWAT team, you've been notified by radio to proceed Code 3 to a location where there is an armed suspect barricaded with a hostage. You have taken a shortcut on a seldom-used narrow rural road. On your left side is a vertical canyon wall. On your right side is a vertical drop of 500 feet. Suddenly, a small child darts across your path. With insufficient braking time, you are faced with either killing the child and arriving at the SWAT operation in time to save the hostage or sacrificing your life and possibly that of the hostage by swerving to miss the child and plunging over the side of the cliff. Write down your decision and why you made it.

Now imagine the same set of conditions except that you are driving the SWAT van and it contains all ten members of your team. Does your decision change? If so, how? Write it down.

Again imagine the same set of conditions except that you have only one member of the SWAT team in your car. Now what do you decide? Write it down.

What moral standard or ethics program did you employ to make your decisions? Was it the same for each scenario?

of individual character and organizational character produces a department's ethical culture. In most police agencies, what is rewarded, sanctioned, or allowed determines the nature of the results achieved. Given that fact, the sergeant is more likely to avoid deceptive conduct if he believes that integrity and honesty are truly valued and enforced by the department and that severe punishment can be expected if he is caught lying about the facts to enhance the department's productivity statistics. Similarly, the civilian assistant is likely to say no to the sergeant only if convinced that the department will stand behind, and in fact expect, an ethical decision of this nature.

It is a smart leader who understands the culture of his or her department and does whatever is needed to strengthen a sustainable ethical culture that generates trust and emphasizes integrity, fairness, and unwavering accountability. This cannot be achieved by sermonizing, harsh disciplinary actions, or strict codes of ethics alone. The admonitions and rules must be translated into commonly understood expectations and made credible by the actions of the managers and supervisors who demonstrate ethical decisions and are intolerant of ethical shortcuts.

The problem in some police agencies is that stated ethical values are not consistently modeled or enforced. There are a few police departments that don't want to rock the boat. Management looks the other way when employees lie on reports, take credit for the work of others, and supervise by intimidation. Good police officers must be good employees—men and women of principle with the courage to make honorable choices even in the face of adversity.

The basic rules of supervision are (1) whatever you allow you encourage, and (2) whatever employees will do for you, they will do to you.

When supervisors are too timid, lazy, ambitious, or scared to firmly and fairly enforce the rules, they make a mockery of departmental policies and ethical standards. What is worse, they demoralize employees who adhere to a moral code of conduct, planting seeds of inefficiency and corruption. Once a bad police employee is allowed to win, the resolve of dozens of honest, hardworking staff is weakened, leading them to believe that following the rules is just for suckers.

STRUCTURED EXERCISE 3–4

THE ETHICAL CLIMATE SURVEY

Ethical decision making in government is essential to a community's health, vitality, and democracy. Ethical behavior and decisions maintain citizen trust and ensure effective and efficient use of resources. Yet an ethical environment does not happen overnight. Successful police supervisors set the pace for ensuring an ethical police organization and provide the necessary tools and establish the climate.

The first steps toward building and maintaining an ethical organization are assessing the current environment and identifying any changes that are needed. How do you know where to start? What actions are most critical? Do employees think the local government is ethical?

Circle the appropriate response below each question or statement, using the following categories:

SD = strongly disagree   D = disagree   A = agree
SA = strongly agree   DK = don't know

1. Ordinarily, we don't deviate from standard policies and procedures in my department.
   SD   D   A   SA   DK

2. My supervisor encourages employees to act in an ethical manner.
   SD   D   A   SA   DK

3. I rarely have to ask my supervisor before I do something.
   SD   D   A   SA   DK

4. Around here, there is continual encouragement to improve individual and group performance.
   SD   D   A   SA   DK

5. The employees in my department demonstrate high standards of personal integrity.
   SD   D   A   SA   DK

6. My department has a defined standard of integrity.
   SD   D   A   SA   DK

7. Individuals in my department accept responsibility for decisions they make.
   SD   D   A   SA   DK

8. It is wrong to accept gifts from people who do business with my jurisdiction, even if those gifts do not influence how I do my job.
   SD   D   A   SA   DK

9. It is not usual for members of my department to accept small gifts for performing their duties.
   SD   D   A   SA   DK

10. Members of my department do not use their positions for private gain.
    SD   D   A   SA   DK

11. Members of my department have not misused their positions to influence the hiring of their friends and relatives in the government.
    SD   D   A   SA   DK

12. I would blow the whistle if someone in my department accepted a large gift ($ _____ or more in value; this amount varies by local government) from a person who does business with the government.
    SD   D   A   SA   DK

13. Promotions in my department are based on what you know or how you perform on the job, rather than on whom you know.
    SD   D   A   SA   DK

14. I trust my supervisor.
    SD   D   A   SA   DK

15. My jurisdiction has implemented a code of ethics.
    SD   D   A   SA   DK

16. There are no serious ethical problems in my department.
    SD   D   A   SA   DK

17. Coworkers in my department trust one another.
    SD   D   A   SA   DK

18. My superiors set a good example of ethical behavior.
    SD   D   A   SA   DK

19. I feel that I am a member of a well-functioning team.
    SD   D   A   SA   DK

20. All employees have equal opportunities for advancement.
    SD   D   A   SA   DK

21. Performance evaluations accurately reflect how employees have done their job.
    SD   D   A   SA   DK

22. Performance evaluations address ethical requirements as well as other measures.
    SD   D   A   SA   DK

23. Employees share negative information with supervisors without the worry of receiving a negative reaction from them.
    SD   D   A   SA   DK

24. Supervisors are concerned with how employees achieve successful results, rather than just with the results themselves.
    SD   D   A   SA   DK

(continued)

STRUCTURED EXERCISE 3–4 (*continued*)

25. When there is a disagreement between employees and supervisors on how best to solve a problem, the employees' ideas are listened to and considered.

    SD   D   A   SA   DK

26. When employees feel that they are being asked to do something that is ethically wrong, supervisors work with them on alternative ways to do the task.

    SD   D   A   SA   DK

27. In this organization, it is much better to report a problem or error than it is to cover it up.

    SD   D   A   SA   DK

28. When something goes wrong, the primary goal is to fix the problem and prevent it from happening again, rather than to find someone to blame.

    SD   D   A   SA   DK

29. The organization's decisions on how people are treated are clear and consistent.

    SD   D   A   SA   DK

30. The organization's expectations concerning productivity, quality, and ethics are consistent.

    SD   D   A   SA   DK

31. The same set of ethical standards is used in dealing with citizens, employees, and others.

    SD   D   A   SA   DK

32. You can rely on the accuracy of the organization's information about what will or won't happen.

    SD   D   A   SA   DK

33. The organization publicly recognizes and rewards ethical behavior by employees when it occurs.

    SD   D   A   SA   DK

34. Around here, doing what is right is more important than following the rules.

    SD   D   A   SA   DK

35. Ethical standards and practices are routinely discussed in employee meetings.

    SD   D   A   SA   DK

36. If there is suspicion that some employees may be violating ethical standards, the situation is dealt with openly and directly.

    SD   D   A   SA   DK

37. Employees are aware of where to obtain assistance when they need to resolve an ethical dilemma.

    SD   D   A   SA   DK

38. If one employee is doing something unethical, the other employees in the group will usually try to correct the situation before management gets involved.

    SD   D   A   SA   DK

39. Employees are encouraged to report their work results accurately even when the results are less than satisfactory.

    SD   D   A   SA   DK

40. Employees maintain the same ethical standards even when no one is observing their actions.

    SD   D   A   SA   DK

Use the scale below each statement to respond to the following items; circle the number that most closely represents your response.

41. My ethical standards are:

    Very low   Very high
    1   2   3   4   5   6   7

42. The ethical standards in my department are:

    Very low   Very high
    1   2   3   4   5   6   7

Circle the answer that best represents your response to this statement:

43. My behavior as a public employee is regulated by state law.

    Yes   No   Don't know

Ethical Framework

Your answers to the survey should begin to give you a framework that can help guide your next steps and actions. You also may find it helpful to give a survey like this to all members of your staff. This could provide you with more information and further guide your ethical actions.

Analysis of the Ethical Climate Survey

The first forty questions of the Ethical Climate Survey are organized in relation to seven important values that affect the nurturing and sustaining of an ethical work environment.

Values and Related Questions

Accountability	Responsiveness/ Customer Service	Integrity/Honesty
1, 7, 12, 16, 22, 27, 38	4, 19, 28, 30, 34	5, 6, 8, 9, 10, 11, 40
Trust	**Fairness**	**Communication**
3, 14, 17, 32	13, 20, 21, 31	15, 29, 35, 36, 37
Leadership		
2, 18, 23, 24, 25, 26, 33, 39		

(continued)

STRUCTURED EXERCISE 3–4 (continued)

The questions are designed and evaluated based on an ideal and ethically healthy work environment, which would be reflected by "strongly agree" answers. Therefore, a strong ethical work environment would be indicated by an average of the questions within each category with a result as close as possible to 4. An average of all the category averages indicates an overall perception by employees of the total work environment, based on the factors listed.

Rating Values of Survey Responses

1 = strongly disagree	3 = agree	0 = don't know
2 = disagree	4 = strongly agree	

Responses to this survey indicate a local government's ethical strengths and weaknesses. For example, if you gave high responses to the questions under the fairness category, your organization probably treats its citizens and staff in a fair manner. If your scores for the communication category were relatively low, however, it might be in the best interest of your local government to write and implement a code of ethics or routinely discuss ethical issues during departmental meetings.

This survey is only the beginning. It might indicate that some work needs to be done, such as including ethics in the performance evaluation system. And by taking the survey and analyzing the scores annually, it also might help you maintain an organization that already has high ethical standards.

An ethical work environment is reflected in ethical decision making that results in important organizational values being addressed, such as productivity, responsiveness, accountability, and a sense of ownership in how the organization conducts its business. Ideally, the most effective organization has a high level of compatibility between the employees' ethical values and those of the organization. There also is a clear understanding of the manager's expectations of the organization and employee behavior and performance.

Source: Reprinted with permission from the May and June 1999 issues of *Public Management (PM)* magazine, published by the International City/County Management Association (ICMA), Washington, D.C.

WHAT KIND OF A PERSON DO YOU WANT TO BE?

There is no pillow so soft as a clear conscience.

—French proverb

Your response to this question—"What kind of a person do you want to be?"—dictates what kind of a supervisor you will be! I have never heard of anyone who is miserable, mean-spirited, and deceitful at work but is the complete opposite at home. Undoubtedly, who you are or want to be as a person translates into who you are or want to be as a police supervisor.

Keep in mind that only good people feel guilty. Unethical people rarely feel guilty because they deny, they justify, they rationalize, and they refuse to accept their share of responsibility. Only ethically aware people struggle with the distance between who they are and who they know they ought to be.

STRUCTURED EXERCISE 3–5

You are a police sergeant, and a business owner describes the following situation. He owns several coin-operated newspaper vending machines. Customers insert 50 cents, open the door, and take a paper. The problem is that once the door is open, some people are taking more than one newspaper. He has decided to place one of the following three signs on the machine to discourage people from stealing. The owner asks you which of the following signs is likely to be the most successful:

1. This machine is under surveillance. If you take more than one newspaper, you will be subject to arrest. Stealing is against the law.
2. I depend on the income from this machine to support my family. Please don't steal from us.
3. Please don't take anything you haven't paid for. What kind of a person are you?

Which of these signs will be most effective for most people? And which of them would be most effective for you personally?

Sometimes police employees (supervisors too) do wrong because doing what they know to be right is too hard for them or because the advantage to be gained by taking an ethical shortcut is just too tempting. They may believe that circumventing what's right just gives them an even chance of winning and that this is okay.

Sometimes employees who have done a misdeed are so remorseful about it that they follow up with another wrongful act to keep the first violation from being discovered.

Sometimes people behave badly out of anger. They may feel that life or society or their department or their supervisor is unfair or dishonest, so why should they be fair or honest?

Sometimes employees feel compelled to support and defer to authority even when that authority orders them to perform an act that they find ethically troubling.

What Kind of People Are We?

Are we naturally good until external circumstances compromise our goodness? Or are we naturally bad, requiring outside authority to constrain us? The obvious answer is that we are both. All of us have right and wrong tendencies—sharing versus selfish, truthful versus lying, helpful versus harmful, and fair versus cheating. All of this is because we are human. And our humanness does not start or stop once we achieve the position of a police supervisor.

Yes, good employees do bad things. Good employees are those who keep their bad notions within due bounds. The true measure of a person's character is what that person would do if he or she were sure nobody could see.

Good People Will Do Good Things

Yes, good people will do good things—lots of them. Unfortunately, they will do bad things because they are human. We make mistakes of the heart and mistakes of the mind. And frequently, we pay the price for these errors on our part. With fortitude and resilience, we will not be overwhelmed by guilt when egotistic impulse defeats our moral resolve. Conversely, we will understand that moral victory is temporary when we cast aside temptation. Granted, it is an ongoing struggle for all of us—daily, hourly, minute by minute.

The question remains, "What kind of person do you want to be?" The clarity and the certainty of your answer to this question provide a definitive and cogent answer to the question posed earlier in this section, "What kind of supervisor do you want to be?"

COURAGEOUS CHOICES

To know what is right and not do it is the worst cowardice.

—Confucius

Courage is what gives ethics vibrancy. So many people espouse ethics about integrity, trust, loyalty, and the like until the dilemma is theirs. Then, because of their particular circumstances, selfish needs, and uncomfortable feelings, the ethics become negotiable. Clearly, to resist the inner drive toward self-interest over character requires an ethical code that judges some behaviors as better than others—along with a value known as courage. Yes, it takes enormous courage to stand firm against the pressure and temptation of self-interest and make a decision in line with moral principles.

Moral Courage

Courage comes in different forms. Most often, we think of physical courage or bravery. That's the kind of courage demonstrated by those who risked their lives trying to help others during the terrorist attacks of September 11, 2001, and by others who fought against acts of terrorism. It's right and proper that we call these people heroes and acknowledge their valor.

But there's another form of courage that's just as important: moral courage. It's the kind of courage C. S. Lewis referred to when he said, "Courage is not simply one of the virtues but the form of every virtue at the testing point." The testing point is the place where living according to moral principles may require us to put our comfort, possessions, relationships, and careers at risk.

For most of us, the need for physical courage is rare, but our moral courage is tested almost every day. Being honest at the risk of disapproval, lost income, or a maimed career; being accountable when owning up to a mistake that can get us in trouble; making tough decisions with and demands of coworkers at the cost of their friendship; being fair when we have the power to be otherwise; and following the rules while others get away with whatever they can—these things take moral courage, the inner strength to do what's right even when it costs more than we want to pay.

The sad fact is that people with moral courage rarely get medals. Instead, they risk ridicule, rejection, and retaliation. Yet this sort of courage is the best marker of one's true character and a life that others who know you can be proud of.

A Public Office Is a Public Trust

A public office (e.g., the role of a police sergeant) is a public trust. This axiom, supported by the related idea that participatory democracy requires public confidence in the integrity of government, lays the very foundations for the ethical demands placed on police personnel and the laws establishing baseline standards of behavior. Laws and rules are especially useful when faced with choices about brutality, stealing, perjury, and bribe taking. Although the choice here is not always easy, it's clear and straightforward. Laws are needed to define minimum standards of conduct.

Referring to such laws and rules as "ethical laws" or "ethical standards" is misleading and actually counterproductive. It is misleading because the laws deal only with a narrow spectrum of ethical decisions that police employees face. It is counterproductive because it encourages us to accept only existing laws as ethics. We accept narrow technical rules as the only moral criteria of conduct. Hence if it's legal, it's ethical. It would be like using the penal code as a substitute for the Bible, Talmud, or Koran.

Easier Said Than Done

One reason ethics are much easier said than done is that legal albeit unethical behavior has become so very ordinary, as we can see from these generic examples:

- Embellishing claims
- Scapegoating personal failures
- Shirking distasteful responsibilities
- Knowingly making unreasonable demands
- Stonewalling questions
- Acting insincerely
- Reneging on promises
- Covering up
- Making consequential decisions unilaterally
- Malingering
- Lying

None of these behaviors is scandalous. But each, nonetheless, violates a sense of what is the morally correct behavior (e.g., the behaviors of personal responsibility, honesty, and fairness), increases cynicism and distrust, undermines integrity, and can be a stepping-stone to wrongful behavior.

Though laws can secure compliance within limited margins, they are far too narrow or minimal to act as a substitute for ethics. We expect too much from laws and demand too little from people.

Easy versus Courageous Choices

The easy choices typically involve clear-cut laws and rules. You take a bribe, and the choice may result in the obvious—you're fired and go to jail. The hard choices deal with moral issues and ethical considerations such as an indiscretion, a rule infraction (e.g., sleeping on duty), deception in police investigations, the use of deadly force, the use of physical force, and off-duty behavior that may or may not be job related.

Ethical decisions—courageous choices—are much more difficult than we would like to think. It is not simply a matter of character or upbringing. Ethical decision making requires an alert and informed conscience. It requires the ability to resist self-deception and rationalization. It requires courage and persistence to risk the disapproval of others and the loss of power and prestige. Finally, it requires the capacity to evaluate incomplete or confusing facts and anticipate likely consequences under all kinds of pressure.

When there is a gap between reality and ethical standards, people of character do not surrender their standards. They fight for them. They work to change the way things are to the way they ought to be. And much more than we realize, corrupt systems and people are prone to collapse at the first sight of principled resistance.

Some of us overestimate the costs of being ethical and underestimate the costs of compromise.

—Michael Josephson

ETHICAL DECISION MAKING

> Bad choices create bad consequences, and no matter how much good a police supervisor does, he or she will be judged by that last, worst decision.

Given the potential impact of every little decision a leader makes, it is obviously wise to think ahead. Though few things turn out exactly as we plan, the better we understand how our choices start a chain reaction of events, the more likely we are to get what we want—an ethical decision.

Ethical decision making is a skill that can be learned. The first step is to know what the ethics are. Figure 3–1 presents an ethical code. If you're a law enforcement officer (public or private), you should know it. Take a few minutes to read it now; you'll find it loaded with ethical values that are much broader than a set of criminal laws.

When faced with a decision that involves ethics, ask the following questions of yourself or your work unit:

1. Will the decision I make violate the rights or goodwill of others?
2. What is my personal motive and spirit behind my actions?
3. Will it add to or detract from my reputation?
4. If I were asked to explain my decision in public, would I do so with pride or shame?

Law Enforcement Code of Ethics

As a law enforcement officer, my fundamental duty is to serve the community; to safeguard lives and property; to protect the innocent against deception, the weak against oppression or intimidation and the peaceful against violence or disorder; and to respect the constitutional rights of all to liberty, equality and justice.

I will keep my private life unsullied as an example to all and will behave in a manner that does not bring discredit to me or to my agency. I will maintain courageous calm in the face of danger, scorn or ridicule; develop self-restraint; and be constantly mindful of the welfare of others. Honest in thought and deed both in my personal and official life, I will be exemplary in obeying the law and the regulations of my department. Whatever I see or hear of a confidential nature or that is confided to me in my official capacity will be kept ever secret unless revelation is necessary in the performance of my duty.

I will never act officiously or permit personal feelings, prejudices, political beliefs, aspirations, animosities or friendships to influence my decisions. With no compromise for crime and with relentless prosecution of criminals, I will enforce the law courteously and appropriately without fear or favor, malice or ill will, never employing unnecessary force or violence and never accepting gratuities.

I recognize the badge of my office as a symbol of public faith, and I accept it as a public trust to be held so long as I am true to the ethics of police service. I will never engage in acts of corruption or bribery, nor will I condone such acts by other police officers. I will cooperate with all legally authorized agencies and their representatives in the pursuit of justice.

I know that I alone am responsible for my own standard of professional performance and will take every reasonable opportunity to enhance and improve my level of knowledge and competence.

I will constantly strive to achieve these objectives and ideals, dedicating myself before God to my chosen profession . . . law enforcement.

FIGURE 3–1   Police code of conduct. (*Source: Reprinted with permission of the International Association of Chiefs of Police.*)

5. Even if what I do is not illegal, is it done at someone else's personal expense?
6. Does what I do violate another's reputation?
7. If it were done to me, would I approve or would I take offense and react in pain?
8. What are the basic principles that govern my actions and decisions?
9. When I am in doubt, to whom will I go to check my decisions?
10. Will my decision give other people any reason to distrust me?
11. Will my decision build the credibility of my work or profession?

If you have time for only one thought, imagine that your decision is being made with your mother, father, and a newspaper reporter watching you. Most police personnel want to do the right thing. In fact, this desire is so compelling that some will unintentionally engage in rationalizations to justify ethically doubtful behavior. It is possible to increase the likelihood that police employees will act more ethically more often if they're trained. In fact, the better and more frequent the training, the higher the likelihood that an employee will opt for the courageous choice: acting ethically.

STRUCTURED EXERCISE 3–6

Read the Law Enforcement Code of Ethics that appears in Figure 3–1. Underline all the values that you discern in it. Next, highlight all the values that you deem to be ethics. Compare your findings with those of others in your class or study group.

Do you agree or disagree that it is better to lose than to sacrifice integrity? One person quipped, "The trouble with the rat race is that even if you win, you're still a rat." We cannot turn moral commitment on and off as it suits us or the situation.

> An ethically based person cannot win by being dishonest, disloyal, or unfair any more than one can truly win a tennis match by cheating.

The liar's punishment is not in the least that he is not believed, but that he cannot believe anyone else.

—George Bernard Shaw

IT'S NOT EASY

Integrity means being whole, unbroken, individual. It describes the character of a person who has united the various facets of his or her personality so that there is no longer any quarreling within about what is right—ethics. Having integrity means you are blessed with wholeness and peace. Having integrity means the courageous choices become the easy ones.

It's Not Easy

Let's be honest. Ethics is not for wimps. It's not easy being a good person.

It's not easy: to be honest when it might be costly. To keep inconvenient promises or to put principles above comfort.

It's not easy: to stand up for your beliefs and still respect differing viewpoints.

It's not easy: to be on time. To control anger. To be accountable for attitudes and actions. To refrain from gossip and hurtful words. To tackle unpleasant tasks. Or to sacrifice the now for later.

It's not easy: to bear criticism and learn from it without getting angry. To take advice. Or to admit error.

It's not easy: to really feel sorry and apologize sincerely. To accept an apology graciously. Or to forgive and let go.

It's not easy: to not complain. To stop feeling like a victim. To avoid disheartening cynicism. To make the best of every situation. Or to be cheerful for the sake of others.

It's not easy: to share. To be consistently kind. To think of others first. To judge generously. To give the benefit of the doubt. To give without concern for gratitude. Or to be grateful.

It's not easy: to fail and still keep trying. To learn from failure. To risk failing again. To start over. To lose with grace. Or to be glad for the success of another.

It's not easy: to avoid excuses. To resist temptations. Or to listen to our better angels.

No, being a person of character is not easy. That's why it's such a lofty goal and an admirable achievement.

Source: Permission to use and reprint this passage is granted by the Josephson Institute of Ethics.

KEY POINTS

- Ethics focus on moral duties and how we should behave.
- Ethos is the distinguishing quality, moral nature, or guiding beliefs we hold.
- Certain values serve as ethical values.
- There is no such thing as police ethics. Ethics are ethics and must not be qualified.
- There are three very different approaches to handling ethical problems: neglect, compliance-based programs, and values-oriented programs.
- The Six Pillars of Character are trustworthiness, respect, responsibility, fairness, caring, and civic virtue and citizenship.
- The decisions of employees will be strongly influenced by the department's ethical culture.
- What kind of a person you want to be determines what kind of a police supervisor you will be.
- Being a police supervisor is a public trust.
- Obeying the law is easy compared with making an ethical decision, which can be hard.
- Self-deception and rationalization will make hard choices even more difficult.
- Some of us overestimate the costs of being ethical and underestimate the costs of compromise.
- Ethical decision making can be learned.
- Integrity means you are integrated, whole, and at peace with your inner world, but it's not easy.

EXTENDED LEARNING

1. What does ethos mean to you? Cite a guiding belief that you believe represents your police agency.
2. Obeying the law is a relatively easy choice. Making ethical decisions is a hard choice. Why? Give examples.

3. Identify a recent motion picture that portrays moral courage. Describe an act or activity. Why did you select it? What does it tell us?

4. What has this chapter not covered? Where did it push or sermonize? Where did it seem uncertain or lacking?

5. Do you agree with the proposition that "there is no such thing as police ethics"? Why do you agree or disagree?

6. Which one of the three approaches to handling ethical dilemmas does your agency use?

7. Describe the most recent courageous choice you made.

RESPONSIBILITY 4

Vision

The police supervisor is responsible for ensuring that his or her team shares in crafting a vision, setting goals, and building a strategy for providing high-quality police work.

Responsibility 4 draws from and builds on Responsibilities 2 and 3. A vision is individual values and ethics put into mission. Supervisors are responsible for leading people in the creation of a vision statement for their work unit. Through communications (Responsibility 5) and time management (Responsibility 6), the vision becomes a reality.

An old story tells of three stonecutters who were asked what they were doing. The first replied, "I am making a living." The second kept on hammering while he said, "I am doing the best job of stonecutting in the entire country." The third one looked up with a visionary gleam in his eyes and said, "I am building a cathedral."

Have you ever held a job where you didn't have a clue about its purpose? You performed tasks but couldn't see how they fit into a meaningful pattern? If so, what you—and probably the people you worked for—lacked was a vision.

Small but important choices that you make in your work life add up to one big choice to perform as a police leader in such a way that you make a difference. Unless you have a vision of where you want to lead others, you'll never be able to judge whether you have made a difference.

STRUCTURED EXERCISE 4–1

As you read the three vision statements that appear below, highlight the values and ethics contained in each. In doing so, you'll appreciate even more the critical importance that values and ethics serve, not just individually but universally. We are what we value, and so are our police organizations.

LOS ANGELES COUNTY SHERIFF'S DEPARTMENT MISSION AND VALUES

Our Mission

The quality of neighborhood life, its safety and welfare, comes from the commitment to each of its citizens. The Los Angeles County Sheriff's Department takes pride in its role as a citizen of the community; partners with its members in the delivery of quality law enforcement services. We dedicate our full-time efforts to the duties incumbent upon every community member. As we act, we are universal citizens deriving our authority from those we serve. We accept our law enforcement mission to serve our communities with the enduring belief that in so doing, we serve ourselves. As professionals, we view our responsibilities as a covenant of public trust, ever mindful that we must keep our promises. As we succeed, our effectiveness will be measured by the absence of crime and fear in our neighborhoods and by the level of community respect for our efforts. In accomplishing this all-important mission, we are guided by the following principles:

> To recognize that the primary purpose of our organization is not only the skillful enforcement of the law, but the delivery of humanitarian services which promote community peace.
>
> To understand that we must maintain a level of professional competence that ensures our safety and that of the public without compromising the constitutional guarantees of any person.
>
> To base our decisions and actions on ethical as well as practical perspectives and to accept responsibility for the consequences.
>
> To foster a collaborative relationship with the public in determining the best course in achieving community order.
>
> To strive for innovation, yet remain prudent in sustaining our fiscal health through wise use of resources.
>
> To never tire of our duty, never shrink from the difficult tasks and never lose sight of our own humanity.

Our Core Values

We shall be service oriented and perform our duties with the highest possible degree of personal and professional integrity. Service Oriented Policing means:

> Protecting life and property
> Preventing crime
> Apprehending criminals
> Always acting lawfully
> Being fair and impartial and treating people with dignity

Assisting the community and its citizens in solving problems and maintaining the peace.

We shall treat every member of the Department, both sworn and civilian, as we could expect to be treated if the positions were reversed.

We shall not knowingly break the law to enforce the law.

We shall be fully accountable for our own actions and failures and, when appropriate, for the actions or failures of our subordinates.

In considering the use of deadly force, we shall be guided by reverence for human life.

Individuals promoted or selected for special assignments shall have a history of practicing these values.

HOUSTON POLICE DEPARTMENT

Mission Statement

The mission of the Houston Police Department is to enhance the quality of life in the City of Houston by working cooperatively with the public and within the framework of the U.S. Constitution to enforce the laws, preserve the peace, reduce fear and provide for a safe environment.

Values

Preserve and Advance Democratic Values

We shall uphold this country's democratic values as embodied in the Constitution and shall dedicate ourselves to the preservation of liberty and justice for all.

Improve the Quality of Community Life

We shall strive to improve the quality of community life through the provision of quality and equitable services

Improve the Quality of Work Life

We shall strive to improve the working environment for the department's employees by engaging in open and honest communication and demonstrating a genuine concern for one another.

Demonstrate Professionalism

We shall always engage in behavior that is beyond ethical reproach and reflects the integrity of police professionals.

Principles

Life and individual freedoms are sacred.

All persons should be treated fairly and equitably.

The role of the police is to resolve problems through the enforcement of laws—not through the imposition of judgement or punishment.

The neighborhood is the basic segment of the community.

Because law enforcement and public safety reflect community wide concern, the police must actively seek the involvement of citizens in all aspects of policing.

(continued)

STRUCTURED EXERCISE 4–1 (*continued*)

The fundamental responsibility of the police is provision of quality services.

The department's employees are its most valuable asset.

Employee involvement in departmental activities is essential for maintaining a productive working environment.

Employees should be treated fairly and equitably in recognition of basic human dignity and as a means of enriching their work life.

NEW YORK CITY POLICE DEPARTMENT

Mission

The MISSION of the New York City Police Department is to enhance the quality of life in our City by working in partnership with the community and in accordance with constitutional rights to enforce the laws, preserve the peace, reduce fear, and provide for a safe environment.

Values

In partnership with the community, we pledge to:

- Protect the lives and property of our fellow citizens and impartially enforce the law.
- Fight crime both by preventing it and by aggressively pursuing violators of the law.
- Maintain a higher standard of integrity than is generally expected of others because so much is expected of us.
- Value human life, respect the dignity of each individual and render our services with courtesy and civility.

Points to Ponder . . .

1. What did you learn from the preceding statements?
2. How are they alike? How do they differ?
3. Which one did you relate to the most? Why?

THE CONSTANCY OF CHANGE

The police leader is challenged by a need for constancy of purpose, progress, change, and teamwork. Did you note the juxtaposition of *change* and *constancy*? One term seemingly conflicts with the other. One paradigm might insist that you can't achieve both. My paradigm is this:

> Change is a constant.

Change never ceases; it keeps coming at us, knocking us off course, confusing us, and fatiguing us. When we understand the paradigm effect, we learn that the only constant in our life is change.

Our values, ethics, and visions flow through paradigms and are automatically subjected to incoming considerations for change. Once a set of values, a code of ethics, or a vision statement has tested valid by the paradigm effect and supported by the staff of a work unit or the police department, then constancy of vision is established.

The police leader is in a pivotal position for conceiving, refining, and implementing a paradigm—a vision that others are able to get excited about working on. Revisit the opening story about the three stonecutters. Which paradigm/vision would compel you as a police supervisor to become a leader?

Everything Changes

When police employees at any level have had an opportunity to actively consider what vision and purpose have real meaning for them, everything changes. Having gone through the hard work and ultimate satisfaction of creating a shared vision for their immediate team, they become more devoted to building shared vision and shared meaning for the entire police organization. As that process is repeated among many teams and multiple pairings, the whole department is engaged and enriched, and multiple strands of shared meaning begin to bind the organization together.

Many police departments have vision statements. Sometimes they are labeled "value" or "mission" statements. Regardless of the title,

- All contain values.
- All express the purpose of the organization.
- Frequently they explain how they intend to make their vision a reality, and sometimes they cast the values into measurable goals.

VISION: THE CONSTANCY OF PURPOSE

Responsibility 2 dealt with individual values, ethics, and personal vision. Here we will focus on group values, ethics, and organizational visions.

Since a vision usually consists of several values and ethics, it is relatively stable over time. If an organization frequently changes its vision, it can cause chaos for the participants.

Visions, like values, are enduring. They will change, but only with considerable time and an enormous amount of thinking. Visions create a consistency of purpose for a police organization.

Vision: An Image of Our Desired Future

Assume a virtue, if you have not.

—William Shakespeare

A vision is a paradigm of the virtue you seek to create, described in the present tense as if it were happening now. A statement of "our vision" shows where we want to go and what we will be like when we get there. The better you see it, the more richly detailed and visual the image is, and the more compelling it will be.

Because of its tangible and immediate quality, a vision gives shape and direction to the department's future or the future of a division, bureau, or work team. And it helps people set goals to take the organization closer to reality.

A vision is not idle daydreaming or casual reflection on the "what if." It reflects a lot of practical thinking about why we're here (purpose) and where we should be headed.

Values and Ethics: What We Are Doing to Get Where We Want to Go

Values and ethics describe how we intend to operate on a day-to-day basis as we pursue our vision. A set of governing values and ethics might include how we want to behave with one another, how we expect to regard our community, and the lines that we will and will not cross. Values and ethics are best expressed in terms of behavior: If we act as we should, what would an observer see us doing? How would we be thinking?

When values and ethics are articulated but ignored, a critical part of the shared vision is destroyed. By contrast, when values and ethics are made a central part of the police organization's shared vision effort and put out in full view, they become a guiding symbol of the behavior that will help the organization's members move toward the vision.

Purpose or Mission: What the Organization Is Here to Do

Whether you call it a mission or a purpose, it represents the fundamental reason for the organization's existence. What are we here to do together? You will never get to the ultimate purpose of your organization, but you will achieve many visions along the way.

Goals and Objectives: Milestones We Expect to Reach before Too Long

Every shared vision effort needs not just a broad vision, but also specific realizable goals. A goal is long-range—one to five years. An objective is short-range—something we seek to accomplish within a year.

BUILDING A SHARED VISION

The following recommended steps will prove helpful as you create a vision and cast it into a vision statement.

Although your agency or division may have a vision or mission statement, this should not discourage you and your staff from generating your own. As a leader, you are responsible for doing so.

- *Listening.* Choosing to continually listen for a sense of emerging purpose is a critical decision that shifts a supervisor and his or her crew from a reactive orientation to a creative one.

- *Linking.* Police mission or purpose statements often lack depth because they fail to connect to the agency's overarching reason for existence. When this connection is made forcefully, an employee's commitment and energy can be increased for fulfilling the department's purpose.
- *Inclusiveness.* To be genuinely shared, visions must emerge from everyone reflecting on the department's purpose.
- *Openness.* At the heart of building shared vision is the task of designing and implementing ongoing processes in which police employees at every level of the agency, in every role, can speak from the heart about what really matters to them and be heard—by police management and one another.
- *Personal vision.* When a shared vision project begins with personal vision, the police organization becomes a tool for the employees' self-realization, rather than an impersonal structure to which they are subjected. They stop thinking of the organization as a thing to which they are subjugated.
- *Equality.* In the department, the top brass wield the policy-making power, but in this exercise, a boss should get only one vote. Similarly, no one team should get more votes than any other. During these exercises, discourage status differences.
- *Unity.* By interface and dialogue, all issues, concerns, and views should be brought to the surface and resolved. Do not expect uniformity; that is groupthink and will produce a seriously flawed vision.
- *Interdependence.* When team members begin talking about their vision, avoid telling them what other teams have said. Instead, ask each team first, "What do we really want?" As teams become curious about each other's visions, two or more teams may discover a strategic value in meeting together, comparing notes, and creating a shared vision.
- *Participation.* To conserve resources, many police chiefs opt to sample the thoughts of their employees. This undermines opportunities for employees to take on ownership.
- *Self.* Participants are permitted to speak only of their ideas and not to allude to those that may be held by missing members.
- *Phasing.* A compelling vision takes time to craft. Cast it into phases, with pauses between each one.
- *Power.* The process is more important than the product. Participants actively instill meaning and inspiration into words and give them symbolic value; the words on their own mean nothing. That's why the benchmark of vision is not in the statement, but in the directional power it instills in the agency.

TWO APPROACHES FOR BUILDING A VISION STATEMENT

First, note the word in the heading above: *vision.* I use the term *vision statement* to encompass vision, value, and mission statements.

Second, conceiving a vision is rigorous work, often perplexing and sometimes frustrating. Once you've got your vision, though, building a written vision statement is relatively easy. Vision thinking is tough; vision writing is straightforward.

Third, your department may not have a vision statement, or it may have one that is corny or that does not reflect the shared vision that you and your staff have of your duties. If so, lead your employees in the creation of another to meet your specific desires. In other words, a vision statement must not be the sole property of the top brass.

Approach 1: Top Down

Since the mid-1980s, many police managers have created vision statements and worked hard to communicate them down to their employees. Many of us have accepted the notion that vision must come from the top. In that case, a meeting is convened so the top managers can develop a vision statement and plan for its distribution. The intent is sincere, and the content is always appealing. Each police management team affirms its uniqueness by declaring that it:

- Is committed to being a professional department
- Believes in its people
- Stands firm for quality
- Cares for citizens
- Affirms honesty and integrity
- Supports teams
- Is innovative

But there are problems: ownership and implementation!

Ownership.   The buy-in resides with those who create a vision and with them alone. The employees do not own a statement created for a police agency to endorse. An even more fundamental defect is that, in most cases, the vision statement is created for the rest of the organization to implement. Notice that the top-down vision is used to define a set of values to be lived. This is different from top management's rightful task of defining and setting operational goals.

The belief that brainstorming the vision is primarily a leadership-at-the-top function defeats, right at the beginning, the intent of empowering those close to the work and the community. Creating vision is an ownership function, and if we want ownership widely dispersed, then each person needs to struggle with articulating his or her own vision for the police function or work unit.

Implementation.   There is something in us that wants a common vision articulated by those at the top. This longing for a common vision is the wish for someone else to create the unity and purpose we seek. The desire for vision from the top is a subtle way of disclaiming any responsibility for its implementation. We continue to want strong leadership from police management even though it steals accountability from those below. Visions are implemented when each police supervisor and assigned staff define vision for their area of responsibility.

STRUCTURED EXERCISE 4–2

Read through the five stages below, and objectively assess which stage best describes your police organization now.

1. *Telling.* The chief knows what the vision should be, and the organization is going to have to follow it.
2. *Selling.* The chief knows what the vision should be but needs the organization to "buy in" before proceeding.
3. *Testing.* The chief has an idea, or several ideas, about what the vision should be and wants to know the organization's reactions before proceeding.
4. *Consulting.* The chief is putting together a vision and wants creative input from the organization before proceeding.
5. *Sharing.* The chief and members of the police department, through a collaborative process, build a shared vision together.

Approach 2: Bottom Up

Moving from approach A to approach B hinges on shared ownership and accountability. The operative word is *shared.* I know of police agencies that reinforce ownership and accountability by conforming their performance-appraisal system to their vision statement. They link the envisioned ideals to the measurement of performance. The department vision becomes an operational reality. (More on this in Responsibility 12, Performance.)

Police chiefs and sheriffs surely need a vision statement, but not for themselves alone to live out and be accountable for.

> Unless a vision statement has a shared beginning and ending, it will remain an ignored and lofty set of well-intentioned values that fail to materialize.

GOAL SETTING: THE CONSTANCY OF PROGRESS

Our beginning should be with an end in mind. In other words, before we start our journey, we should have a destination or goal set for ourselves. By keeping the end clearly in mind, you can make certain that whatever you do on any particular day does not stray from the goal you have set as supremely important and that each day of your life contributes in a logical way to the vision you have of your life as a whole. Hence we are able to maintain our constancy of progress.

A while ago I conducted a three-day team-building workshop for a large full-service sheriff's department. The sheriff is a tall, rugged, red-headed, affable guy. At that time, he'd been the sheriff of the 1,800-person organization for twelve years. The workshop was attended by an undersheriff, four assistant sheriffs, a coroner, and fifteen captains. The second day started with a discussion of a pending shift in the allocation of sworn personnel. Within a few minutes, the fifteen captains were adamantly defending their assigned turfs. The sheriff sensed this and asked, "Hey, what are our goals?" No one said a word. I saw his face start to match the color of his hair. In a louder voice, he stated, "I guess there's no reason to ask you: What are our priorities?" Then there was silence—perhaps sixty seconds, which seemed like an hour.

Finally, one brave captain ventured, "Sheriff, in my opinion, our number one priority and goal is corrections. After all, about one half of our personnel are assigned to it." In a second, the sheriff's obvious anger switched to puzzlement. He dropped his head and then looked up and scanned the group. He proceeded to surprise us by saying, "I apologize. I thought you knew. It's my mistake for not telling you and then retelling you. Our goals, in order of their priority, are (1) drug abuse enforcement, (2) contract cities, (3) corrections, (4) county patrol areas, and (5) the coroner's office. Now, don't forget them." I'm confident no one has; I certainly haven't.

It is very easy to get in an "activity trap" in the business of police work, to work harder and harder at producing results only to discover that they're unnecessary. A police organization without goals can be highly efficient and very ineffective. The police organization that lives without goals will spend its future in the present.

> The police supervisor who supervises without goals is not positioned to lead.

A goal is something we desire; it is something we hope for in the future. An objective is a goal that is more finite and time-certain. For example, a police supervisor may set a goal of developing his or her assigned personnel to the maximum of their innate strengths. An objective that would support fulfillment of this goal could be this: All personnel within my purview will have attended an officer survival course within the next six months. Note that the goal is broader in scope, while the objective is specific with an assigned time frame.

At first glance, it might appear that organizations have a singular objective—for police departments to apprehend criminals. But closer analysis demonstrates that all organizations have multiple goals. Police agencies also seek to increase public safety and provide general government services. No one measure can effectively evaluate whether an organization is performing successfully. Emphasis on one goal, such as reducing crime, ignores other goals that must also be achieved if long-term safety is to result. Additionally, the use of a single goal almost certainly will result in undesirable practices, since supervisors will ignore important parts of their job in order to look good on the single measure.

Real versus Stated Goals

Stated goals are official statements of what an organization says and what it wants various publics to believe are its objectives. But stated goals, which can be pulled from the organization's charter, annual report, public relations announcements, or public statements made by a police chief, are often conflicting and excessively influenced by what society believes police organizations should do.

The conflict in stated goals exists because police organizations respond to a vast array of constituencies. Unfortunately, these constituencies frequently evaluate the organization using different criteria. As a result, the police are forced to be different things to different groups.

STRUCTURED EXERCISE 4–3

This is a simple but powerful exercise to help you understand the significance of distinguishing between real and stated goals.

- Imagine learning that you have to retire in one year. List three things you'd like to accomplish during this last year.
- Assume that eleven months have passed. List three things you would like to do in your last month.
- Make a new list assuming that you have one week left, and another assuming that you have only forty-eight hours left.
- Examine what you've written. If your list includes activities you're not currently pursuing, what's stopping you from pursuing them now? Get on track!

This exercise can be easily modified to focus on your personal life. Merely assume that you have one year to live. List three things you'd want to do within the year, and so on.

Given the diverse constituencies to which the police are required to respond, it would be a surprise to find a department with a set of objectives stated to everyone that actually describes what the organization seeks to achieve.

There is visible evidence to support the fact that police chiefs give much attention to their social responsibilities in the decisions they make and the actions they take. The overall goals that top management expresses can be real, or they can be fiction. If you want to know what a police department's real objectives are, closely observe what members of the organization actually do. It is behavior that counts.

> If we are to develop comprehensive and consistent plans, it is important to differentiate between stated and real objectives.

The police supervisor should be able to articulate the real goals of the department. The supervisor should understand existing values and possess a clear vision of the future. This ensures the consistency of progress.

STRATEGY: THE CONSTANCY OF CHANGE

> The twentieth century began by changing the old constancies. The twenty-first century begins with change being the only constant.

How well a police agency negotiates the hurdles of change is the key to its survival and success. Some change is external (e.g., Americans with Disabilities Act, terrorism, population mix). Some is internal (e.g., organizational structure, management style, labor relations). Regardless of its source, any change poses two questions:

- Does it challenge our vision?
- How does it affect our goals?

Incessant and avalanching changes can modify a goal, which means reexamining and perhaps recasting it. Or these changes can alter how the goal will be implemented. In both cases, the police supervisor must think strategically.

Strategic thinking is the basis for developing strategic plans and operational plans. It is a supervisory tool for making better choices about how to implement departmental goals in the face of chronic and random changes. Strategic thinking always

- Uncovers the causes versus the symptoms of problems
- Hammers conventional thinking
- Depends more on intuition than on intellect
- Seeks to anticipate
- Points out more than one approach for accomplishing a goal

Step 1: Recognizing Insight

Recognizing insight in yourself or others begins with increased comprehension of the characteristics that insightful police leaders share. Don't look for once-in-a-lifetime brilliant flashes! Deep insight is a basic and abiding skill that continually guides the thinking of a winner. Most often, you'll find insightful police leaders engaged in the following behaviors:

- They prefer tackling problems that do not have precise answers, asking questions like "In what ways can we improve our police services for our community?"
- They spend more time synthesizing information than gathering it, relishing the process of breaking information down into its component parts and then reconfiguring those parts to expose the essence of a problem.
- They can easily drop an approach to a problem that isn't working, forcing their way out of habitual methods of thinking or analyzing.
- They doggedly pursue difficult problems over long periods of time, never feeling frustrated when the solution isn't readily apparent.
- They don't worry about asking questions that might display their ignorance.
- They usually think up more ideas more rapidly than anyone else in brainstorming sessions because their disciplined but flexible mind thrives on such exercises.
- They have made meditation a habit, not an occasional exercise, and set aside time each day for it.
- They read voraciously to satisfy a thirst for knowledge and the experience of others.
- They entertain new ideas enthusiastically. They help their associates and staff come up with innovative approaches.

With these attributes in mind, let's test your level of insight with the Leader Insight Self-Examination (Structured Exercise 4–4).

STRUCTURED EXERCISE 4–4

LEADER INSIGHT SELF-EXAMINATION

	Always	Often	Seldom	Never
1. You are stimulated by complex problems and situations that tax your thinking.	4	3	2	1
2. You dislike the sort of rigid problem solving that attacks every problem with the same mechanical approach.	4	3	2	1
3. You encourage open discussion and disagreement in your work unit.	4	3	2	1
4. You read voraciously to expand your experience.	4	3	2	1
5. You entertain new ideas with enthusiasm rather than skepticism.	4	3	2	1
6. You ask numerous questions, never worrying about whether they reveal your ignorance.	4	3	2	1
7. You look at things from a variety of viewpoints before making a decision.	4	3	2	1
8. You surround yourself with people who promote distinctly different orientations and points of view.	4	3	2	1
9. You make decisions others call "innovative."	4	3	2	1
10. You search for new and better ways of approaching work within your organization.	4	3	2	1

How did you fare? A score of 40 marks you as a deeply insightful leader, while anything below 30 indicates a need for improvement. Your improvement will occur when you take the next two steps.

Step 2: Asking the Right Questions

The majority of us function daily with paradigms that constrain our creativity. There are six in particular that limit our powers of imagination:

- *Resistance to and avoidance of change.* Many of us who cling to the status quo for safety are consciously or unconsciously blocking new insights.
- *Dependence on rules and conformance.* Some supervisors emphasize conformance over performance by enforcing strict adherence to rules, procedures, and structures.
- *Fear and self-doubt.* Some police supervisors become immobilized by insecurity, lack of confidence, and fear of criticism.

- *Fixation on logic and hard data.* Some police supervisors have more of a commitment to mechanics than to results. Some expect problems and solutions to fit snugly into neat compartments. This hampers our intuitive powers.
- *Black-and-white viewpoints.* The maturity that comes with experience tends to change previously black-and-white judgments to varying shades of gray. Regretfully, some police supervisors hold to an either/or approach, which reduces their options to a few oversimplified solutions.
- *Narrow-minded dedication to practicality and efficiency.* Some police supervisors refuse to consider wild alternatives and ideas. Every idea for them must fit into some logical scheme.

Here are five exercises that will help free up your creativity and be more innovative in your role as a police leader.

Creativity Training.   Numerous training programs are available to help you increase your creativity. For example, contact Princeton Creative Research in Princeton, N.J. An excellent guide on the subject is Roger Von Oech's *A Whack on the Side of the Head* (Warner Books).

One New Idea a Day.   Supervisors are usually idea getters; hence you should find it natural to get one more idea every day. At first, it may seem difficult, even frustrating. But once in motion, you'll find that ideas flow with ease. New visions of alternative futures for yourself and your department will outcrop.

Wild Thinking.   Wild thinking helps us break the locks of mechanistic approaches. Whenever you find yourself bogged down with formal, technical processes for solving problems, pause for a little wild thinking. Look for historical successes that can be retested. Look for other technologies, such as robotics, and see how they fit in your operation. Ask this question: What is impossible to do right now, but if it could be done, it would significantly change my work?

Make the Obvious Strange.   Instead of relying on the tried-and-true perspective on a problem, force yourself to see two or more strikingly different solutions. Before making any decision, step back to view the full richness of the situation. Look for multiple meanings and possibilities. Once a day for a month, pick at least one situation or problem and make it complex and ambiguous. The quick and simple answer to a problem can be both quick and wrong!

Push the Artist; Restrain the Judge.   An overdependence on being practical and getting to the bottom line hurries you into making an evaluation. At least once a week for three months, deliberately postpone a new idea, discussion, strategy, or plan by reserving judgment until it becomes unavoidable. Don't think you're procrastinating. Rather, allow a little further discussion, initiate an experiment, or demand a follow-up report. Once your creative juices have ebbed, the practical you—the judge—can step in to evaluate the ideas.

Step 3: Tuning In

In police supervision, "tuning in" means letting your intuition, your years of experience, your awareness of challenges, your sensitivity to the community, and your understanding of cold, hard facts flow together in a calm and natural way. Most of us seldom tap the full reserve of our knowledge and experience. When we encounter problems, we suffer anxiety because problems pose dangers, as well as opportunities. In our anxiety, we forget to trust our most valuable intuitive resources. Insight, like great poetry, music, or art, arises from the quiet depths of the unconscious from a source that lies beneath words, deeds, thoughts, and figures.

With the integration of your insight, experience, and knowledge, you're armed to build an operational paradigm. An operational paradigm enables a leader to accurately and quickly move to the heart of strategic issues confronting his or her work unit, meanwhile dodging bureaucratic barriers and vaulting mountains of minutiae.

> *Whatever you can do or dream you can, begin it. Boldness has genuis,*
> *power and magic in it.*
>
> —Johann Wolfgang von Goethe

THINK SLOWLY; ACT QUICKLY!

Police organizations and police supervisors are inclined to make two major blunders when it comes to crafting a vision, defining goals, and developing a strategy:

- Not making the three processes a shared or team effort
- Taking far too much time in their accomplishment

Both are killer bullets to vision statements, goal setting, and strategic plans. I underscored earlier the importance of everyone sharing in the three-part effort. In terms of time commitments, I concur with the Greek proverb "Think slowly." Only I would add, "Do it now!" Some believe that establishing a vision, goals, and strategies demands months of brainpower. Nonsense. Get everyone into a room, and do it! Allow twenty-four hours maximum.

More Later . . .

Visioning, goal setting, and strategic thinking set the stage for planning and managing by objectives (MBO). The latter two move from thinking about who we are to showing others who we are. Planning and MBO will be discussed in Responsibility 12, Performance.

KEY POINTS

- The way we envision our world and our job is determined by our paradigms.
- A key paradigm is that change is a constant.
- Without a vision, a supervisor will never be able to determine whether he or she made a difference.

- The vision encompasses its values, purpose, and goals.
- There are two approaches for building a vision: top down and bottom up.
- The bottom-up or shared approach is, by far, preferable.
- Goal setting is an effort to translate a vision into measurable benchmarks of progress.
- Strategic thinking is intended to keep organizational goals operable.
- Act now on a vision, a set of goals, and a strategy for their realization.

EXTENDED LEARNING

1. What is the primary purpose of a local police department in today's modern world?
2. What is wrong with the top-down approach for building a vision statement?
3. Why build a shared vision of what you are and where you want to go?
4. Why are goals important? How do they relate to a vision?
5. How does strategic thinking affect goal attainment?
6. What does "Think slowly; act quickly" mean to you as a police supervisor?

RESPONSIBILITY 5

Communications

> The police supervisor is responsible for communication with others in such a manner that employee understanding, trust, and mutual support are engendered.

> At this point, we have explored your values (Responsibility 2) and ethics (Responsibility 3) for the purpose of developing your capacity to create a vision for your work team (Responsibility 4). The next step is to accurately convey your vision.

If you cannot express yourself on any subject, struggle until you can.
If you do not, someone will be the poorer all the days of his life.

—Oswald Chambers

> Communication is our most important and learnable human skill.

Everything that we have done, are doing, and wish to do revolves around our ability to communicate. Everything a police supervisor does involves communicating. Not a few things, but everything! You can't make a correct decision without information. That information has to be communicated. Once a decision is made, communication must again take place. Otherwise, no one will know a decision has been made. Supervisors, therefore, must have effective communication skills. I am not saying that solid communication skills alone make a successful police supervisor. I am saying, with confidence, that ineffective communication skills can lead to a continuous stream of problems for the supervisor.

The success of any relationship—whether work, marriage, or friendship—hinges on trust. And trust depends on communication. As you read what follows, keep in mind that communication and trust are tied to one another. If one rises or drops, so will the other.

As a supervisor you've got to be trusted; hence you've got to communicate. The good news is that communication skills can be learned.

We'll start here by asking why, and we'll eventually conclude this chapter by asking an additional why.

WHY DO WE COMMUNICATE?

> Our ability to communicate openly and clearly determines our success in becoming a leader, our success in making accurate decisions, and our success in being trusted.

When I use the term *communications,* I am referring to it in its most dynamic, pervasive, and expansive dimensions: words written, spoken, and not spoken. First of all, why do we communicate?

- To be a leader
- To make decisions
- To establish trust

Leadership

Communication is the vehicle for supervisory leadership. The police supervisor is a key person in building and maintaining effective organizational communications. It is the supervisor who links the line employee to management.

Decision Making

A police supervisor assesses issues based on information received in conjunction with previously developed strategies, procedures, or rules. Consequently, the communication process is necessary because the flow of proper information to the decision points throughout the organization is such a vital requirement for task accomplishment. In fact, if supervision were thought of primarily as decision making, and if the decision process were considered essentially a communication process, including a network of communication systems, then supervision could be viewed as a communication process. The closer we look at leadership and decision making, the more we become aware of the significance of information exchange.

Trust

In a future chapter we'll cover the concept of a trust bank account (TBA). The most important ingredient we put into any relationship is not what we say or what we do, but what we are. We do this by communicating. How do you react to people who do not share with you their ideas, values, hopes, and ethical standards? Do you grow to trust them?

Probably not. They either refuse to make or are incapable of making deposits into your TBA. In fact, if these individuals persist in being closed, they'll likely make withdrawals from your TBA. Trust and communication are linked. For one to be high, the other must be high. If you lower one (reduced communication), you'll lower the other (reduced trust).

WHAT IS COMMUNICATION?

Communication is the

- Transfer of meaning between two or more people in order that . . .
- Understanding will occur within an . . .
- Environment—in this case a police organization.

Transfer of Meaning

Communication is the transfer of meaning. If no information or ideas have been conveyed, communication has not taken place. The supervisor who is not heard or the writer who is not read does not communicate. For communication to be successful, the meaning must be not only sent but also comprehended. Therefore communication is the movement and understanding of meaning. Perfect communication, if such a thing were possible, would exist when a transmitted thought is perceived by the receiver exactly as envisioned by the sender.

Understanding

Good communication is often erroneously defined by the communicator as agreement, rather than clarity of understanding. If someone disagrees with us, it's not unusual to assume that the person just didn't fully understand our position. What happens is that many of us define good communication as having someone accept our views. But a supervisor can very clearly understand what you mean and not agree with what you say. In fact, often when observers conclude that a lack of communication must exist because a conflict has continued for a prolonged time, a close examination reveals that there is plenty of communication going on.

Yes, there is a lot of communication, but unfortunately little or no understanding. First, there must be understanding; then there is a basis for agreement. Without mutual understanding, two people may actually agree and not know it. Worse yet, without it two people may think they agree but be on opposite sides of an issue.

Environment (the Setting)

A communication—or, in terms of an organizational setting, a communication system— provides the means by which information, vision, values, and instructions are transmitted through a department. Although one often speaks of the "flow" of communications, this flow actually consists of a series of discrete messages of different length, form, and content. These messages are transmitted through certain channels (or lines of communication), which make up the communication system or network. Each message is sent by a transmitter (an individual, a group, a division, a computer) to a receiver or several receivers.

WHAT WE KNOW ABOUT COMMUNICATIONS

What knowledge exists about communications is scattered over numerous disciplines and fields and is often contradictory. In many ways, what we know about communications has been derived from our failures, rather than from our successes. Sufficient evidence is now before us to conclude that communications (1) is perception; (2) is expected; (3) makes demands; (4) is related to, but different from, information; (5) is marginal when one-way; and (6) is best when accomplished by example. These six dimensions are explained next.

Perception

Paradoxically, it is the recipient who communicates, rather than the person who initiates the message. (Hence the truism—a leader cannot lead until he or she has a follower.) While the communicator speaks, writes, or gesticulates a message, communication does not occur until the receiver perceives it. Keep in mind that perception is a total experience, as opposed to logic. And receivers vary in their sensory and mental capacities to perceive data inputs. Hence the first question that the communicator must ask before sending a message is "Can the receiver perceive it?" That is, is the receiver sensorially and cognitively capable of accepting and conceptualizing the message? The second question concerns the values, attitudes, and emotions of the recipient. Thus the query, "What is the receiver's particular mental set at this time?" The communicator is therefore dealing with psychophysiological paradigms that determine whether the message is received and how it is interpreted.

Expectations

In most instances, we perceive what we expect to find in the message. The unexpected or unwanted data is frequently ignored or filtered in line with our expectations. Basically, our human mind seeks to fit incoming data into a preestablished pattern of expectations. Consequently, before we attempt to communicate, we must predict what the recipient expects to hear or see. And we should keep in mind that minor incongruities will probably be rejected or distorted to fit the pattern. Thus if the data is important, the communicator may find it necessary to apply sufficient "shock" or drive to the message so that it disturbs the pattern and alerts the recipient that the unexpected is occurring.

Demands

The prime usage of communications is to make decisions. Therefore it is always making demands on us to change or continue to do what we are doing, believe or not believe, and act or not act. Usually, such demands are gradual or subliminal in that major demands are frequently resisted because they do not comply with the existing pattern of expectations.

Information

Information and communication, although different, are nevertheless interdependent. Information is formal and logical. Conversely, communication is personal and psychological. Indeed, communications can occur without information. As an example, we can share in an experience while not receiving the logic of information. Also of interest is the difference between effective information and effective communication. The former is specific, terse, and structured; the latter is subjected to varying perceptions, expectations, and demands. It is debatable whether information, once freed from these three conditions, becomes more informative or whether, on the contrary, it tends to lose its meaning.

Two-Way Is Good

One-way communication typically fails. It is ineffective for the obvious reason that we do not know if or how the recipient has perceived the message. Listening is important, but not sufficient to ensure that one has communicated. Moreover, the answer to better communications is clearly not more information. Usually, more information tends to widen the communication gap between the sender and the receiver (information overload). Aren't most of us today in need of more communication and less information?

> E-mail and fax messages are one-way communications.

By Example Is Much Better

The clearest, most convincing message to the receiver is the one conveyed by an example. The leader relies on furnishing examples of what is intended. The message in some way is demonstrated. It is experienced. If the subject matter is a complete and well-written crime report, then the supervisor will show the officer what one looks like along with an explanation and a two-way conversation. There are hundreds of written procedures, but rarely do they impart precisely what is expected. Good and bad police officer behavior is learned. Much of it is learned—by example—from the person's supervisor.

> Producing examples today is more and more difficult and frustrating for the supervisor. Mounds of paperwork, pervasive technology, and invasive procedures dictate the supervisor's time and attention. Field supervisors are being tied to their desks and captivated by their computers. Simultaneously they will know that first-line leaders, to be leaders, must be visible. Examples of what is expected are next to impossible to convey by e-mail, fax, telephone, or roll call conversations. "Tell me" doesn't cut it; "Show me" does.

It is the courageous supervisor who daily battles bureaucratic baloney and technological entrapments. This person realizes that to communicate and therefore provide leadership, you must provide examples. Being visible is a prerequisite for leadership by example. Being visible today is not easy, but then again neither is supervision, per se. If you're going to lead, then you've got to communicate successfully with your potential followers. This can't be accomplished from behind your desk while fixated on a computer screen and processing paper. If your priority is to be a leader, then you've got to be seen.

COMMUNICATION CHANNELS AND DIRECTIONS

Supervisors communicate in two channels that flow in three different directions.
The channels are

- Formal
- Informal

The directions are

- Down
- Up
- Across/diagonal

Formal channels are primarily configured for the downward and upward movement of information, although there is some across and diagonal movement of formal information. Informal channels use all four directions equally.

Formal Communication Channels

All organizations develop formal communication channels as a response to large size and the limited information-handling capability of each individual. The formal channels adhere to the recognized official structure of the organization. Accordingly, the formal communication channels transmit messages expressive of the legitimate structure of authority. Hence one usually sees formal orders and directives, reports, official correspondence, standard operating procedures, and so on. Those persons who emphasize going through channels are doing so in deference to the unity-of-command principle within the formal hierarchy.

Strict compliance with formal channels can be disruptive. These are disruptions primarily of time, creativity, and experience. First, it takes a long time for a formal message from a supervisor in one division to pass to another supervisor in another division. Second, formal messages are on the record and thus restrict the free flow of ideas. As an example, police officers may not want to expose their ideas to their supervisors for the time being, even in rough form yet any formal communication is immediately routed through the originator's supervisor. Third, in practice a formal communication system cannot cover all informational needs. Informational needs change quite rapidly, while the formal channels change only with considerable time and effort. The most urgent need for informal communication channels is to plug the gaps in the formal channels.

Informal Communication Channels

Regretfully, there are some who consider formal communication channels as the only way to transmit information necessary to the functioning of the organization. However, this precept is no longer as sacred as it once was. We are witnessing an interest in acquiring a better understanding of the informal organization along with its potential use. This interest and awareness quite naturally lead to a different perspective on the structuring of communication flow. This perspective does not confine organizationally useful communication to purely formal channels. It includes all the social processes of the broadest relevance in the functioning of any group or organization. Consequently, we now treat informal and personal communications as a supportive and frequently necessary process for effective functioning.

It is futile for police administrators to establish formal channels and assume that those channels will carry most of the messages. Ironically, the more restricted the formal channels, the greater the growth of informal ones.

We next proceed to an analysis of three kinds of informal communication channels.

Subformal. Subformal channels carry those messages arising from the informal power structure existing in every police organization. Every member of the department must know and observe informal rules and procedures about what to communicate and to whom. Such rules are rarely written down and must be learned by experience and example, a necessity that causes difficulties for newcomers.

There are two types of subformal communications: those that flow along formal channels, but not as formal communications, and those that flow along purely informal channels. Both types have the distinct advantage of not being official; therefore they can be withdrawn or changed without any official record being made. As a result, almost all new ideas are first proposed and tested as subformal communications. The vast majority of communications in police organizations are subformal.

Subformal channels become all the more necessary under certain conditions. First, the greater the degree of interdependence among activities within the department, the greater the number and use of subformal channels. Second, the more uncertainty about the objectives of the department, the greater the number and use of subformal channels. When the environment is relatively unpredictable, people cannot easily determine what they should be doing simply by referring to that environment. Consequently, they tend to talk to one another more to gain an improved understanding of their situation. Third, when a police organization is operating under the pressure of time, it tends to use subformal channels extensively because there is often no time to use the formal channels. Thus police administrators reach out for information whenever they can get it from whatever channel is necessary. Fourth, if the divisions of a police organization are in strong competition, they tend to avoid subformal channels and communicate only formally. Conversely, closely cooperating sections rely primarily on subformal communications. Fifth, subformal communication channels are used more frequently if departmental members have stable, rather than constantly changing, relationships with one another.

Personal Task-Directed. A personal task-directed communication is one in which an employee deliberately reveals something of his or her own attitude toward the activities of the agency. While personal, this communication also relates to the goals or activities of the organization. Thus we can refer to it as task-directed. It possesses the following characteristics: First, task-directed personal channels are nearly always used for informing, rather than for directing. Second, before a person acts on the basis of information received through personal channels, he or she usually verifies that information through either subformal or formal channels. Third, this channel transmits information with considerable speed because there are no formal mechanisms to impede its flow. Fourth, because personal task-directed messages are transmitted by personnel acting as individuals, they do not bear the weight of the position emitting them. To this extent, they differ from subformal messages, which are transmitted by individuals acting in their official capacity—but not for the record.

Personal Non-Task-Directed.   This form of communication apparently does not contain information related to the task of the police department. Note the word *apparently.* Paradoxically, this channel may on occasion handle information far more valuable to the achievement of organizational goals than does any other channel, including the formal ones. An example of this channel is the supervisor learning through a friendly subordinate of the reasons for growing job dissatisfaction. First, non-task-directed channels furnish a vehicle for an individual to satisfy his or her social needs. In doing so, a person experiences a certain degree of need fulfillment that carries over into the job. Second, this channel provides a way for an individual to blow off steam over things that are disturbing. Third, non-task-directed channels frequently supply useful feedback to the management and supervisory levels. This feedback normally comprises unexpected information not obtainable in any other way. Fourth, personal channels offer the best medium for a person to become socialized in the organizational setting. Unwritten standards, group values, and "the way we do things here" are conveniently expressed through non-task-directed channels.

Downward Communications

Communications from supervisor to staff are primarily of five types:

- Job instructions: specific task directives
- Information needed to produce the understanding of the task and its relation to other organizational tasks: job rationale
- Information concerning organizational procedures and practices
- Feedback to the subordinate officer about his or her performance
- Information to instill a sense of mission: indoctrination of goals

1. *Job instructions.* The first type of message is most often given priority in police organizations. Instructions about the position of police officer are communicated to the person through direct orders from the supervisor, training sessions, training manuals, and written directives. The objective is to ensure the reliable performance of every police officer in the organization.
2. *Job rationale.* Less attention is given to the second type, which is designed to provide the police officer with a full understanding of his or her position and its relation to related positions in the same organization. Many police officers know what they are to do, but not why. Withholding information on the rationale of the job not only reduces the loyalty of the member to the organization but also means

that the organization must rely heavily on the first type of information, detailed instructions about the job. If a person does not understand why he or she should do something, or how his or her job relates to other jobs performed by coworkers, then there must be sufficient repetition in the task instructions so that the individual behaves automatically.

3. *Procedures and practices.* Information about organizational procedures supplies the role requirements of the organizational member. In addition to instructions about the job, the police officer is informed about other duties and privileges as a member of the police organization.

4. *Feedback.* Feedback is necessary to ensure that the organization is operating properly. It is also a means for motivating the individual performer. However, feedback to the individual about how well he or she is doing in the job is often neglected or poorly handled, even in police organizations in which the managerial philosophy calls for such evaluation.

5. *Organizational goals.* The final type of downward-directed information has as its purpose to implant police department goals, either for the total organization or for a major unit of it.

Size of the Loop. The size of the loop in downward communication affects organizational morale and effectiveness. In terms of morale, communications about the goals of the police organization cover in theory a loop as large as the agency itself. In practice, however, the rank-and-file officers are touched only minimally by this loop. Their degree of inclusion within the loop depends mainly on how they are tied into the police organization. If they are tied in on the basis of being rewarded for a routine performance, information about the goals and policies of the overall structure will be of no interest to them.

Next, the size of the loop affects the degree of understanding contained in a communication. Messages from top management addressed to all police personnel often are too general in nature and too far removed from the daily experiences of the line police officer to convey their intended meaning.

Upward Communications

Communications from subordinate to supervisor are also of chiefly five types:

- Information about his or her performance and grievances
- Information about the performance and grievances of others
- Feedback regarding organizational practices and policies
- Feedback concerning what needs to be done and the means for doing it
- Requests for clarification about goals and the mission

1. *Performance and grievances of the employee.* By our very nature, we want to know why. This is especially so when it comes to performance evaluations. Good, bad, or standard, we want to know the reasons for such judgments about our work. We

want examples, the facts about our rating. To get this information, we have to communicate upward. Similarly, when it comes to feeling unfairly treated, we seek an upward appeal—a second opinion—about what befell us.

2. *Performance and grievances of others.* We likewise want to ask similar questions about our coworkers. This is a touchy one because in some cases it may not be any of our business. However, if we're reprimanded for a mistake, and someone else commits the same one and is not reprimanded, we'll want to know why.

3. *Feedback on policies and practices.* Feedback is one form of two-way communication. Indeed, it may be the most important. "Do I understand this policy or practice correctly?" is a critical inquiry deserving the singular attention of the person being asked.

4. *Feedback on objectives and methods.* Later on I'll be covering managing by objectives (MBO) and how it motivates people into action. You'll find that without feedback, it crashes. The supervisor should be in a position to clarify, explain, and justify the objectives of the work unit and how the police employees ought to proceed to accomplish these objectives.

5. *Goal clarification.* Similar to the above, the police supervisor should be able to clarify, explain, and justify the overall goals and mission of the department.

Upward Is Tough.   There are enormous constraints on free upward communication, for a variety of reasons. Most prominent is the structure itself. Simply stated, bureaucracies or highly formalized police organizations tend to inhibit upward informal communications. In doing so, a tremendous amount of important information never reaches the upper-level decision centers.

Other factors adversely affect the upward flow of messages. Supervisors are less in the habit of listening to their staff than of talking to them. Furthermore, information fed up the line is often used for control purposes. Hence the supervisor is not likely to be given information by team members that would lead to decisions adversely affecting the staff. They tell the supervisor not only what they want to hear, but also what they want him or her to know. Employees do want to get certain information up the line, but generally they are afraid of presenting it in the most objective form. Full and objective reporting about one's own performance and problems is difficult.

For all these reasons, the upward flow of communication in police organizations is not noted for spontaneous and objective expression, despite attempts to formalize the process of feedback up the line. Importantly, it is a problem not of changing the communication habits of individuals, but of changing the operational conditions responsible for these habits.

Across and Diagonal Communications

Communications between police employees must occur out of necessity between work units that are located in different divisions. "Across" means a sergeant in patrol speaking to a sergeant in investigations. It also means a dispatcher in communications talking to a lieutenant in training. Communicating across and diagonally in a police organization ensures seamless operations. There are four reasons for across and diagonal communications:

- Information necessary to ensure teamwork
- Information for identifying and defining common problems to be solved through cooperation
- Feedback from coworkers that fulfills individual needs
- Information needed to provide professional guidance for a group so that it can maintain the members' compliance with its standards and values

1. *Teamwork.* Confusion, conflict, and frustration result from a lack of coordination between work units. If teamwork is not emphasized, detectives and narcotics officers could be investigating the same crime, one patrol unit could be messing up the operations of another, and so on.
2. *Common problems.* Weak horizontal and diagonal communications nearly guarantee that the root causes of a police problem will go undetected. When I discuss problem-oriented policing in a subsequent chapter, you'll gain an appreciation for a comprehensive (versus narrow) view of a police problem.
3. *Feedback on individual needs.* Most of us want to know what others think about our efforts. "Am I doing a good job?" "Am I trusted?" The answers to questions like these concern us. Some of this feedback occurs within the work unit. Clearly, it is also valued from coworkers in other work units.
4. *Professional guidance.* The sharing of information among police work units increases the probability that the various groups are acting in concert with approved service values and quality standards.

A Balance.   Organizations face one of their most difficult problems in procedures and practices concerned with lateral communication. A working balance must be found between unrestricted and overrestricted communications among peers in an organization. Unrestricted communications of a horizontal and diagonal character can detract from maximum efficiency because too much irrelevant information may be transmitted. At the opposite extreme, efficiency suffers if an employee receives all his or her instructions from the person above, thus reducing task coordination.

Communication across boundaries is usually overrestricted. If I had to choose between too much or too little, I would opt for the former. Teamwork depends on the speed and ease of movement of information from one departmental sector to another.

The type and amount of information that should be circulated on a seamless basis are best determined by answering the question "Who needs to know, and why?" To put it another way, the information transmitted should be related to the objectives of the various units in the police organization, with the primary focus on their major task. An interesting hang-up in horizontal communications occurs when people overvalue peer communication and neglect those below and above them: sergeants talking only to sergeants, lieutenants only to lieutenants, and so on.

HOW WE COMMUNICATE

The four major ways that we endeavor to communicate messages are

- Orally
- In writing
- Nonverbally
- Electronically

The four avenues of communication produce the total volume of messages received and sent by a police supervisor.

Oral Communication

The method most used by people to communicate with one another is the spoken word. Popular forms of oral communication include speeches, formal one-on-one and group discussions, and the informal rumor mill or grapevine.

The advantages of oral communications are speed and feedback. A verbal message can be conveyed and a response received in a minimal amount of time. If the receiver is unsure of the message, rapid feedback allows for early detection by the sender, and for correction.

The major disadvantage of oral communication surfaces whenever the message has to be passed through a number of people. The more people a message must pass through, the greater the potential for distortion. In a police agency where decisions and other information are verbally passed around the hierarchy, considerable opportunity exists for messages to become distorted.

Spoken messages are of two varieties: meetings (face-to-face communication) and telephone conversations (ear-to-ear communication).

- *Meetings.* A meeting involves a discussion among two or more people. Meetings have four purposes: (1) to provide a means for exchanges to take place quickly; (2) to provide a job environment in which members are stimulated to new ideas by the rapid exchange of views between individuals; (3) to reduce the amount of semantic difficulties through face-to-face interaction; and (4) to get the members attending the meeting committed more strongly to given proposals or procedures than they would be otherwise.

  There are two types of meetings: routine meetings, such as those of permanent committees, and ad hoc meetings, called to discuss particular issues. The difference between a routine meeting and an ad hoc meeting is similar to that between a routine report and a memorandum. Like a routine report, a routine meeting can be either time- or event-triggered, whereas an ad hoc meeting may either be called in regard to a request to consider a particular problem or be triggered by an event.

- *Telephone conversations.* Many of the comments made about meetings are pertinent to telephone communications. The distinction made earlier between routine and ad hoc communications may be useful here. There are, however, some noteworthy differences between the two media: (1) A telephone conversation is generally confined to two participants, and (2) it lacks certain unique characteristics of interaction that take place in a face-to-face exchange. The preceding two differences are being rapidly erased by technology that supports videoconferencing.

Words are the primary stock-in-trade of leadership, and all leaders use them to attract, hold, inspire, and galvanize their followers.

To be sure, the written word can sometimes be effective in motivating people. But the spoken word is by far the most powerful form of communication between a police supervisor and his staff. Nothing comes close to direct oral communication in terms of offering as wide a range of opportunities for a leader to inspire his followers and to learn what is on their minds. Any supervisor who thinks that an e-mail or a written memo is as meaningful as a face-to-face meeting is just dead wrong. There is a reason for this fact. Humankind has been communicating orally for hundreds of thousands of years, while the written word is a much more recent form of communication. Our brains are "prewired" in favor of the spoken word.

> If you want to really inspire your staff and reach them at their emotional core, you must speak to them in person.

Written Communication

Written communications include memos, letters, organizational periodicals, bulletin boards, and any other device that transmits information via written words or symbols.

Written messages have advantages because they are permanent, tangible, and verifiable. Typically, both the sender and the receiver have a record of the communication. The message can be stored. If there are questions concerning the content of the message, it is physically available for later reference. This is particularly important for complex or lengthy communications. A final benefit of written communications comes from the process itself. More care is taken with the written word than with the spoken word. Written communications are more likely to be well thought out, logical, and clear.

Of course, written messages have their drawbacks. They're time-consuming. You could probably say the same thing in ten to fifteen minutes that it takes you an hour to write. Thus while writing may be more precise, it also consumes a great deal more time. The other major disadvantage is feedback, or lack of it. Oral communications allow the receivers to respond rapidly to what they think they hear. However, written communications do not have a built-in feedback mechanism.

There are six basic characteristics of a well-written report, and each of these is equally important. A well-written report is

- *Accurate.* An accurate report is in exact conformity to fact.
- *Clear.* A clear report is plain or evident to the reader; the meaning is unmistakable.
- *Complete.* Reports must have all the necessary parts and include the who, what, when, where, why, and how. Crime reports must include the elements of the crime.
- *Concise.* A concise report expresses all the necessary information in as few words as possible, but it does not leave out some of the facts in the interest of brevity.
- *Factual.* A fact is something real and presented objectively. Facts are things the officer can prove or disprove. Inference and unsubstantiated opinion are not facts and must not be written in police reports. Unsubstantiated opinions are usually based on premises; however, they are sometimes based on prejudice and bias.

- *Objective.* Objective police reports are not influenced by emotion, personal prejudice, or personal opinion. Officers should record all the facts, remembering that
there is more than one side to each story.

Nonverbal Communication

Some of the most meaningful communications are transmitted neither verbally nor in
writing. These are nonverbal communications. A loud siren at an intersection tells you
something without words. A supervisor instructing a group of officers doesn't need words
to tell when the trainees are bored. The size of a person's office and desk and the clothes
a person wears also send messages to others. However, the most well-known areas of
nonverbal communication are verbal intonations and body language.

Verbal intonations are how we use the voice to emphasize words or phrases. A pleasant, smooth tone creates a different meaning than an intonation that is abrasive with
strong emphasis placed on the last word. Body language includes everything from facial
expressions to our sitting or standing posture.

Electronic Communication

Old communication paradigms are being replaced by new technologies and application dynamics. The Internet is generating unprecedented data traffic, and customers
are no longer tolerant of routine network downtime. But this evolution is about more
than data. It's about optical networking, which is creating virtually unlimited capacity
and mind-boggling speed. It's about wireless systems that offer mobility without
sacrificing quality or reliability. And it's about the need for networks of networks that
can handle data or voice, wired or wireless, and optical or electronic signals with
equal aplomb. It's not just a data-networking revolution or a voice-networking
revolution. It's a communications-networking revolution, and police agencies are at
the center of it.

> The communications revolution is really about liberating communications from the
> confines of one medium or protocol. It's about how and where and why we com-
> municate, and it will change forever the way we work, play, shop, and socialize.

The industrial age manufactured things, whereas the communications age is
intended to provide knowledge. The computer, and especially the personal computer
(PC), is presently the driving force. The PC has given us new applications, online
systems, Internet connections, electronic mail, multimedia titles, and a host of games.

Technological advancements are racing toward us all, creating a world in which
information is both advantage and freedom. This is a world where time and space are
decreased, where computers operate faster, taking up a fraction of the space and communicating across networks without borders. We hear it every day: "cyberspace,"
"wired," "on demand," "seamless access," and "virtual reality." But what does it all really
mean to you? Does it make your job easier? Does it make your life better? We are
becoming a society that is in touch, but . . . not touched!

Microsoft's Bill Gates asserts that the current information revolution, with all of its unresolved confusion and challenges, is but a porous foundation for the incoming second revolution in communications. (In fact, he refers to the present global information highway as more like a lot of country lanes.) The dimensions of the second revolution are less vague and will involve increasing speeds, inexpensive communications, global interconnections, and customer-driven applications. The most fundamental difference we'll see in future information is that almost all of it will be digital. The latter point means that the cyber-executives will ask us what we want and then they'll build it for us. Bill Gates sees technology as responsible for providing us with more flexibility and efficiency.

Forward-looking police leaders will have numerous opportunities to perform better in the years ahead if they are able to strike a balance between "high-tech" and "high-touch." An overconcentration on high-tech will cost them leadership; an overemphasis on high-touch will cause them obsolescence. While the Internet, e-mail, and fax machines have enhanced the movement of information, they in turn are impeding interpersonal communication. There is no substitute for face-to-face communications. We see "fax potatoes" emerging. They'll fax or e-mail you a message, rather than walk a few feet to communicate with you in person. Technology is frequently sold as the panacea of all work-related problems. It is alluring and habit-forming to the detriment of much-needed person-to-person contacts.

> We're getting tons of information with only a few pounds of knowledge.

WHY DON'T WE COMMUNICATE BETTER?

We started this chapter with the three main reasons why we communicate with one another:

- To be a leader
- To make decisions
- To establish trust

After covering what communication is, what we know about it, and where and how we do it, we've arrived at an end point of again asking why. Why aren't we doing a better job of understanding one another? We have the need; we have the training and education; we know it's vital for the supervisor, and we have incredible technology. But we're not as successful as communicators as we should or could be.

There are a few reasons and hundreds of excuses. I'll cover the reasons.

Failure to Listen Actively

The average person suffers from three delusions: (1) that he is a good driver, (2) that he has a good sense of humor, and (3) that he is a good listener. Despite these widely held beliefs, most supervisors (indeed, most people) are terrible listeners. Most prefer to talk rather than to listen.

> Good leaders are artful listeners, and vice versa.

The police leader who can turn listening into an art is one who, rather than listening passively, encourages others to speak and actively listens to what is being said. In the process, this type of leader not only receives the information being conveyed but also gains valuable insights into the filters, biases, and opinions of the speaker. For the police supervisor who aspires to excellence in leadership, artful listening isn't just an asset; it's a necessity.

Active listening, accompanied by relevant questioning of the speaker, helps the leader determine the quality of the information being reported and the degree of accountability of the person reporting it. In turn, through the active listening process, the speaker is led to the realization that he will be held accountable for his ideas and recommendations.

> Artful listening also means knowing when to stop listening and make a decision to tackle a problem, delegate it, or do nothing about it.

Understand First—Empathic Listening.   The key to influencing another person is first to gain an understanding of that person. As a supervisor, you must know your staff to influence them. Most of us are prone to want the other person to open his or her mind to our message. Wanting to understand the other person requires that we open our mind to him or her.

Consider this scenario. Sergeant Ker says to Sergeant Paulson, "I can't understand Officer Hooper. He just won't listen to me." Sergeant Paulson replies, "You don't understand Hooper because he won't listen to you?" Ker answers, "That's what I said." Paulson remarks, "I thought that to understand another person, you needed to listen to him!" Ker realized that he didn't communicate with Hooper because he didn't understand him!

When we seek to understand, we are applying the principle of empathy. *Empathy* is a Greek word. The *em-* part of *empathy* means "in." The *-pathy* part comes from *pathos,* which means "feeling" or "suffering." Empathy is not sympathy. Sympathy is a form of agreement, a form of judgment. We have empathy, then, when we place ourselves within the other person, so to speak, to experience his feelings as he experiences them. This does not mean that we agree but simply that we understand the other viewpoint.

Once we understand, we can proceed with the second step of the interaction: seeking to be understood. But now it is much more likely that we will actually be understood because the other person's drive to be understood has been satisfied.

> • To understand another person, we must be willing to be open to that person's thoughts.
> • When we are open, we give people room to release their fixed positions and consider alternatives.
> • Seeking first to understand lets us act from a position of knowledge.
> • By seeking to understand, we gain influence in the relationship.
> • Seeking first to understand leads us to discover other options.

When we seek to understand, people become less defensive about their position. They become more open to the question "How can we both get what we want?" As they get their position out of the way, they begin to see their values more clearly so that they can use them as guidelines for creating and evaluating other options.

STRUCTURED EXERCISE 5–1

Complete this exercise by yourself. Then, if others are available, brainstorm the possible answers as a group.

1. Identify a situation in which you should use the skill and attitude of empathy.
2. What benefit might occur from your use of empathy in this situation?
3. What might happen if you don't use empathy?
4. Would it be helpful to inform the other person of your intention to try to be a better listener and to ask for his or her support as you try out this approach? Explain.

Empathic listening is particularly important under three conditions:

- When the interaction has a strong emotional component
- When we are not sure that we understand
- When we are not sure the other person feels confident that we understand

The following three techniques will assist you in listening with an empathetic ear:

- *Listen with the eyes.* To truly understand, we must listen to more than words. Words are weak compared with the richness and complexity of the ideas that we need to express. They are particularly poor at expressing feelings, for example, and yet feelings are often the thing that people most want us to understand. So when we seek to understand, we must look beyond the surface issues that the words describe to consider how people feel.

- *Develop a win-win attitude.* The most vital part of empathic listening is developing a win-win attitude. Win-win requires a nexus of courage and consideration. It will give us success even when we are not adept at the skill. As we learn the skill, we will be that much better.

    Empathic responses will destroy understanding if the attitude behind them is wrong. The danger of empathic listening is that we may use it because we believe that it "works." We may see it as a tool for getting what we want or for manipulating people. If we use it with wrong intentions, we corrupt the skill. Empathic listening creates positive results only when we accept it as a useful principle and use it solely with the intent to understand.

- *Now be understood.* Once we understand, we can then proceed to be understood. This is related to the earlier comment that win-win is a balance between courage and consideration. Understanding the other person shows consideration. Being understood takes courage. Both are necessary conditions for win-win agreements.

If, in the course of being understood, we sense resistance, we have another opportunity to choose again either to be defensive or to seek to understand. So we may find ourselves moving back and forth between seeking to understand and seeking to be understood. The process is complete when both parties feel understood and when their interaction has given them a foundation for discovering other options. This provides a basis for empowerment. (See Responsibility 8.)

Communication Overload

Communication is costly. Every message involves the expenditure of time spent deciding what to send, the time spent composing the message, the cost of transmitting the message (which may consist of time or money or both), and the time spent receiving the message. Consequently, the volume of messages in an organization is of real concern to everyone. The more information there is, the more difficult it is for communication to succeed.

Every individual has a saturation point regarding the amount of information that can be usefully handled in a given time period. In this case, both the volume and the length of the message can overload an individual beyond the saturation point. When overloaded, a person will be unable either to comprehend the information provided or to use it effectively. The methods used by a police organization to collect, select, and transmit information are critically important determinants of its performance.

The volume of messages in a police agency is determined by seven basic factors:

- The total number of members in a work unit
- The nature of its communication networks (downward, upward, or seamless)
- The transmission regulations controlling when and to whom messages are sent
- The degree of interdependence among the organization's various activities
- The speed with which relevant changes occur in its external environment
- The search mechanisms and procedures used by the agency to investigate its environment
- The amount and type of communications technology in the department (e.g., everyone has a cell phone)

The greater the message volume, the more the overloading. Police supervisors can react to this situation in one or more of the following ways. First, they can slow down their handling of messages without changing the organization's network structure or transmission rules. This action will cause the police department to reduce its speed of reaction to events and thereby lessen its output. Second, they can change the transmission rules so that their subordinates screen out more information before sending messages. This reaction also reduces the quantity of the department's output. Third, they can add more channels to the existing network to accommodate the same quantity of messages in the same time period. This reaction provides more opportunities for messages in the same time period. This reaction provides more opportunities for message distortion and is more expensive. Fourth, they can relate tasks within the department so that those units with the highest message traffic are grouped together within the overall communications system. This action reduces the volume of messages sent through higher levels in the network and facilitates the coordination of effort. Fifth, they can improve the quality of the messages in order to reduce the time needed for receiving, composing, and transmitting them. Currently the major culprit causing information overloads is "infotech."

Infotech Abuse

Supervisors' energy is being suffocated and their time trapped by infotech. They're being buried in an avalanche of paper, accosted by more and more telephone calls, and bombarded by incessant e-mail. Many are also being burdened by "collateral" assignments. Now the kicker: They're expected to lead others, which means being visible, being in front, and serving as an example to their team members. Something's got to give here.

It's not easy to develop trust and attain understanding in an e-mail or fax message. One-way messages are typically impersonal. Worse still, such infotech encourages us to be the great communicator. "With one touch of a key I can send my message to tens, hundreds, or more people." This thinking is the cause of overloads and confusion. Infotech has its place. If used properly, it promises many advantages. If abused, it reduces the supervisor's chances of becoming a leader. Use infotech as necessary, but remember—it is not leadership.

Diversity

One's culture consists of such prominent factors as demographics, language, mores, art, music, and religion. Culture differences usually present a challenge to achieving mutual understanding. Think about it; you're a police supervisor, and your new team member is from a different culture. English is a second language, and the mores, music, and art are "diverse." Now, add religion to this mix. You have a definite challenge in bridging cultural diversity while cementing foundations of understanding.

In respect to gender differences, the French say, "Vive la différence." Across the world, men and women continue to seek answers to our inability to better understand each other. Researchers are concentrating on the reduction of eons of confusion. (See, for example, John Grey's *Men Are from Mars, Women Are from Venus*.) As more women engage in police work, supervision, and management, miscommunication is exacerbated. Many of us are prone to rationalize or outright ignore the situation. By now you may be looking for a pat answer to centuries of gender-driven misunderstanding. There isn't any.

Little attention is paid to the many generations that must coexist in our world as being not just an issue but a major problem in our quest for better understanding. We hear and read about such generations as "Baby Boomers," "Gen-Y," "Gen-X," and the venerated "Great Generation." Each one has its own paradigms on values, ethics, family, happiness, and so on. The older generations typically disparage the younger ones. At times it seriously injures mutual understanding.

The police sergeant of one generation thinks, "The new officers are all screwed up." The officer thinks, "Wow, are these supervisors out of touch." Each generation reaches for the easy explanation; it must be a difference (conflict) in our race, gender, or culture. Thus ignored is how enormous and incredibly complex our generational differences are. And how powerful they are in messing with our need and ability to learn from one another.

STRUCTURED EXERCISE 5–2

This is an awareness exercise. The questions require thoughtful answers—no rationalizations, wishes, or "sounds good to me" allowed. The exercise also encourages feedback. (Leaders thrive on feedback.) Circle the number that reflects where you are now on a particular dimension, and box the number where you hope to be in twelve months.

	Miss a Lot					Very Active	
Listening	1	2	3	4	5	6	7
	Misuse It					Use Properly	
Infotech	1	2	3	4	5	6	7
	Unaware					Very Aware	
Race	1	2	3	4	5	6	7
	Unaware					Very Aware	
Culture	1	2	3	4	5	6	7
	Unaware					Very Aware	
Gender	1	2	3	4	5	6	7
	Unaware					Very Aware	
Generation	1	2	3	4	5	6	7

The next step is important. Ask someone whom you respect and who is candid to respond to each question for you. Compare your responses. What have you learned about your ability to communicate with other people?

KEY POINTS

- Communication is our most important and learnable human skill.
- The supervisor communicates to be a leader, to make decisions, and to establish trust.
- Communication is the transfer of meaning so that understanding will occur within a particular environment.
- Communication is influenced by our perceptions and expectations. It makes demands on us and is related to but different from information. It is best when not "one-way," and better still by example.
- Communication channels are of two types (formal and informal), and they flow in three directions: down, up, and across/diagonal.
- We transmit messages four ways: orally, in writing, nonverbally, and electronically.
- The spoken word is by far the most effective type of communication.

- The volume of messages received and sent by supervisors affects their effectiveness. Too many is as harmful as not enough.
- The barriers to improved understanding within a police agency center on failure to listen actively, communication overload, infotech abuse, and diversity.

EXTENDED LEARNING

1. What are other reasons we communicate besides those cited at the beginning of the chapter?
2. What information do we usually find moving in a formal channel, as compared with informal channels?
3. Of the four main methods for communicating, which is best? Why?
4. In which direction is it most difficult for a supervisor to communicate (up, down, or across/diagonally)? Why?
5. Of the five communication networks, which is best? Why?
6. What have you or your organization done recently to improve the communication process?
7. When have you either performed or observed empathic listening? What did the listener actually do?
8. How has communication technology helped you in your job? How has it caused you problems?
9. Review with others the results of Structured Exercise 5–2. Afterward, generate an action plan for correcting any deficiencies in the group members' ability to understand one another.

RESPONSIBILITY **6**

Time Management

> The police supervisor is responsible for self-discipline, which ensures precious time for making prudent decisions on job-related matters.

> Now that you have acquired a greater understanding and appreciation of your values (Responsibility 2) and ethics (Responsibility 3) and of how to communicate (Responsibility 5) a vision (Responsibility 4), you are prepared to manage yourself, and in turn your time, in their application.

Nine-tenths of wisdom is being wise in time.

—Theodore Roosevelt

> My time is very important to me. When I waste my time, I'm frustrated, even sore. I'm sure you feel the same. Time is one of our top values, yet it seems we have so little of it. This chapter will help you master time as a police supervisor.

Imagine there is a bank that credits your account each morning with $86,400. It carries over no balance from day to day. Every evening the bank deletes whatever part of the balance you failed to use during the day. What would you do? Draw out every cent, of course!

Each of us has such a bank. Its name is Time. Every morning it credits you with 86,400 seconds. Every night it writes off, as lost, whatever of this you have failed to invest to good purpose. It carries over no balance. It allows no overdraft. Each day it opens a new account for you. Each night it burns the remains of the day. If you fail to use the day's deposits, the loss is yours. There is no going back. There is no drawing against "tomorrow." You must live in the present on today's deposits. Invest your time to get from it the utmost in health, happiness, and success! The clock is running.

Have you ever heard or used the expression "I'll save some time by taking this approach"? Or "I really lost a lot of time by doing it that way"? Time is not ours to bank or spend. It is a precisely measured period of seconds, minutes, and hours that eventually become a day.

> On May 6, 1954, Roger Bannister achieved a major breakthrough in time: He ran a 3:59:6 mile. Now many track athletes have run a sub-four-minute mile. Will this year see a sub-three-and-a-half-minute mile or a sub-two-minute-mile marathon? The athletes who will eventually succeed in doing so will not be managing time; they'll be managing themselves.

Once you've finished this chapter, you'll be managing your time by better managing yourself. If you truly intend to manage your time, this responsibility will require much more thought and effort than the mere number of pages would suggest. You'll discover that much of what you will do depends on the accomplishment of the last four responsibilities. If you have those well in mind, you'll find the steps necessary for fulfilling Responsibility 6 to be richly rewarding and even fun. Moreover, you'll be closer to what you seek to become—a police supervisor and a leader.

A COUPLE OF QUESTIONS FOR YOU

On a sheet of paper, write down short answers to the following questions. (Later on you'll find that your responses are important, so be certain to write down your answers.)

First, what one thing could you do consistently (but are not doing now) that would make a significant change in your personal life?

Second, what one thing would cause similar results in your career life?

A PURPOSE-DRIVEN LIFE

> We gain control of time and events by understanding how they relate to a purpose-driven life.

Responsibility 6 is the exercise of our independent will to become a more effective supervisor, which automatically means a more effective person. We do not lead a compartmentalized life. The various roles that we play out in life definitely overlap and influence one another. If you spot a wise time manager at work, you'll probably discover that this individual also prudently manages time as a father or mother, family member, sports participant, hobby enthusiast, and so on. Conversely, the worker who is managed by time, misses deadline dates, is late for work, or is unprepared to do the tasks is probably the same way in attempting to fulfill other life roles.

> Your approach to time management must involve the total you. Dealing with your role of supervisor exclusively would be meaningless, or at best a long list of "to-do's," many of which would never get done. Obviously, we'll concentrate on making your time at work more productive. At the same time, remember that when I use the term *purpose*, I mean your purpose-driven life—the total you.

PEOPLE, PEOPLE, PEOPLE

A nationally recognized business leader wrote, "My firm basically is comprised of manufacturing, service, and people. In order of importance they are: people, people, people."

If you accept the preceding premise that people are a police agency's greatest asset, then supervisors must understand how to bind them together in a culture wherein they feel truly motivated to achieve high goals. Face-to-face communication, ongoing training and development, creative incentive programs, and job security all display the sort of sensitivity that nurtures strong departmental cultures. Every strong culture derives from management's sensitivity. Without it, police employees feel unmotivated, underused, and even exploited. Building the kind of work culture and work team you want obviously takes time. Quality time. Priority time.

THE TIME DIMENSION

> Time\tim\n[Me,fr]: the measured or measurable period during which an action, process, or condition exists or continues.

One complexity is ever-present in every supervisory job: Every decision, every action demands due consideration of the time dimension. Supervisors have to assess both today and tomorrow—the present and the future. Little Orphan Annie sang in the musical of the 1980s, "Tomorrow, tomorrow, tomorrow is only a day away."

The challenge of harmonizing today and tomorrow exists in all areas—and especially with people. The time dimension is inherent in supervision because supervisors are concerned with decisions for action. The time dimension influences decisions for progress (e.g., crime reduction, crime prevention). Finally, the supervisor's time dimension entails the future. The successful police supervisor constantly prepares for the future—the next event, the next decision, the next risk—all the while knowing that they'll be different. A time for action, a time for progress, and a time for tomorrow—you've got to get a grip on this threefold time dimension.

SELF-MASTERY OF TIME

One of Albert Einstein's brilliant contributions to modern physics was his intuition that linear time, along with everything happening in it, is superficial. Time seems to flow and move; clocks tick off their seconds, minutes, and hours; eons of history unfold and disappear. But ultimately, Einstein held, this vast activity is all relative, meaning that it has no absolute value.

Einstein displaced linear time with something much more fluid—time that can contract and expand, slow down and speed up. He often compared this to subjective time, for he noted that a minute spent sitting on a hot stove seems like an hour, while an hour spent with an attractive companion seems like a minute. What he meant by this is that our perception of time depends on our situation.

We all have a sense that time expands and contracts, seeming to drag one moment and race the next, but what is our constant, our absolute? It is "me," our core sense of self. The clock doesn't lie about how much linear time has elapsed "out there." But subjective time, the kind that exists only "in here," is a different matter. If you're bored, time hangs heavy; if you're desperate, time is running out; if you're exhilarated, time flies; when you're in love, time stands still.

> Whenever you take an attitude toward time, you are really saying something about yourself. Time, in the subjective sense, is a mirror.

Time Pressure = Stress

Time pressure causes stress hormones to be released into the body, which in turn elevates heartbeat. If the person struggles against this reaction, the situation only gets worse. Now his heart has to put up with time pressure and frustration. When heart patients are given demanding tasks under a deadline, a significant number grow so agitated that their heart muscles actually suffer "silent" heart attacks ("silent" meaning that damage is occurring but without any sensation of pain).

The element of time pressure also alters behavior, attitudes, and physiological responses. Subjective time can be an incredibly powerful force. It's no accident that the word *deadline* contains the word *dead*.

Some people are much more sensitive to stress than others. One feels time pressure as a threat; the other feels it as a challenge. One feels thrown out of control; the other feels impelled to test his or her sense of control and improve on it. You'll learn more about this issue in Responsibility 10, Vitality.

Boundaryless Time

We are the only creatures on earth who can change our biology by what we think and feel. Being able to identify with a reality that is not bounded by time is extremely important; otherwise, there is no escape from the tyranny that time inevitably brings. Linear time

STRUCTURED EXERCISE 6–1

Choose a time of day when you feel relaxed and unpressured. Sit quietly in a comfortable chair and take off your watch, placing it nearby so that you can easily refer to it without having to lift or move your head very much. Now close your eyes and be aware of your breathing. Let your attention easily follow the stream of breath going in and out of your body. Imagine your whole body rising and falling with the flow of each breath. After a minute or two, you will be aware of warmth and relaxation pervading your muscles.

When you feel very settled and quiet inside, slowly open your eyes and peek at the second hand of your watch. What's it doing? Depending on how relaxed you are, the second hand will behave in different ways. For some people, it will have stopped entirely, and this effect will last up to perhaps three seconds. For other people, the second hand will hesitate for half a second and then jump into its normal ticking. Still other people will perceive the second hand moving, but at a slower pace than usual. Unless you have tried this little experiment, it seems very unlikely, but once you have had the experience of seeing a watch stop, you will never again doubt that time is a product of perception. The time you are aware of is the only time there is.

(the clock) fools us into thinking that one minute follows another with equal spacing, but change your reference for a moment to *subjective time*. You can catch a glimpse of timelessness with a simple mind-body exercise.

Eastern philosophy and Western science together inform us that:

- While perception appears to be automatic, it is in fact a learned phenomenon. The world you live in, including the experience of your body, is completely dictated by how you learned to perceive it. If you change your perception paradigm, you change the experience of your body and your world.
- Time does not exist as an absolute, but only in relationship to eternity. Time is quantified by eternity, timelessness chopped up into bits and pieces (seconds, hours, days, years) by us. What we call "linear time" is a reflection of how we perceive change.

TIME AND PRODUCTIVITY

Most of us want to feel productive. Those who do feel this way do not want to waste their time. After all, time is our most perishable resource. There is nothing less productive than the idle time of equipment (patrol cars) or the wasted time of highly paid and able police employees. Equally unproductive—even counter-productive—may be jamming more work effort into time than it will comfortably hold—for instance, the attempt to provide full patrol coverage by repeatedly paying overtime to officers who are daily becoming more fatigued and less quality-conscious.

Time and productivity are causally linked. You have to pay attention to both factors. However, solid time management is the forerunner of highly productive supervisors.

OVERLOADS

You will never find time for anything. You must make it.

—Charles Buxton

Many years ago you would hear police supervisors complain, "I don't get enough information to do my job." The 1950s started to flip such statements around, and today we hear, "Good grief! There's just too much information. I don't have the time to process it!"

There have never been more media—websites, blogs, new television networks and channels, video and film, magazines, newsletters, journals, and newspapers—dedicated to delivering you the changing news of the day. Compounding this is the computer—desktops, laptops, in-car terminals, and PDAs. You don't have to look for telephones today—they're in airplanes, trains, and automobiles and frequently on a person's hip. We have e-mail and voice mail. Then there is the omnipresent fax.

What are you absorbing? Do you have the time to process the multitude of incoming messages, much less add yours to the information glut? Incidentally, have you noticed that the so-called paperless society actually has more paper than before? And while you're receiving and sending more information much faster, much of it doesn't make sense, or you haven't the time to make sense out of it.

> Without a structure, a frame of reference, the vast amount of data that comes your way each day will probably whiz right by you.

Nearly four thousand years ago, probably in reaction to the overloads of his day, Lao Tzu wrote to the leaders of China,

> Endless drama in a group clouds consciousness. Too much noise overloads the senses. Continual input obscures genuine insight. Do not substitute sensationalism for learning.
>
> Allow regular time for silent reflection. Turn inward and digest what has happened. Let the senses rest and grow still.
>
> Teach people to let go of their superficial mental chatter and obsessions. Teach people to pay attention to the whole body's reaction to a situation.
>
> When group members have time to reflect, they can see more clearly what is essential in themselves and others.

It takes time for reflection. Overloads attempt to block such time allocation. The supervisor must assign reflection a high priority. Otherwise, any endeavor to manage one's time is doomed to fail.

TIME-OUT!

When we use or hear the term *time-out,* we commonly think of an athletic event (e.g., football) or perhaps parenting (e.g., "If you don't behave, I'm going to give you a time-out!"). For the police supervisor, a time-out equates to leisure time. And all police leaders are in desperate need of leisure time.

> The most valuable time is your own.

Leisure time is not a passive, nondirected, lackadaisical use of one's precious time. It's not "goofing off." On the contrary, leisure time, taking a time-out, is a period of active personal, fun, restful time. It is a time to relax, recreate, and recharge one's batteries.

We have been programmed to believe that fatigue is a sign of courage, that feeling exhausted and beat up makes us a hero. We've become a generation of people who worship their work and work at their play. Unfortunately, most police leaders schedule all sorts of work and even family time but woefully neglect their personal or leisure time. They forget the importance of time-outs. Granted, we should not put off until tomorrow what we can do today, but nor should we cram into today all of tomorrow and the next day. Leaders must learn the lesson of leisure. When was the last time you told yourself, "Time-out"?

Leisure is not idle time. Some of the most valuable work done in the world has been done at "leisure" and has never earned a salary. Leisure is activity undertaken by choice. In contrast, labor is compulsory. Most leisure time is spent doing what we enjoy; labor is doing what we must. In our on-duty time, we meet the needs and demands of others—managers, fellow supervisors, officers, and community members. But it is in our leisure time that we often encounter the opportunity to accomplish what is truly meaningful and purposeful in our lives. In leisure time, our minds and our emotions are free of the tyranny of immediate necessity, and we are able to think and act outside of the grit and grind of our routine obligations.

> A time-out to explore leisure activities will greatly enhance creativity, happiness, and vitality in all aspects of our personal and professional lives.

The word *leisure* comes from the Latin word *licere,* which means "to be permitted." If we are ever going to include leisure time in our daily lives, we must give ourselves permission to do so. It's a personal choice.

Dost thou love life? Then do not squander time, for that is the stuff
life is made of.

—Benjamin Franklin

STRUCTURED EXERCISE 6–2

HOW DO YOU EXPERIENCE TIME?

Read the following sentences, and check off each one that applies to you fairly often or that you generally agree with. Some of the statements in Part I may seem to contradict others in Part II, but that doesn't matter. Even if you have seemingly opposed traits and opinions, answer each statement on its own.

Part I

_____ 1. There's barely enough time in the day to do all the things I have to do.

_____ 2. I'm sometimes too exhausted at night to get to sleep.

_____ 3. I've had to abandon several important goals I set for myself when I was younger.

_____ 4. I'm less idealistic than I used to be.

_____ 5. It bothers me to let unpaid bills sit around.

_____ 6. I'm more cautious now about making new friends and entering serious relationships.

_____ 7. I've learned a lot from the school of hard knocks.

_____ 8. I spend more time and attention on my career than on my friends and family.

_____ 9. I could be a lot wiser about how I spend my money.

_____ 10. Life is a balance of losses and gains; I just try to have more gains than losses.

_____ 11. In a loving relationship, the other person should be counted on to meet my needs.

_____ 12. It sometimes hurts to remember the people I have let down.

_____ 13. Being loved is one of the most important things I can think of.

_____ 14. I don't like authority figures.

_____ 15. For me, one of the most frightening prospects about old age is loneliness.

Part I score: _____

Part II

_____ 1. I do what I love. I love what I do.

_____ 2. It's important to have a greater purpose in life than just family and career.

_____ 3. I feel unique.

_____ 4. Near-death experiences are very real.

_____ 5. I often forget what day it is.

_____ 6. I would describe myself as a carefree person.

_____ 7. It's a good thing to bring sexual issues out in the open, even when they are disturbing.

_____ 8. I work for myself.

_____ 9. It doesn't bother me to miss reading the newspaper or watching the evening news.

_____ 10. I love myself.

_____ 11. I've spent time in therapy or other self-development practices.

_____ 12. I don't buy into everything about the New Age, but it intrigues me.

(*continued*)

STRUCTURED EXERCISE 6–2 (continued)

_____ 13. I believe it is possible to know God.

_____ 14. I am more leisurely about things than most people.

_____ 15. I consider myself a spiritual person: This is an area of my life I work on.

Part II score: _____

Evaluating Your Score

Although everyone usually checks at least a few answers in both sections, you will probably find that you scored higher in one section than the other.

If you scored higher in Part I, you tend to be time-bound. For you, time is linear; it often runs short and will eventually run out. Relying on outside approval, motivation, and love, you have not grappled with your inner world as much as with the external one. You are likely to value excitement and positive emotions more highly than inner peace and nonattachment. You may cherish being loved by others too much and lose the opportunity to find self-acceptance.

If you scored higher on Part II, you tend to be timeless in your awareness. Your sense of loving and being loved is based on a secure relationship with yourself. You value detachment over possessiveness; your motivations tend to be internal rather than external. At some time in your life, you developed a sense of being larger than your limited physical self; your life may have been shaped by decisive experiences of a spiritual nature or your higher self. Where others fear loneliness, you are grateful for your aloneness. Solitude has developed your ability to know who you are.

IF IT'S WORTH DOING, IT'S WORTH DOING POORLY

Take a moment to reread the title of this section. This comment was made by a very successful person. Think about it. Before reading further, develop an argument for refuting or confirming "If it's worth doing, it's worth doing poorly."

Let us now add—to make the best use of your time, you have to make a habit of using it flat out. Conversely, do you not agree with the proposition that working hard is not necessarily the same as working smart? One more thought—are working hard and working fast synonymous?

Many of us prefer fast decisions to slowness and wrong ones to none at all. Throughout his writings, Tom Peters challenges us to "move, move, move." The preceding heading essentially means that if something is vitally important, make a decision quickly. It may cause less-than-perfect results (even poor results), but the fact remains that someone is taking on the problem. It's the quick and timely response, with the underlying knowledge that you're doing the best you can. Now the big "but"—slow decisions are usually better than fast ones. It has been demonstrated again and again that shared or participative decision making produces significantly better results. Further, shared decision making typically builds in a commitment on the part of those involved to implement it.

Fast or slow—which should it be? No doubt both approaches have an impact on your truly irreplaceable commodity: time. I believe the answer to this puzzle is both—sometimes a fast, sometimes a slow application of time. Both have their place in police organizations. An emergency situation (e.g., a robbery in progress) obviously requires quick decisions, a fast time frame. Many supervisors make all decisions quickly, when in most cases there is ample time to involve those who are going to be affected by the decisions. Getting one or two really good ideas normally requires getting a lot of ideas at first. Later we'll consider empowerment. Fast decisions impede empowerment.

I'm not against fast decisions. At times they're needed. What I am arguing for is flexibility. Sometimes fast, sometimes slow—it all depends on the situation.

> *The tyranny of the urgent will always outshout the essential nature of the important . . . if you let it.*
>
> —Charles R. Swindol

FOUR GENERATIONS OF TIME MANAGEMENT

According to Steve Covey, a management consultant, there are four generations of time management. Each one builds on the other. The first three conform to this axiom: Organize and execute around priorities. The first generation is characterized by notes and checklists. It essentially recognizes the varying demands made on our time. The second generation is epitomized by calendars and appointment books. Here we see an endeavor to schedule ahead. The third generation reflects the most prevalent form of time management. It takes the above two and adds the dimension of prioritization. It focuses on values toward which time and energy are allocated. (The higher the priority of a value, the more time spent.) It is planning with a purpose. The emerging fourth generation recognizes that time management is misconstrued! The challenge is not to manage time; after all, time by its very nature manages itself. Rather than concentrating on activities and time, the fourth generation emphasizes preserving and enhancing relationships and getting results through teamwork.

Time Management Matrix

The matrix in Table 6–1 categorizes activities or things as fast or slow and as critical or noncritical. Fast activities press us to respond now. Critical matters have to do with results, the fulfillment of our job duties.

Category I is both fast and critical. All of us operate on occasion in this area. Regretfully, some become habitual crisis people. Push, push, faster, faster. These people are frequently task-driven and aggressive. Unfortunately, they beat themselves up while tackling the crises. They experience stress, burnout, and overloads; they are always putting out fires. When exhausted, they often retreat to Category IV, with little attention paid to Category II. There are others who spend a lot of time in Category III, believing that they're in Category I. They are confronting crises all right, only the issues are relatively unimportant in terms of their mission. In fact, they are likely responding to the values and expectations of others. Those of us who spend most of our time in Categories III and IV basically lead irresponsible lives.

Category II is the crux of managing ourselves. It deals with things that do not require a fast response but are critical, such as trust building, enhancement of candid communications, long-range planning, physical exercise, preparation, and renewal. These are high-leverage, capacity-expansion activities.

TABLE 6–1   *Time Management Matrix*

FAST	SLOW
Critical Activities	
I	**II**
Crises (shots fired)	Prevention of conflicts
Pressing problems (computers down)	Relationship building
Deadline-driven projects (staff reports)	Recognition of new opportunities
	Planning, recreation
	Team building
Noncritical Activities	
III	**IV**
Interruptions, some calls (open door)	Trivia, busy work
Some mail, some reports (in-basket)	Some mail
Some meetings (roll call)	Some phone calls
Proximate, pressing matters (evaluation)	Time wasters
Popular activities (code 7)	Pleasant activities

Now take a look at the two answers you wrote down earlier. What category do they fit in? They probably relate to Category II, but because they do not require a ready-aim-fire response, we neglect them. Your effectiveness will grow measurably if you focus on them. They will make a tremendous positive difference in your professional and personal lives.

Just Say No

The only place to get time for Category II in the beginning is from Categories III and IV. You can't ignore the urgent and important activities of Category I, although it will shrink in size as you spend more time with prevention and preparation in Category II. But the initial time for Category II has to come out of III and IV. You have to be proactive to work on Category II because Categories I and III suck you in. To say yes to critical Category II priorities, you have to learn to say no to other activities, sometimes apparently urgent things. We expect kids to "just say no to drugs"; as adults, we are equally capable of just saying no to the time wasters.

Time Wasters

Complete Structured Exercise 6–3 before reading further.
    Now compare your list with those that are most commonly cited (in rank order):

1. E-mail
2. Internet
3. Telephone interruptions

STRUCTURED EXERCISE 6–3

The major contributors to wasting my time at work are as follows:

1. _____
2. _____
3. _____
4. _____
5. _____
6. _____
7. _____
8. _____
9. _____
10. _____

Compare your time wasters with those cited in the text. Look for similarities. Discuss what might be done to lessen their adverse impact on you and others in the group.

4. Drop-in visitors
5. Meetings (scheduled and unscheduled)
6. Crises
7. Lack of objectives
8. Ineffective delegation of responsibilities and too much involvement in routines and details
9. Too much work attempted at once and unrealistic time estimates
10. Lack of self-discipline

BECOMING A CATEGORY II POLICE SUPERVISOR

The objective of Category II supervisors is to manage their life effectively—from a center of sound principles, from a knowledge of their overall (career and personal) mission, with a focus on the "critical" as well as the "fast," and within the framework of maintaining a balance between increasing their actual production and increasing their capability for producing.

Category II organizing requires you to

• Produce an individual mission statement
• Identify your roles
• Select your goals
• Use weekly scheduling
• Take action and be flexible

Your Mission Statement

Return to Responsibility 2, Values, and write down on a separate sheet of paper the top six or seven values that you identified. Using those values, create a one-page mission statement for yourself. (It is likely this will take three or four drafts before you are pleased with it.)

Here's a hypothetical example: Phillip Clark, police sergeant, age 27, is married and has two children. Clark's core values are, in rank order, (1) integrity, (2) spouse, (3) children, (4) parents, (5) police work, (6) house, (7) financial security, and (8) physical and mental health. Here is what he might have written.

Mission Statement

Phillip D. Clark, age 27

My mission in life is to demonstrate integrity consistently in myself and with others as follows:

- I will love and care for my wife, being certain that she is receiving top-priority time.
- I will serve as an example of responsible citizenship for my children. They will be daily recipients of my love and help. . . .

Once you've finished your mission statement, you're ready to move to identifying your various roles in life.

Your Roles

The first step is to record your main roles. Write down what immediately comes to mind. You have a role as an individual. You may want to list one or more roles as a family member—husband or wife, mother or father, son or daughter, member of the extended family of grandparents, aunts, uncles, and cousins. You certainly want to list a few roles in your police job, indicating different areas in which you wish to invest time and energy on a regular basis. You may have roles in church or community affairs. (Your mission statement will coach you on what they are.)

You don't need to worry about defining the roles in a way that you will live with forever. Just preview the week, and write down the roles you expect to play during the next seven days. For example, our Sergeant Clark might list the following seven roles:

- Husband
- Father
- Son and brother
- Police sergeant—human relations
- Police sergeant—production
- Self-growth—mental and physical
- Investor

Note how Clark's values, mission statement, and roles are integrated, systematic, and indeed logically compelling. Complete this step for yourself now, and then proceed to the next.

Your Goals

It's late Sunday afternoon, and Sergeant Clark has set aside thirty minutes for managing himself during the coming week. He lists the following:

ROLE	GOALS
Husband	Discuss vacation plans; review life insurance; schedule dinner and a movie; ask about her job.
Father	Discuss schoolwork; play one group game; play one individual game; develop a new sport skill.
Son and brother	Phone parents; send photographs of family; write sister.
Police sergeant— human relations	Complete performance evaluations; counsel Officer Mead; meet with each officer for coffee (15 minutes each).
Police sergeant— production	Analyze called-for services; prepare a problem-oriented approach to a major need; assess assigned equipment.
Self-growth— mental and physical	Read assigned textbook chapters; read *Time* and fifty pages in fiction book; exercise five times for fifty minutes; read national newspaper daily.
Investor	Paint interior of small bathroom (first coat); read *Money* magazine; assess CDs.

You're probably wondering how in the world Clark is going to accomplish all of the preceding goals. At this point it is straightforward, and all he has to do is schedule. It is now your turn to specify your goals for the next week. Stop reading and do it now.

Your Schedule

Now you can look at the week ahead with your goals in mind and schedule time to achieve them. For example, if your goal is to telephone your parents, you may want to set aside a 15-minute block of time on Sunday to do it. Sunday is often the ideal time to plan your weekly organizing.

If you set a goal to become physically fit through exercise, you may want to set aside an hour three or four days during the week, or possibly every day during the week, to accomplish that goal. There are some goals that you may be able to accomplish only during work hours or some that you can do only on Saturday when your children are home. Do you now see some of the advantages of organizing the week instead of the day? Having identified roles and set goals, you can translate each goal to a specific day of the week, either as a priority item or, even better, as a specific appointment.

Let's return to our Sergeant Clark to illustrate what must be done at this juncture. To begin with, he has to (1) divide up the goals by day and (2) assign each goal a priority. We'll cover Monday and Tuesday as examples of what you'll soon be doing:

	MONDAY	**TUESDAY**
Priorities	**Complete Performance Evaluations**	**Meet with Officers**
	Meet with officers	Assess equipment
	Analyze called-for services	Counsel Mead
	Read assigned text	Read assigned text
	Exercise fifty minutes	Exercise fifty minutes
	Schoolwork	College class
Time	**Activity**	**Activity**
0500–0600	Awaken 0530	Awaken 0530
0600–0700	Jog	Drive to work
0700–0800	Drive to work	Lift weights
	Audiotape on current affairs	
0800–0900	Briefings/roll call	Briefings/roll call
0900–1000	Meeting with officers	Meeting with officers
1000–1100	Performance evaluations	Meeting with officers
1100–1200	Performance evaluations	Review reports
1200–1300	Lunch/read text	Lunch/read text
1300–1400	Analyze called-for services	Assess equipment
1400–1500	Field supervision	Counsel Mead
1500–1600	Field supervision	Field supervision
1600–1700	Report review	Report review
1700–1800	Drive home	Drive to college/dinner
1800–1900	Dinner	College course
1900–2000	Review schoolwork	College course
2000–2100	Games with children	College course
2100–2200	Alone time with wife	Drive home/wife

Action and Flexibility

With Category II weekly organizing, daily action becomes more of a response to daily adaptations, prioritizing activities and adjusting to emergent circumstances, relationships, and experiences in a systematic way. As mentioned earlier, you can analyze each incoming day and fine-tune your schedule as appropriate. You're now organizing and executing around your goals and priorities.

> While you cannot actually manage time, you can certainly manage yourself—if you choose to.

STRUCTURED EXERCISE 6–4

JOB-TIME ANALYSIS FORM

Take a few moments to concentrate on the key tasks that make up your job. The Job-Time Analysis Form will help you assess the specific areas of time management in which you need improvement. List the individual tasks you perform on the job, and complete each column for each task.

Job task	What percentage of my time does it consume?	What is its priority (high, medium, or low)?	Do I like or dislike performing it?	Can I delegate it?	Is it discretionary or nondis-cretionary?

After completing the Job-Time Analysis Form, review it for accuracy. Showing the analysis to colleagues at work and learning their opinion might be helpful in this respect. After ensuring the accuracy of the completed analysis, answer each of the following questions:

1. What unnecessary tasks am I performing?
2. On which tasks am I spending too much time?
3. On which tasks am I spending too little time?
4. What tasks am I performing that could be performed better by others?
5. What specific changes do I plan to make in the way I manage my time?

Turn to Structured Exercise 6–5, and fill in the blanks. (Remember to prioritize your goals before scheduling the specific activities.) For future time management planning, you're welcome to copy and use the form or design one of your own. Obviously, the time frames will vary according to night-shift or early-morning-shift work. Remember to keep the Category II activities prominent in your goal setting, prioritizing, and scheduling. (See Figure 6–1.)

There is only one moment in time when it is essential to awaken.
That moment is now.

—Buddha

Managing Priorities and Scheduling

WEEKLY WORKSHEET

Week of: _____

Roles	Goals	Weekly Priorities	Sunday	Monday	Tuesday	Wednesday	Thursday	Friday	Saturday
					Today's Priorities				
		Appointments/Commitments							
			8	8	8	8	8	8	8
			9	9	9	9	9	9	9
			10	10	10	10	10	10	10
			11	11	11	11	11	11	11
			12	12	12	12	12	12	12
			1	1	1	1	1	1	1
			2	2	2	2	2	2	2
			3	3	3	3	3	3	3
			4	4	4	4	4	4	4
			5	5	5	5	5	5	5
			6	6	6	6	6	6	6
			7	7	7	7	7	7	7
			8	8	8	8	8	8	8
			Evening	Evening	Evening	Evening	Evening	Evening	Evening

FIGURE 6–1   Fourth–generation management: five steps to effective management of priorities.

KEY POINTS

Fourth-generation management is devoted to ensuring that as we manage ourselves, we more effectively supervise others. It is a constant reminder that people are always more important than things. It has been successful for several reasons:

- It is value-laden; it encompasses our driving forces.
- It is conscience-focused; it helps us make the correct choices about what comes first, second, and so on.
- We can change our experience with time by changing what we think and feel.
- Time does not exist as an absolute.
- It defines our individual mission, including values and goals that are prioritized.
- It aligns various life roles, allowing us to schedule time accordingly.
- It provides an expanded framework for organizing by scheduling weekly activities.

EXTENDED LEARNING

1. If working as a group, divide into subgroups of five to six people, and review your responses to Structured Exercise 6–3. Then share the contents with one another. Attempt to identify one or two common time wasters.
2. At the beginning of this chapter, you wrote down the answers to two questions that I had posed. (See "A Couple of Questions for You.") Share your responses with your group. What are some interesting similarities? What are some unusual considerations?
3. Review the types of overloads that individuals in your group are experiencing both at work and in their personal life. Develop some tactics for handling or avoiding overloads.

4. What decisions should receive a fast response? Conversely, what decisions can and should take more time?

5. Reevaluate the Category II activities that I listed earlier. Expand on that list by adding activities. Next, identify one or more examples of each activity.

6. Share with your group your successes in developing and using a fourth-generation time management form.

7. What is meant by subjective time? Have you experienced it? If so, in what way?

PART 2

Team Building

RESPONSIBILITIES

Team Leadership

The police supervisor is responsible for cultivating the qualities of a team leader and then applying them in a productive, rewarding, and caring manner.

Responsibilities 2 through 6 covered the basics for building a team of employees. Responsibility 7 involves team leadership.

To lead in the twenty-first century, you'll need both competence and character.

—H. Norman Schwarzkopf

Police leaders really don't *run* organizations (although we often use that term in describing leadership). Rather, leaders lead individual followers, and team leaders lead teams of people. Regardless of a leader's approach to his or her staff—as individual officers or a team of officers—each staff member is a unique human being who must be respected and treated with dignity if the department is to flourish. An effective leader never forgets that it is the followers who give the leader credibility. It is they who define the leader.

Police work of this century will not belong to "supervisors" or those who make the members dance. It will belong to passionate, driven team leaders—those people who not only have enormous amounts of energy but who also can energize those whom they lead.

Controlling people, stifling them, keeping them in the dark, and wasting their time on trivia and reports are traits I associate with supervising. You can't implant teamwork in people. You have to nurture it and let it grow in them by allowing them to win and then rewarding them when they do. I never associate the word *supervisor* with passion, and I've never seen a leader without it. Above all else, team leaders are open. They go up, down, and around their agency to reach people. They're informal. They're straight with their team. They're inevitably accessible.

Before D-day, June 6, 1944, General Dwight D. Eisenhower joined the forces of several nations, made up of military personnel with different upbringings and conflicting ideas about fighting a war, and he forged them into a team. His emphasis on teamwork and his never-flagging insistence on working together were the most important reasons for his being selected as Supreme Commander of the Allied Expeditionary Force.

TEAM LEADERSHIP AT THE TOP

Since the mid-1980s, police organizations have grown more interested in encouraging high-quality teamwork. Despite the focus on the heroic personality of a police chief or sheriff, these organizations are moving toward being led by a team of managers and supervisors.

It is becoming less frequent that the individual sitting at the top of the pyramid is the sole leader. Rather, we see a group of people with shared responsibilities and clear accountabilities strategizing together, reaching decisions by consensus, coordinating implementation, and generally performing many, if not all, the functions previously performed by a police chief. Through this team leadership at the top, these police agencies are seeking ways of realizing all the talent and intelligence of all the employees.

There are at least two good reasons why the management/supervision team leadership form is on the rise. First, the problems our police organizations face today are enormously complex. The most difficult issues that a leadership team faces are often cross-disciplinary or cross-functional. They require a deep expertise in specific areas, complemented by insight into the interrelationships between functions. Few, if any, individuals have the intelligence and breadth to deal with this kind of complexity on their own, yet it must be dealt with. Consequently, major breakthroughs in teamwork are required.

Second, within the past decade there has been a change in the management of police organizations. Managers and supervisors, reconceiving their own job as setting forth broad visions and strategies, now empower their staff much more to plan and implement. In a police organization led by example, people are moved and convinced when they see a group of people at the top truly sharing a vision and strategy and modeling them in their behavior. When they don't see that commitment and congruency, their confidence and commitment will be less.

> Creating a competent team of police employees is a new dimension of supervision—and a demanding one. It may be a discipline in its own right. Collective leadership is as different from individual leadership as collective learning is different from individual learning. Mastering team leadership means mastering a larger and more complex learning agenda.

THE POLICE DEPARTMENT AS A VOLUNTARY ORGANIZATION

Authority flows from the bottom up! If you really do not want to work for an organization anymore, you can quit. You have that freedom of choice. (There are a few select organizations, such as prisons, where quitting is not an option.)

When you commence working as a police officer, you temporarily loan the department authority over you. If the department abuses it or fouls up in some way, you can merely take it back. As Johnny Paycheck sings, "Take this job and shove it. I ain't workin' here no more." Granted, finding another job may be difficult, but you do have a choice.

THE POLICE SUPERVISOR AS LEADER

Most police supervisors strive to be a leader. When approaching team leadership, however, many revert to their underlying beliefs about control and direction. They agree that leadership can be taught and learned, but they suspect that team leadership is just a fleeting fad. Supervisors get things done; police employees obey supervisors. Team leaders instill heart, passion, spirit, and vision in the work team.

- Police supervisors-as-leaders reinforce the idea that work accomplishment comes from great individual acts (usually theirs), rather than teamwork.
- Police supervisors-as-leaders want their subordinates to rely on them.
- Police supervisors-as-leaders begin to own their power and their successes.
- Police supervisors-as-leaders are expected to choose service over self-interest, but it seems the choice is rarely made.
- Police supervisors-as-leaders attempt to recreate themselves in "their people" so that their beliefs and actions become reproducible.

The current view of leadership does not leave much room for the idea of team leadership. We need a way to hold on to the initiative and accountability and vision of the team leadership idea and to abandon the inevitable baggage of superiority and self-centeredness.

THE POLICE SUPERVISOR AS TEAM LEADER

Team leadership asks us to be accountable for the outcomes of a work unit without acting to define purpose for others, control others, or take care of others. The current leadership theory is very different. When we train police supervisors or leaders, the topics of defining purpose, maintaining control, and taking care of others are at the center of the curriculum. We were raised to believe that if we are to be accountable, we need the authority to go with it. How many times have we heard the cry, "How can you hold me accountable without giving me authority?"

Team leadership questions the belief that accountability and empowerment go hand in hand. We can be accountable and empower police officers, operating from the belief that in this way police work is better served. Instead of deciding what kind of culture to create and thus defining purpose, team leaders can ask that each member of the work team decide what the workplace will become. Team leadership also asks us to forsake caretaking (mentoring is not caretaking), which is an even harder habit to give up. We do not serve other adults when we take responsibility for their well-being. We continue to care, but when we caretake, we treat others, especially those at the line level, as if they were not able to think for themselves. In our working relationships, we have begun to understand the downside of caretaking and the dominance that defining purpose for others can represent. What we have not yet done is to apply these concepts to the structure of how we supervise others.

> We are reluctant to let go of the belief that if we are to care for something, we must control it. There must be a way for us to be accountable for outcomes of a group of police employees without feeling that we must dominate them.

To want to see team leadership as simply a different form of leadership is to miss the key distinction. When we hold on to the wish for leaders, we are voting for control and accountability at the top. Looking for leadership is some blend of wanting to get on top or stay on top plus liking the idea that someone up there in my police department (my chief or my captain) is responsible for my well-being.

STRUCTURED EXERCISE 7–1

A team leader is, by definition, a highly adaptive person, open to change and free from conditioned responses. If you want to see whether you have learned the skills that make someone adaptable (e.g., a team leader), answer the following questions as they apply to you, assigning the following points:

Almost never applies	0 points	Usually applies	2 points
Sometimes applies	1 point	Almost always applies	3 points

1. When I am first confronted with a problem and have no idea how it can be solved, I take the attitude that the right answer will emerge.
2. Events in my life happen with their own right timing.
3. I feel optimistic about my future.
4. When someone rejects me, I feel hurt, but I accept that the decision was theirs to make.
5. I feel the loss of family and friends who have died, but the grief resolves itself and I move on. I don't try to bring back what cannot be brought back.
6. I feel committed to ideals larger than myself.
7. When I'm arguing with someone, I defend my position, but I also find it easy to acknowledge the rightness in the other side.

8. I vote the person, not the party.
9. I donate time to worthwhile causes, even if they are unpopular.
10. I am considered a good listener. I don't interrupt others when they talk.
11. If someone has a lot of emotion at stake in something, I will hear them out without expressing my views.
12. Given a choice between a high-salaried job that is fairly boring and a job I like doing at half the pay, I'll take the job I love to do.
13. My style of supervising other people is to allow them to do what they want rather than try to control them. I interfere as little as possible.
14. I find it easy to trust others.
15. I am not prone to worry; the ups and downs of difficult situations affect me less than most other people.
16. In a competitive situation, I am a good loser. I will say, "Good game," not "I wasn't at my best."
17. Being right in every situation isn't all that important to me.
18. I feel comfortable playing games and laughing.
19. I don't think about my moods very much.
20. I can easily feel what someone else is feeling.
21. Quiet people make me feel comfortable. Nervous people don't make me nervous.

Total score: _____

Evaluating Your Score

50 Points or Over. You are an exceptionally adaptable person. Others seek you for guidance. You place a high priority on your ability to remain comfortable under pressure. You pride yourself on being able to resolve conflicts well.

30–49 Points. You are reasonably adaptable to everyday challenges. You are the kind of person whom others consider easygoing, but you are likely to have some worries and regrets. Conflicts upset you, and you tend to fall under the influence of people with emotions stronger than yours.

20–29 Points. You have definite ideas of right and wrong behavior and put a high priority on defending your point of view. You are likely to be well organized and decidedly goal oriented. If you find yourself in a situation of conflict or competition, you really want to be on the winning side.

Under 20 Points. Your sense of self needs considerable work. You fear rejection and become upset or critical when others disagree with you. You have your way of doing things and do not like surprises. You are likely to be obsessively orderly, with lots of hidden worry, or else very disorganized, reacting strongly to one external event after another.

The purpose of the findings is not to make anyone feel superior or inferior, but to spur conscious growth. The common denominator of all team leaders is that they actually work, on a daily basis, at having an open mind.

TEAM LEADERSHIP AND EMPOWERMENT

Because it exercises accountability, but centers on service rather than control, team leadership is a means to affect the degree of empowerment each employee feels for the success of the work team and even the police agency.

> Empowerment has to be felt strongly at every level—from bottom to top—for community-oriented policing to succeed. Team leadership gives us the guidance system for navigating this intersection of supervision, followership, and empowerment.

What is troubling about an idea like team leadership is that even though it is intuitively appealing, it seems removed from the heart of the way we run our police organizations. There needs to be a clear connection between the idea of team leadership and the achievement of measurable results (e.g., crime reduction) for the department. If we do not have a strong reason to initiate significant improvement in our police agencies, no real progress will take place.

AUTHORITY AND POWER

Authority

In one police agency, I noticed that the police chief managed and that his assistant chief managed and led. Briefly, the chief used the authority of his office to gain compliance and provide direction for achieving results. Authority is the right to command. The assistant chief had the same right and executed it at times. However, he more often relied on his leadership, or his individual capacity for managing. Although both were successful managers, the assistant chief demonstrated more effectiveness in achieving results than did the chief.

All police supervisors have authority, the right to command. As a police supervisor, your authority originates in your position. Your position grants you the right to reward and sanction the behavior of those who work for you. In other words, all three—position + rewards + sanctions—provide you with authority. And when you exercise your authority, you are attempting to influence the attitudes and behavior of others. If they comply, then your authority is working well.

Position.   By its very definition, your position is to command or influence the acts of others. The statement of your duties, your stripes, your salary, your training, and so on attest to the responsibilities of the job.

Rewards.   Your authority to reward is based on the right to control and administer rewards to others (such as money, promotions, or praise) for compliance with the agency's requests or directives.

Sanctions.   Your authority to sanction is based on the right to control and administer punishments to others (such as reprimands or termination) for noncompliance with the agency's requests or directives.

Power

Supervisors, because of the responsibilities of their position, acquire the right or the authority to command. With this right or authority comes influence. Hence police supervisors are strategically located for moving an agency toward goal attainment. It is the effective supervisors who develop their talent for leading others and consequently possess a significantly enhanced influence (authority + power) for achieving results— for achieving results effectively.

Fundamentally, your power is person-based as opposed to position-based. Your power to lead others is derived from your expertise and example. Both combine to attract others to follow you.

Expertise.   Expert power is based on a special ability, skill, expertise, or knowledge exhibited by an individual. For example, a new police sergeant may have some questions regarding the functioning of a piece of equipment. Rather than asking the lieutenant, the sergeant contacts the individual who previously held the sergeant's position for assistance, because of their knowledge of or expertise with the equipment.

Example or Referent.   Referent power is based on the attractiveness or the appeal of one person to another. A leader may be admired because of certain characteristics or traits that inspire or attract followers. (Charisma is an example.) Referent power may also be based on a person's connection with another powerful individual. For example, the title of "assistant" has been given to people who work closely with others with titles such as sheriff or police chief. Although the title of assistant to the sheriff may not have reward or coercive (or legitimate) power, other individuals may perceive that this person is acting with the consent of the boss, resulting in their power to influence. The sheriff's assistant is perceived as the sheriff's alter ego. Many will wonder if the assistant is acting for the sheriff or on their own. Rather than taking a chance, one typically opts in favor of the former possibility.

- Power is the capacity to command.
- All police supervisors have it.
- Not all police supervisors use it.
- Hence, only some police supervisors are leaders.

FORMAL AND INFORMAL TEAM LEADERS

Not all police leaders have sergeant's stripes or lieutenant's or captain's bars. For a number of reasons, there are informal leaders. These people surface in all organizations to fill a one-time or ongoing need. For example, if a particular expertise is required, then the person who possesses it will provide leadership. This could occur if the victim of a crime can communicate only in Spanish. A Spanish-speaking officer thus may temporarily lead in an investigation. Another occurs when the supervisor fails to establish followership because of either inadequate expertise or a poor example. The work team will commonly fill this void by creating an informal leader.

The reasons for an informal leader's emergence determine if it is helpful or harmful to the work team. Informal leaders are a normal phenomenon in an organization. They can be extremely useful to a supervisor if they act in concert with and support of the group's goals.

Leadership is a relationship between two or more people in which one attempts to influence the other(s) toward the attainment of a goal or goals. The key to the concept of leadership is to look at it as an influence process. It is a process that includes the elements of the power base of the person and the authority of the position.

A Productive Team Leader–Team Follower Relationship

Team followers and team leaders concentrate on the mission of the police department; followers do not concentrate on the leader. A common purpose pursued with decent values is the heart of the healthy leader-follower relationship.

Follower is not synonymous with *subordinate*. A subordinate reports to an individual of high rank and may in practice be a supporter, an antagonist, or indifferent. A follower shares a common purpose with the leader, believes in what the agency is trying to accomplish, and wants both the leader and the department to succeed.

Like the team leader, the follower is a steward of the resources a police organization can draw on to carry out its work. The resources of a group include its leaders. Thus a team follower is the leader's cohort every bit as much as a team leader is the follower's cohort.

MANAGING YOUR BOSS

The phrase "managing your boss" sounds unusual, even suspicious. Because of the traditional top-down emphasis in police organizations, it is not obvious why you need to manage relationships upward—unless, of course, you would do so for selfish or political reasons. I am using the term to mean the process of consciously working with your superior to obtain the best possible results for you, your boss, and, most importantly, the police department.

Some police sergeants behave as if their bosses were not very dependent on them. They fail to see how much the boss needs their help and cooperation to do his or her job effectively. These people refuse to acknowledge that the boss needs cooperation, dependability, and honesty from them.

Some supervisors see themselves as not very dependent on their bosses. They gloss over how much help and information they need from the boss in order to perform their own jobs well.

A supportive working relationship requires that

- You have a good understanding of the other person and yourself, especially regarding strengths, weaknesses, work styles, and values

STRUCTURED EXERCISE 7–2

There are several excellent motion pictures that portray leadership characteristics and strategies. The HBO movie *Band of Brothers* is one example. Identify a movie that you can borrow or rent. (Be certain the movie depicts an actual leader.) View the movie and analyze it for leadership characteristics. Look for the successes and mistakes that the leader experienced. Record what you see. When the movie is finished, discuss with others what you saw in the leader's behavior (values, vision, positive self-regard, integrity, etc.).

- You use this information to develop and maintain a healthy working relationship, one that is compatible with both people's work styles and assets, is characterized by mutual expectations, and meets the most critical needs of the other person (and that is essentially what we have found good leaders doing)

At a minimum, you need to appreciate your boss's goals and pressures, strengths and weaknesses, and values. What are your boss's organizational and personal objectives, and what are the pressures on him, especially those from his boss, and the degree of acceptance of his characteristics, needs, and decisions by his staff? What are your boss's strong suits and blind spots? What is her preferred style of working? Does she like to get information through memos, formal meetings, or phone calls? Does your boss thrive on conflict or try to minimize it?

Without this information, a police supervisor is flying blind when dealing with the boss, and unnecessary conflicts, misunderstandings, and problems are inevitable.

The boss is only one half of the relationship. You are the other half, as well as the part over which you have more direct control. Developing an effective working relationship requires, then, that you know your own needs, strengths and weaknesses, personal style, and values.

With a clear understanding of both your boss and yourself, you can usually establish a way of working together that fits both of you, that is characterized by unambiguous mutual expectations, and that helps both of you to be more productive and effective. Above all else, a good working relationship with a boss accommodates differences in work style. Work style differences include the boss's (1) preferred way of receiving information; (2) preferred method of making decisions; (3) degree/type of expectation; (4) amount of information required; and (5) willingness to delegate.

No doubt, some police supervisors will resent that on top of all their other duties, they also need to take time and energy to manage their relationships with their bosses. Such supervisors fail to realize the importance of this activity and how it can simplify their jobs by eliminating potentially severe conflicts.

> Seeing themselves as ultimately responsible for what they achieve in a police organization, supervisors know they need to establish and manage relationships with everyone on whom they are dependent, and that includes the boss.

THE LOYALTY OF A TEAM FOLLOWER

Team leaders and team followers need to find a mutual place for their loyalty that transcends their relationship yet bonds them in a framework of trust. This is the importance of the contemporary emphasis on vision, values, and mission statements: Well formulated, these define the loyalty that leaders and followers pledge to those who have a stake in the group. (See Responsibility 4.)

The values statement evokes a focused loyalty—to fairness, to quality, to honesty, to service, to a common purpose. Focused loyalty to worthy values avoids the pitfalls of unlimited loyalty. Both team leaders and team followers enter into a contract to pursue the common purpose within the context of their values. The loyalty of each is to achieving the purpose and to helping each other stay true to that purpose. Loyalty—being loyal to a purpose, a profession, or one's integrity—takes a lot of courage.

COURAGEOUS FOLLOWERSHIP

The term *follower* causes some of us discomfort. It conjures up images of conformity, weakness, and failure to succeed. Often, none of this is the least bit true. The sooner we move beyond these images and get comfortable with the idea of powerful team followers supporting powerful team leaders, the sooner we can fully develop dynamic, self-responsible, mutually supportive relationships in our police agencies.

Rudyard Kipling wrote, "The opposite of courage is not cowardice. It is conformity." It's the courageous followers who openly communicate agreement and disagreement with their bosses. They refuse to engage in groupthink. They are loyal, but not compliant. They strive for unity but will not submit to uniformity.

If you want to be a courageous follower and if you want the members of your assigned team to be the same, then you must do the following five things:

- *Assume responsibility.* Courageous followers assume responsibility for themselves and their police department. They do not view their team leader as paternalistic or wait for the team leader to give them permission to act. Courageous followers discover or create opportunities to fulfill their potential and maximize their value to the agency. The pronoun they most frequently use is *we,* and they rarely use *me, I,* or *they.* (When *they* is used, it involves praise for the work of others.)
- *Work hard.* Courageous followers use the words "I'm going to work," and not "I have to work" or, worse yet, to a coworker, "Don't work too hard." They assume new or additional responsibilities to unburden the team leader and serve the organization. They stay alert for opportunities in which their strengths supplement the leader's, and they assert themselves in these areas. Courageous followers endorse their leader and the tough decisions a leader must make if the police department is to fulfill its mission.
- *Challenge.* Courageous followers challenge bad ideas, poor conduct, and dysfunctional procedures. They are willing to stand up, to stand out, and to risk rejection. Courageous followers value their relationship with the team leader, but not at the expense of the overall mission and their own integrity.

- *Champion change.* Courageous followers recognize the need for change. They champion it and stay with the team leader and work team while they mutually struggle with the difficulties of real change. They examine their own need to change and do so as appropriate.
- *Separate.* Courageous followers know when it is necessary to transfer to another team or flat out quit the department. They are prepared to withdraw support from and even to disavow or oppose destructive bosses, despite high personal risk.

BECOMING A TEAM LEADER

Team leaders share seven common traits and practices. They

- Accentuate the positive
- Know what's going on
- Get attention through vision
- Create meaning through communication
- Build trust through integrity
- Deploy through positive self-regard
- Master change

Accentuate the Positive

During World War II, General Eisenhower realized that optimism and pessimism are infectious and that they spread more rapidly from the head downward than in any other direction. He learned that a commander's optimism has a most extraordinary effect on all with whom he comes in contact. He said, "With this clear realization, I firmly determined that my mannerisms and speech in public would always reflect the cheerful certainty of victory—that any pessimism and discouragement I might ever feel would be reserved for my pillow."

Optimism does not mean being foolish about taking on challenges. It means pursuing your adversaries with an abundance of faith and hope in your resources.

Know What's Going On

One of the most difficult tasks for a team leader is to know with great accuracy what is going on within the work unit. Information-gathering mechanisms seem to evolve in ways that result in the top of the system having a limited, incomplete, and even biased understanding of reality. Team leaders develop methods that surface and rectify these mechanisms so that, for example, bad news is as likely to come to their attention as good. Face-to-face, two-way communication is developed deep into the department, and a norm is established of responsibly surfacing and exposing the truth as completely as possible.

Get Attention through Vision

Vision grabs. At first, it grabs the team leader, and if effectively projected, it convinces others to get on board. The leader's vision is intended to be magnetic. Winning coaches transmit an unbridled clarity about what they want from their players. If coaches can do it, so can police supervisors—if they want to.

The first thing you do with your vision is convey it to others. Your staff has to know what you see. Second, they must understand it. The understanding may be vague or incomplete, but they have to have at least a fundamental concept of what you're proposing. Third, the people must be convinced that the vision is of paramount importance, even if it initially appears impossible. It excites people and drives them. Fourth, you have to pay close attention to the vision and use it as a transaction between yourself and your followers. It becomes a subtle link that forges you and your followers as one—coach and team, sergeant and officers.

Once the preceding steps have been taken, the team leader must:

- Live the enabling vision closely
- Use it to prioritize (quality first, quantity second, etc.)
- Adapt the vision of changing needs and new opportunities

If you understand your values, the values of your department, and the values of your profession, then visioning is possible for you. You merely allow your imagination and conscience to take charge. Through imagination, you can visualize the uncharted wealth of potential that lies within yourself and others. Through conscience, you can compare your ideas with universal laws or principles, as well as with your personal standards.

Create Meaning through Communication

Responsibility 5, communications, provides expansive coverage of this strategy. I underscore it here because research has demonstrated that all team leaders master communication. It is inseparable from effective leadership. It isn't just information or facts; it is the context of presentation, the overall meaning.

All police organizations depend on the existence of shared meanings and interpretations of reality, which facilitate coordinated efforts. Meaning surpasses what is typically meant by "communication." Meaning has little to do with facts or even knowing. Facts and knowing pertain to technique, tactics, and "knowing how to do things." That is useful and often necessary. But thinking is much closer to what we mean by "meaning" than knowing is. This is not a subtle difference. Thinking prepares us for what ought to be done.

To depend on facts, without thinking, may seem all right, but in the long run it is dangerous because it lacks direction. The distinctive characteristic of leaders (especially in a volatile police environment) is that the "know-why" occurs before the "know-how." This logic shows, once more, one of the basic differences between leaders and supervisors.

Leadership, by communicating meaning, generates a confederation of learning, and this is what successful police agencies proudly possess. Lack of clarity makes police organizations little more than simple devices for the avoidance of responsibility.

I have conducted more than two thousand team-building workshops for police and sheriff's departments. (I also have conducted similar workshops for fire departments, city councils, and a variety of business firms.) With rare exception, the number one issue in the workshop is the failure to communicate with one another. Far too often the participants state with detectable anger: "I never got the word." "Everything moves, but there's no feedback." "I've expressed my ideas before, but they could care less." And the worst one is, "I don't know our priorities, let alone our goals."

If our body's arterial system does not touch base with our cells, they'll eventually die. Similarly, if a police organization's communication system does not contact, with meaning, its human resources, the staff may not be dead, but they might as well be.

Build Trust through Integrity

Effective leaders must establish their integrity first and their vision and ideas second.

Trust encompasses accountability, predictability, reliability, and integrity. To achieve it, there must be a mental or physical act. Something must happen for me to trust you, or vice versa. If you tell me that you'll be at work on time, and you are, I start the trust process.

Trusting involves a trust bank account (TBA). You consistently arrive at work on time, and your TBA prospers. You make many daily TBA deposits in a variety of ways. You open new TBAs with people whom you meet. Depending on your working relationships, family members, and friends, you may have hundreds of TBAs in existence. You could be trust-rich. Conversely, you could be trust-poor.

It takes a lot of deposits to build a strong TBA with another person. Making a mistake—for example, lying to another person—can wipe out your TBA. It can send you into indefinite, maybe permanent, bankruptcy with the other party. It can also destroy a working relationship, a marriage, a friendship. TBAs take considerable time to build and only one second—in some cases, one word—to dissolve.

Leaders who are trusted are known for their integrity. Followers do not stay with shiny ideals and cute words. Only relentless dedication to integrity on the part of a police leader will engage trust.

Just as trust is the key to all relationships, so also is trust the glue of organizations. It is the cement that holds the bricks together. For a police organization to foster trust, it first must present a vision of what it is and what it is to do. The police leader is responsible for seeing to it that the integrity of the department is known to employees and community members alike. This is not easy because people have different perceptions. The police leader may see the integrity of the department as X, the employees as Y, and the citizens as Z. If the three viewpoints are contradictory, then trust is hard to achieve.

The greater the integrity of the leader, the more one is able to trust him or her. If I know what you stand for, and believe in it, I'll trust and follow you.

The vast majority of all leadership failures are integrity failures.

STRUCTURED EXERCISE 7–3

ESSENTIAL QUALITIES OF A LEADER

Rank the following leadership characteristics in terms of their relative importance, using a scale from 1 (high) to 12 (low). When you have finished, turn to the Extended Learning section at the end of this chapter, and read question 9.

_____ Caring		_____ Dedicated	
_____ Integrity		_____ People focused	
_____ Communicator		_____ Decision maker	
_____ Model		_____ Visionary	
_____ Motivator		_____ Courageous	
_____ Expert		_____ Other: _____	

Deploy through Positive Self-Regard

The higher you advance in a police organization, the more interpersonal and relational the working environment is. This deployment of self makes leading a profoundly personal activity. Such a deployment depends on one's positive self-regard. Positive self-regard is a triangle consisting of (1) competence, (2) positive other-regard, and (3) the Wallenda factor.

Competence.   Positive self-regard is not self-aggrandizement, conceit, or egomania. Essentially, it is confidence in who you are and what you are capable of doing. It is prudent self-esteem and self-respect.

The first step in building positive self-regard is recognizing your strengths and compensating for your weaknesses. The next step involves the constant nurturing of skills. The final step is evaluating the fit between your perceived skills and what the job requires. Being good at your job, and knowing why, makes up one side of positive self-regard. I label this "competence."

Other-Regard.   Those who have high regard for themselves typically have the same for others. Having positive self-regard is contagious. Potentially everyone can catch it. Positive self-regard creates it in others. It seems to exert its force by generating in others a sense of confidence and high expectations.

Positive self- and other-regard encourage the development of five key people skills:

- The ability to accept individuals as they are, not as you would like them to be. This ability is fundamental to leading a culturally diverse workforce.
- The capacity to approach people and problems in relation to the present, rather than the past.
- The ability to deal with those who are close to you with the same active listening ear and courtesy that you give to citizens and casual acquaintances.

- The ability to trust in another person's dedication and capabilities.
- The ability to function without constant approval or even support from others.

Wallenda Factor.   Team leaders do not think about failure. In fact, they reject the concept. The closest they identify with it is through terms such as "learning experience," "setback," or "delayed success."

Failure to them is like learning to ski. At first, you're destined to fall; with persistence and perspiration, you'll eventually master the art of skiing. It's the same with leadership. Team leaders use their mistakes as a lesson on what not to do as well as what to do next.

Failure and mistakes can open us up to self- or other-criticism, which can erode positive self- and other-regard. The more valid it is, the more bothersome it is to us. The successful leader accepts it but then twists it into a useful message. Remember, feedback is the breakfast of champions.

Karl Wallenda was one of the premier high-wire aerialists. He fell to his death in 1978 while walking a 75-foot-high tightrope. After his fall, Mrs. Wallenda commented that for three straight months before the accident, all he thought about was not falling. He substituted thinking about falling for his past thinking about successfully walking the tightrope.

Karl Wallenda would likely tell the police supervisor to pour his or her energies into success (walking the tightrope) and not failing (falling). To worry places barriers in the path of clear thinking. An absence of clear thinking can cause mistakes for those who possess positive self-regard. An absence of clear thinking can cause failures for those who do not have it.

Three Sides of Positive Self-Regard.   The three sides combined look like Figure 7–1. Your positive self-regard is a direct derivative of

- Your competence (you have what it takes, and you know it)
- Your capacity for instilling competence in others by having high other-regard for them
- Your conviction of an outcome (the expectation of success)

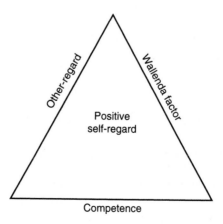

FIGURE 7–1   Three sides of positive self-regard.

STRUCTURED EXERCISE 7–4

I've described above seven critical characteristics or strategies of proven team leaders. What would you add to this list? Which, if any, are unimportant? Create your own list; then along with your colleagues, reach a consensus on a joint list of strategies.

For team leadership to occur, there has to be a fusion of competence, capacity, and conviction. It is similar to the archer who builds his prowess to the point where the zeal to hit the center of the target is obliterated and man, bow, arrow, and target become one, united. Positive self-regard magnetically attracts and gradually empowers people to join the police supervisor, the police leader, in a quest for quality services that are good for police departments and for society.

Master Change

As a team leader, you must master organizational change—design, structure, and implementation. This must be accomplished through methods that get the entire work team engaged and committed, both in favor of the shared vision and in a rigorous search for the truth. If you want to create an organization committed to a new way of being and a new set of operational procedures, then the processes that must be employed must foster commitment. Team leaders are superb at anticipating. They get ahead of the learning curve and make an early and easy adjustment to it.

TWO BIG MISTAKES A TEAM LEADER CAN MAKE

The worst mistake a leader can make is ducking accountability. If others see the leader attempting to slide away from a bad situation or, worse yet, trying to blame others for it, the leader's TBA is zero. Leadership is down the tubes and is extremely difficult to restore.

A second common trap for even those leaders who have the seven characteristics is taking too much credit. In fact, a good leader rarely takes credit. We've found that the people who most quickly generate trust, loyalty, excitement, and energy in an organization are those who pass on the credit to the people who have really done the work.

Most good team leaders have strong character and positive self-regard, but they shouldn't let their egos get too big. Your ego needs to be strong enough to handle the kind of anger or abuse you will sometimes incur and to appreciate contrary feedback. But your ego should not be so big that you lose your associates' respect. Positive self-regard does not preclude being humble.

A THIRD BIG MISTAKE: GROUPTHINK

Groupthink is a mode of thinking that people engage in when they are deeply involved in a cohesive in-group, when the members' striving for unanimity overrides their motivation to realistically appraise alternative courses of action. It is a clear case of something productive (teamwork) being carried to an extreme and leading to something unproductive (poor-quality decision making).

Groupthink is a shared reality that we create. As a result, the team's decision becomes the sum total of the things its members won't look at. Groupthink is fostered by

- A team that is highly insulated with limited access to outside feedback
- A stressful decision-making context
- Unreasonable external pressure

Symptoms of Groupthink

There are eight symptoms of groupthink. The greater the number that are present in a work team, the greater the likelihood that the team will succumb to groupthink.

- *Illusion of invulnerability.* The feeling of power and authority is important to any decision-making team. It gives team members confidence that they will be able to carry through on any decisions reached. However, if the team members come to believe that any decision they reach will, therefore, be successful, then they have fallen prey to an illusion of invulnerability.
- *Belief in a sacred mandate.* Team members need to believe in the rightness of their decisions. Taken to the extreme, they may defend a decision by pointing to a moralistic code or philosophy "for the good of all." Basically, this relieves them of the responsibility for rationally justifying an action. The protection of the team's self-esteem becomes more important than the accuracy of its judgment.
- *Rationalization.* In reaching a decision, it is normal and natural to downplay the drawbacks of a chosen course. The problem occurs when legitimate objections exist within the work team, but they are not voiced due to perceived negative reactions to those raising objections to the team position.
- *Rejection of external groups.* Police teams can fall prey to stereotyping other groups as troublemakers—as enemies. "Don't trust outsiders" is the prevalent attitude in this case.
- *Self-censorship.* As one of the principles on which our country was founded, the ability to express oneself without censorship has always been highly prized. The most common form of censorship is that which we force on ourselves under the guise of group loyalty, team spirit, or adherence to "departmental policy." Group compliance takes precedence over individual courage.
- *Direct pressure.* Pressure on police team members can surface in many forms. The net effect is the same: Team members are conditioned to keep opposing views to

themselves. In addition, they're urged not to believe in differing views because to do so puts them at odds with the team's integrity. Dissent or argument against the team's presumed agreement is considered counter to the team's interests, even an act of disloyalty.

- *Mind guards.* In groupthink, a phenomenon may surface to protect us from disturbing thoughts and ideas—a mind guard. Interestingly, mind guards are typically self-appointed and perform their function not within the team, but rather externally from the group decision. Data, facts, and opinions that might bear directly on the team are deliberately kept out of the purview of the team. Generally, this is done with a variety of justifiable intentions: There is no time, a regular member will "summarize" for the team, the issue is not pertinent, or, saddest of all, the team has already made up its mind.

- *Illusion of unity.* Rationalizations and psychological pressures have their effect: The team coalesces around a decision. Drawbacks are downplayed; the invincibility of the final course is reinforced. And doubting team members may even feel that they have justifiably put their own fears to rest. More likely, it is simply the sense of relief that an indecision has become a decision.

Avoiding Groupthink

Is teamwork immune to the effects of groupthink? As long as teams are constituted of human beings, prone to all the dynamics and pitfalls of human interaction, and therefore vulnerable, the answer is no. Fortunately, it is possible to spot the incipient causes of groupthink and thereby reduce a team's chances of falling into it. The police leader should attempt to

- *Maintain an open climate.* The police supervisor should practice what is called an open leadership style—free discussion, nonjudgmental attitudes, acceptance of divergent thinking—as opposed to a closed management style, characterized by tightly controlled discussion, highly defensive posturing, and lack of tolerance of opposing thoughts in favor of consensus thinking.

- *Avoid group isolation.* At times, it is valuable to bring in outsiders to provide critical reaction to the team's assumptions. In this way, the work team is not isolated with limited data and constrained choices. This is especially helpful with problem-oriented policing. (See Responsibility 14.)

- *Assign critical evaluators.* The police supervisor should assign each team member the role of critical evaluator, giving each the duty to question current practices and uncontested team assumptions. By questioning even areas in which a particular team member may not have special expertise, the team members are forced to rethink their assumptions and rationalizations.

- *Avoid being too directive.* The most important single step a supervisor can take is to avoid being too directive in decision making. (See Responsibility 8 and the section on microdelegation) For some, this may mean occasionally allowing other team members to facilitate a meeting in their presence. In this way, supervisors will lessen undue influence on their team.

- *Remember that silence may mean disagreement, not consent.* Individual and organizational values are under siege by blistering technological and social upheaval. It is time to put away the "silence means consent" notion, which still pervades much of our organizational thinking. Supervisors best assume not that silence means consent but rather that such silence indicates disagreement with proposed team action. Maintaining an open climate via an open leadership style can avoid the supervisor's trap of inferring that an employee's silence means agreement.

Groupthink masks itself as teamwork. It is seductive. It is contagious. And it is very dangerous. Here is what the leader can and should do:

- Understand the significance of groupthink in the team-based decision-making process and how it can subvert the success of group goals and objectives.
- Realize that groupthink—the striving for agreement leading to faulty decision making—can occur in any team, no matter how small or how worthy its intentions.
- Recognize the eight symptoms of groupthink and understand that when more of them are present, it is more likely the team will make an unsuccessful decision.
- Apply the five key strategies for avoiding groupthink:

    Maintain an open climate.
    Avoid group isolation.
    Appoint critical evaluators.
    Avoid being too directive.
    Remember that silence is not always agreement.

> In the long run, the most difficult part of building a diverse team of police officers is integrating people whose interests, values, intellect, and moral principles cover a wide spectrum and are not simply cookie-cutter reflections of the police supervisor.

KEY POINTS

- Team leadership is a new dimension of police supervision.
- Leadership and team leadership are not synonymous.
- Authority is the right to supervise, and power is one's capacity to do so.
- Both authority and power seek to influence the behavior of others.
- There are three types of authority: position, rewards, and sanctions. And there are two types of power: expertise and example.
- All police employees are volunteer employees.
- Informal team leadership is a natural phenomenon in an organization.
- Courageous followership requires: (1) assumption of responsibility; (2) hard work; (3) challenge; (4) willingness to change; and (5) withdrawal.

- Without followers, there would be no leaders.
- Successful team leaders demonstrate seven common patterns of behavior. They consistently (1) accentuate the positive, (2) know what's happening, (3) get your attention through their vision, (4) create meaning through communication, (5) build trust through integrity, (6) deploy through positive self-regard, and (7) master change.
- The greatest mistakes a leader can make are ducking accountability, assuming too much credit for good work, and engaging in groupthink.

EXTENDED LEARNING

1. What's the difference between leadership and team leadership?
2. Discuss authority and power. How do they differ? What is their common bond? If you could only have one, which would you choose?
3. If you, the police supervisor, are a formal team leader, how do you explain the presence of informal leaders in or around your assigned work unit?
4. What is your reaction to the concept of followership? What are the realities involved? Do you have any concerns?
5. What is meant by "managing your boss"? Have you attempted to do so? If so, what occurred?
6. What is meant by "positive self-regard"? How does one acquire it? Whom do you know who has this characteristic?
7. Have you witnessed leaders either avoiding accountability or frequently taking credit? If so, discuss what you saw and what occurred as a result of it.
8. What is groupthink? Have you experienced it? If so, what happened? What have you done to avoid it?

Structured Exercise 7–3 has been conducted with hundreds of police management and supervisory groups. Invariably, they identified integrity as the most essential quality of a leader. The salient message is, "I'm not going to follow you if I don't trust you. Even though I might be coerced into following you for a while, as soon as your back is turned, I'm out of here!"

In many settings today it is out of vogue to speak in terms of integrity. It's become equated with soft, touchy-feely stuff or with someone's religion. Some people wonder if our inner values matter anymore. Many have come to believe that the only things we need for success are talent, energy, and personality. But history has taught us that over the long haul, who we are is more important than who we appear to be.

RESPONSIBILITY 8

Empowerment

The police supervisor is responsible for creating a partnership with his or her work team that is motivated through empowerment and that results in enhanced commitment, better decisions, and good police work.

Responsibility 8 is a logical extension of Responsibility 7, Team Leadership. An empowered employee is typically a motivated one. Additionally, empowered employees take on the role of leader. Training for empowerment is essential, and this is the subject of Responsibility 9.

The best executive is the one who has enough sense to pick good people to do what he wants done, and self-restraint enough to keep from meddling with them while they do it.

—Theodore Roosevelt

The supervisory dynamic of the moment is empowerment. It is alleged to be the cure-all for job dissatisfaction, low morale, employee inefficiency, poor performance, and risk avoidance. Everyone seems to be hailing its virtues and scorning any detractors. But just granting power, without some method of replacing the discipline and order that come out of a command-and-control bureaucracy, produces chaos. We have to learn how to disperse power so that self-discipline can largely replace imposed discipline. That immerses us in the area of culture: replacing the bureaucracy with aspirations, values, and visions.

Empowerment embodies the belief that the answer to the latest crisis lies within each of us and therefore we all buckle up for adventure. Empowerment bets that people at our own level or below will best know how to organize, serve citizens, and get it right the first time. We know that a democracy is a political system designed not for efficiency but as a hedge against the abuse of power. Empowerment is our willingness to bring this value into the workplace. Empowerment enables us to claim our autonomy and commits us to making the organization work well, with or without the sponsorship of those above us. This requires a belief that our safety and our freedom are in our own hands—no easy task!

> To be an empowered police employee one must work for an empowering supervisor. Empowerment is a strong and positive motivating force for doing the right work for the right reasons.

Now we will explore worker motivation, understanding that being empowered creates motivation. We will also cover the topic of job satisfaction, which is an outcome of worker motivation. With these subjects in mind, we are positioned to understand and appreciate the power of empowerment.

MOTIVATION

Imagine a police organization full of people who come to work enthusiastically, knowing that they will grow and flourish, and who are intent on fulfilling the vision and mission of the department. There's an ease, grace, and effortlessness about the way they get things done. Work flows seamlessly among teams and functions. Employees take pleasure and pride in every aspect of the enterprise—for example, in the way they can talk openly, reflect on each other's opinions, and have genuine influence on the decisions being made about what they do. That's a lot of energy walking in each day, accomplishing an ever-increasing amount of work, and having fun along the way.

Is this scenario energizing or frightening? If you don't want police employees to bring this much passion, caring, and focus to their work, then don't practice the recommendations that follow. You will find that they reject the assumption that workers are motivated primarily by money, recognition, and fear. Instead, you must assume that in the right atmosphere people will contribute and make commitments because they want to; they want to do good work for its own sake and to be recognized as individuals.

As a supervisor, you are responsible for motivating your staff to accomplish the mission of your agency. A cursory look at any police agency shows that some personnel work harder than others. An individual with outstanding abilities may consistently be outperformed by someone with obviously inferior talents. Why do officers exert different levels of effort in different activities? Why do some employees appear to be "highly motivated," while others do not? These are some of the issues this chapter addresses.

Why Have Motivated Workers?

Why? The obvious answers to this vital question are

- Job performance . . .
- Job satisfaction . . .
- They deserve it!

A highly motivated worker is more likely to be a top performer. Further, a highly motivated worker is likely to experience good job satisfaction, which spells good morale.

From the individual's standpoint, being motivated is the key to a productive and satisfying job. Work consumes a sizable portion of our waking hours. If this time is to be meaningful and contribute toward the development of a healthy personality, the individual must be willing to devote effort toward a purpose, a mission.

How Does Motivation Start?

> Motivating others starts and stops with you. If you're not motivated to do a good job, then those working for you won't be either.

When I encounter unmotivated police employees, inevitably I see an unmotivated supervisor. I hope for your sake and the sake of those who work for you and your department that you are motivated to make a difference in your life and the lives of others. It takes a lot of energy and enthusiasm, but it's worth it. Everyone benefits.

What Is Worker Motivation?

Worker motivation can be defined as the psychological forces within a person that determine

- The direction of the person's behavior in an organization
- The person's level of effort
- The person's level of persistence in the face of obstacles

See Table 8–1 for further explanation of these three cornerstones of worker behavior.

TABLE 8–1   *Elements of Worker Motivation*

ELEMENT	DEFINITION	EXAMPLE
Direction of behavior	Which behavior does the employee choose to perform in a police organization?	Does the police officer take the time and effort to convince skeptical superiors of the need to change the specifications for the patrol plan?
Level of effort	How hard does the employee work to perform the chosen behavior?	Does the officer prepare a report outlining problems with the original plan, or does the officer casually mention the issue when she bumps into a supervisor in the hall?
Level of persistence	When faced with obstacles, confusion, and conflicts, how hard does the employee keep trying to perform the chosen behavior successfully?	When the supervisor disagrees with the officer and indicates that a change in the patrol plan is a waste of time, does the officer persist in trying to get the change implemented or give up despite her strong belief in the need for a change?

STRUCTURED EXERCISE 8–1

Think for a few moments about the various jobs you've had. Which ones were you the most and least motivated to perform? Now the crucial question: Why? Have you ever worked hard and done good work but with little or no motivation to do so? Are you doing that now? Alternatively, have you ever done very little work but with a lot of motivation? In both instances, why? Share this information with your teammates. Probe for similarities and uniqueness in your discussion. What did you discover?

The Distinction between Motivation and Performance

Because motivation determines what employees do and how hard and diligently they do it, you might think that a worker's motivation to do a job is the same as the worker's job performance. In fact, motivation and performance, though often confused by workers and supervisors alike, are two distinct aspects of behavior in an organization. Performance is an evaluation of the results of a person's behavior. It involves determining how well or how poorly a person has accomplished a task or done a job. Motivation is only one factor among many that contribute to a worker's job performance.

One is apt to expect a highly motivated dispatcher to perform better than one who is poorly motivated. This may not be the case, however. There are other influences at work, such as an innate work ethic or lack of one, amount of training, availability of resources, working conditions, a motivated or unmotivated supervisor, a slave-driver boss, and more.

> Because motivation is only one of several factors that can affect performance, a high level of motivation does not always result in a high level of performance. Conversely, high performance does not necessarily imply that motivation is high: Workers with low motivation may perform at a high level if they have a great deal of ability.

Supervisors have to be careful not to automatically attribute low performance to a lack of motivation, or high performance to high motivation. If they incorrectly assume that low performance stems from low motivation, supervisors may overlook the real cause of a performance problem (such as inadequate training or a lack of resources) and fail to take appropriate actions to rectify the situation so that workers can perform at a high level. Similarly, if police supervisors assume that workers who perform at a high level are highly motivated, they may inadvertently fail to take advantage of the talents of exceptionally capable workers. If workers perform at a high level when their motivation levels are low, they may be capable of making exceptional contributions to the department if supervisors devote their efforts to boosting the workers' motivation.

It ain't what you don't know that gets you into trouble.
It's what you know that ain't so.

—Will Rogers

Intrinsic and Extrinsic Motivation

Another distinction important to a discussion of motivation is the difference between the intrinsic and extrinsic sources of worker motivation. Intrinsically motivated worker behavior is behavior that is performed for its own sake; the source of motivation is actually a deeply personal satisfaction in performing the behavior. Police officers who are intrinsically motivated often remark that their work gives them a sense of accomplishment and that they feel they are doing something worthwhile.

Extrinsically motivated worker behavior is behavior that is performed to gain material or social rewards or to avoid punishment. The behavior is performed not for its own sake, but rather for its consequences. Examples of extrinsic rewards include pay, praise, and status. Both extrinsic and intrinsic rewards either promote or detract from a motivating job climate.

Intrinsic and extrinsic rewards can be considered to be values (Responsibility 2). Hence if an employee is primarily extrinsically oriented, he or she will respond more quickly to salary, benefits, power, status, and job security. The job per se is not a source of motivation. Workers with an intrinsic bent will relate to completing particular assignments, being of service to others, feeling they are achieving to their full potential, and making a difference. In this case, the job itself is a motivator. The majority of us seek to attain both intrinsic and extrinsic rewards from our work. Typically, however, we tend to emphasize one set over the other.

JOB SATISFACTION

When we measure individual job satisfaction and combine the results, it adds up to group morale. Low job satisfaction or low morale is typically the result of poor motivation. A number of causal factors from the earlier theories of motivation have been grouped into four categories, as shown in Table 8–2.

TABLE 8–2 *Primary Causal Factors Influencing Job Satisfaction*

ORGANIZATION-WIDE FACTORS	JOB-CONTENT FACTORS
Pay system	Training
Promotional opportunities	Job scope
Departmental policies and procedures	Role clarity and conflict
Organization structure	Challenge and opportunities
Communications	

IMMEDIATE WORK-ENVIRONMENT FACTORS	PERSONAL FACTORS
Supervisory style	Age
Participation in decision making	Tenure
Work-group size	Personality
Coworker relations	Past experiences
Working conditions	Health
Recognition	
Trust	

STRUCTURED EXERCISE 8–2

Complete the following questionnaire by yourself. Add up your scores when finished, and compare them to the scale at the end. With your group or a class, compare your scores and calculate an arithmetic mean and top to bottom ranges. Do you see any patterns or notice anything unusual? Discuss what can be done to elevate your job satisfaction. (Keep in mind that the group score equals morale.)

1. How satisfied are you with the sort of work you are doing?

   I   2   3   4   5

   Very dissatisfied   Very satisfied

2. What value do you think the community puts on your service?

   I   2   3   4   5

   None   Very great

3. In your daily work, how free are you to make decisions and to act on them?

   I   2   3   4   5

   Not at all   Very free

4. How much recognition does your supervisor show for a job well done?

   I   2   3   4   5

   None   Great deal

5. How satisfied are you with the type of leadership you have been getting from your supervisor?

   I   2   3   4   5

   Very dissatisfied   Very satisfied

6. To what extent do you get to participate in the supervisory decisions that affect your job?

   I   2   3   4   5

   None   Great deal

7. How closely do you feel you are observed by your supervisor?

   I   2   3   4   5

   Too closely   About right

8. How satisfied are you with the department as it now stands?

   I   2   3   4   5

   Very dissatisfied   Very satisfied

9. How satisfied are you with your prestige within the city government?

1	2	3	4	5

Very dissatisfied   Very satisfied

10. How satisfied are you with your chances of being promoted to a better position?

1	2	3	4	5

Very dissatisfied   Very satisfied

11. How satisfied are you with your present salary?

1	2	3	4	5

Very dissatisfied   Very satisfied

12. How satisfied are you with your status in the community?

1	2	3	4	5

Very dissatisfied   Very satisfied

13. Would you advise a friend to join this department?

1	2	3	4	5

No   Yes

14. Do you receive a feeling of accomplishment from the work you are doing?

1	2	3	4	5

No   Yes

15. Rate the amount of pressure you feel in meeting the work demands of your job.

1	2	3	4	5

Great deal   None

The higher the total score, the greater your job satisfaction. A general rule of thumb is

55	Very high	40–44	Average
50–54	High	35–39	Below average
45–49	Above average	15–34	Take this job and shove it

THE INCREASING IMPORTANCE OF RECOGNITION AND REWARDS

Few supervisory practices are firmly founded on the concept that positive reinforcement—rewarding behavior you want repeated—works. But in today's police culture, recognition and rewards have become more important than ever for several reasons:

- Supervisors have fewer ways to influence police employees and modify their behavior. Coercion is no longer an option; supervisors increasingly must serve as mentors to influence rather than compel desired behavior.
- Employees are being asked to do more. To support empowerment, supervisors must create job environments that are both positive and reinforcing.
- Demographics predict that fewer workers will be available after Generation X. The emerging pool of employees has different values and expects work to be both purposeful and motivating.
- With tight budgets, recognition and rewards provide a genuine and low-cost way of encouraging higher levels of performance from employees.

A primary reason why most supervisors do not more frequently reward and recognize police employees is that they think they lack the time and creativity to come up with ways to do it. No longer can police supervisors reject the power and practicality of praising. No longer can they fail to recognize a deserving employee because they couldn't think of something to do to show their appreciation. No longer will police employees accept being ignored or getting feedback only once a year (if at all) during a performance review. No longer will using praise, recognition, and rewards be optional in successfully leading people.

Guidelines

The guidelines for recognizing and rewarding police employees are easily practiced:

- *Be sincere.* Phony attempts to recognize and reward others will be quickly detected. If not genuine, people will see through you. You'll lose credibility. Your trust bank account with these individuals will show a zero balance. If you are sincere and adhere to the following principles, you'll become an even more efficient police supervisor and an effective organizational leader.
- *Fit the reward to the employee.* Start with the individual's personal interest: Reward him or her in ways he or she truly finds rewarding. Such rewards may be personal or official, informal or formal, public or private. The main objective is to ensure that the employee values the reward.
- *Customize the reward to the accomplishment.* Successful reinforcement should be designed to take into account the significance of the accomplishment. An employee who completes a two-year project should be rewarded in a more substantial way than one who does a favor for you. The reward should be an outcome of the amount of time you have to plan and award it.

- *Make rewards timely and specific.* A reward must be given as soon as possible after the achievement. A reward that comes weeks or months later does little to motivate a police employee to repeat his or her actions. You should always say why the reward is being given—that is, provide a reason for the recognition.
- *Be accountable.* Hold yourself accountable for identifying police employees; your department should avoid using blanket approaches to motivation. "Jelly bean" motivation—giving the same reward to every member of the organization—not only does not inspire employees to excel, but also may actually damage performance, as top achievers see no acknowledgment of the job they have done. An exception to this principle is based on team performance. Much like Super Bowl champions, all members of the victorious team receive a winner's ring.
- *Ask.* The ideas in the remainder of this section will be most effective if they are tailored to the individual preferences of the people being recognized. Thus the way to begin is by asking your staff how you can best show appreciation when they have done a good job.
- *Make rewards multidirectional.* Many of us mistakenly think that recognition is always downward. Your boss commends you, and you express appreciation to your staff. This is nonsense. Recognition and rewards should move like communication—downward, upward, diagonally, and horizontally. Sergeants should recognize the good work of their peers. Further, sergeants should be complimenting their bosses. This may sound servile, but bosses possess the same needs and interests as other employees. If they do a really good job, let them know it. They'll probably be motivated to become even better police managers.

No-Cost Recognition

Some of the best types of recognition cost nothing at all. A sincere word of thanks from the right person at the right time can mean more to an employee than a raise, a formal award, or a whole wall of certificates or plaques. Part of the power of such rewards comes from the knowledge that someone took the time to notice the achievement, seek out the employee responsible, and personally deliver praise in a timely manner.

The no-cost recognition is limited only by your imagination. Here are a few examples:

- Tell your staff up front that you are going to let them know how they are doing.
- A good way to personalize any reinforcement is to use the person's first name when delivering the comment. Tell them why the behavior or result is important to you.
- Greet all employees by name.
- When discussing an employee's or a group's ideas with other people, peers, or police management, make sure you give credit.
- Arrange for the police employee to have lunch with the captain or chief.
- Have lunch or coffee with a police employee or a group of employees you don't normally see.
- Make certain that, in addition to your recognition of the employee, the chief or commander telephones the person.

STRUCTURED EXERCISE 8–3

With your group, brainstorm at least twenty additional ideas for no-cost recognition. In your opinion, what are the top five ideas?

- Ask the person which training program they would find most useful, and then see to it that he or she attends it.
- Similarly, ask employees what assignment they are most interested in, and help them get it.
- Recognize (and thank) people who recognize others. Be sure it's clear that making everyone a hero is an important principle in your work unit.
- A great motivational act that you can do for another person is to listen.
- Send information about an accomplishment to a police association publication and the individual's hometown newspaper. Get your employees' pictures in the department's annual report.
- When a team of police employees achieves, the entire team needs to be recognized. If only one officer or the highest performer of the group is recognized, the group is apt to lose motivation.
- Have the person attend a command staff meeting.

RETENTION

Some police personnel decide not to transfer to another agency although the salary or benefits are better. Others decide not to retire although their pension may be 80 percent or more of their salary. Why? When asked, the frequent response is, "I'm having too much fun."

> New studies show that employees rate having a nice, caring boss more highly than they value money or benefits. How long employees remain with an organization, and how productive they are, is directly determined by their relationship with their immediate supervisor.

Police agencies are in dire need of experienced and hardworking personnel. Alternatively, the enticement of improved retirement benefits is compelling. There are now retirement programs that vest at 90 percent or more—meaning that the employee is working for 10 percent of his salary. There are other programs that vest at 3 percent at age 50 (25 years of employment $\times$ 3 percent = 75 percent of salary; 30 years = 90 percent).

More and more agencies are recognizing that the need to motivate people to stay is as important (in some cases, more important) as motivating them to join the department. The supervisor is in the best position to recruit, get the best out of, and retain police employees.

DON'T BE A DAMN FOOL

A frustrated and depressed police sergeant told me, "For six months I've attempted to motivate an officer. I've done everything I can think of, and he doesn't respond. What should I do?" I immediately thought of the words of a great comedian . . .

> *If at first you do not succeed, try and try again. Then if you do not succeed, give up; don't be a damn fool about it.*
>
> —W. C. Fields

I realize that there are some people who enjoy being miserable and thrive on making others miserable too. No matter how hard you try, they will persist in accentuating the negative. They'll gleefully point out every mistake made. They'll ignore and even ridicule all of the positive events and fun associated with police work. They're likely burned out, burned up, or rusted out. And they do not, will not, or cannot change—no matter how hard anyone tries to change them.

When confronted with a person who is always substandard in performance and a chronic naysayer, then face it: Leadership is not the answer. Micromanagement and discipline are the tools needed.

WE DON'T ACT ON WHAT WE KNOW

We already know a lot about service and about empowerment. The books have been written, the experiments have been conducted, and the results are in. We now know, intellectually and empirically, that empowerment is a leadership strategy for creating high-performance workplaces. Empowerment works! The advantages far exceed any downside. Before discussing the benefits associated with empowerment, however, it is best to disclose some of the issues and pitfalls that could trip and surprise you when empowering others.

> If you want community-oriented policing (COP), then you must empower your staff. Without their empowerment, COP will be a great success on paper and an embarrassing failure in reality.

What's the Problem?

The problem is that despite a load of knowledge and evidence supporting worker empowerment, there has been disturbingly little fundamental change in the way police departments manage themselves. Few organizations are working hard to introduce tools and methods to actually help people make more intelligent decisions, especially decisions that improve systemwide performance. This likely will result in organizations that decentralize authority for a while, find that many poor and uncoordinated decisions result, and then abandon the "empowerment fad" and recentralize. This, of course, is precisely what many of the newly "empowered" workers, cynical from past management fads, fear. Even the organizations that are out telling their stories about COP and empowered police personnel have enormous difficulty in capitalizing on their experience. The problem is caused by the following factors:

- *Being unwilling to really open up.* What remains untouched is the belief that power, purpose, and decision making can reside at the top and the police organization can still learn how to better serve its customers via COP. When an innovative program like COP challenges this fundamental belief about how to govern, one of two things usually occurs. Either police management rejects it, and it's power and decision making as usual, or an effort is made to drive new programs across the bottom layers of the department.

> In essence, empowerment is enabling decision making in others. Because empowerment is cutting-edge stuff today, most police managers and supervisors are espousing its magic. But in fact, they are averse to really opening up and sharing their decision-making authority.

- *Ducking responsibility.* When you empower your staff, you share with them successes and failures. Everyone is in the same boat. You can't sign on only for the victories and duck the failures. There are some people who do not want to be empowered! They do not, or cannot, make the commitment to be held accountable. They prefer to gripe about decisions and, when asked for theirs, respond with, "Whatever you say. You're the boss."
- *Not believing.* Empowerment necessitates a strong belief in the integrity of the employees' work ethic. If a supervisor does not truly believe that staff members want to do a good job and enjoy their work, then empowering them is impractical.
- *Risking.* Empowering others is stressful when you lack faith in their ability to make the right decision. Whether unprepared, unskilled, or unanalytical, it matters not. A supervisor would be foolish to chance a set of no-brainer decisions in order to be recognized as an empowerer. Taking a risk and being a fool are not synonymous.
- *Misunderstanding.* A few moments ago you read that "empowerment is enabling decision making in others." Those being empowered could erroneously assume that they own the ultimate decision, that the supervisor abdicated the rights and responsibilities of their rank. Empowerment is not giving away the decision; it is permitting those who are affected by it to contribute their ideas and aspirations. While empowerment is akin to a partnership, the supervisor is the senior partner. The senior partner retains the final authority for saying "yes" or "no." Some see empowerment as a vote on what to do, when it is a voice on what to do. Those who consider empowerment as the "majority rules" will experience frustration and confusion. Those who accept empowerment as a vehicle for expressing, even arguing, their point of view will be grateful for the opportunity and supportive of the final decision. The accountability for its results sticks with the supervisor.

- *Using an "all or none" approach.* The "all or none" approach to empowerment can be mistakenly adopted by a police supervisor. Behind such thinking is equal treatment. While well intentioned, the underlying reasoning is faulty. For example, if a supervisor has a staff of six people and five are ready and willing to share in decisions that affect them, while one is not, such a supervisor decides there is no empowerment. Thus all experience equal treatment—all or none. If equality really counted, then all of us should have the same salary, same rewards, and so on. What really counts is being fair with everyone. Clearly, it is fair to empower those who are ready, while denying those who are incapable of handling expanded decision-making authority.

- *Focusing.* The core focus of COP is a police-customer partnership. This partnership seeks to empower members of the public in making decisions about the quantity and quality of police services they experience. Empowering the citizenry without empowering the staff is not only ridiculous and confusing, but also counterproductive. An empowered public, combined with an empowered police, spells "COP"—real COP!

DELEGATION, PARTICIPATION, AND EMPOWERMENT

Many of us approach some of our most vital ideas and emotions as if they were finite—limited. For example, there is only so much beauty to go around. Fairness can be counted up to 100 percent. Love is like a pie; there are only so many pieces to serve. Loyalty, trust, integrity, and power can be thought of in the same terms. In fact, though, all of these values are unlimited in mind and deed.

Some would agree, as I do, that the more you give away, the more you're likely to possess. Rodgers and Hammerstein wrote in a lyric, "A bell is not a bell till it's rung, a song is not a song till it's sung, and love is not love until you give it away." Similarly, power is not power until you give it away.

> It stands to reason that police supervisors who opt to give a share of their power to others automatically expand their sphere of influence. Basically, these supervisors have empowered others and in turn are in a much better position to accomplish their assigned tasks.

By now, you may see the link between empowerment and delegation. Delegation means sharing power, sharing power leads to empowerment, and empowerment means that employees experience ownership of their jobs. In essence, they are given the opportunity to become 100 percent responsible.

Next, we'll cover delegation in detail and then, later on, its partner in empowering others: participation. Remember the following simple but proven formula:

> Delegation + participation = empowerment

STRUCTURED EXERCISE 8–4

Twenty-seven statements about your job environment follow. Read each statement. If you feel it is true or mostly true of your job environment, mark it "T." If you believe the statement is false or mostly false, mark it "F."

1. The work is really challenging.
2. Few employees have any important responsibilities.
3. Doing things in a different way is valued.
4. There's not much group spirit.
5. There is a fresh, novel atmosphere about the place.
6. Employees have a great deal of freedom to do as they like.
7. New and different ideas are always being tried out.
8. A lot of people seem to be just putting in time.
9. This place would be one of the first to try out a new idea.
10. Employees are encouraged to make their own decisions.
11. People seem to take pride in the organization.
12. People can use their own initiative to do things.
13. People put quite a lot of effort into what they do.
14. Variety and change are not particularly important.
15. The same methods have been used for quite a long time.
16. Supervisors encourage employees to rely on themselves when a problem arises.
17. Few people ever volunteer.
18. Employees generally do not try to be unique and different.
19. It is quite a lively place.
20. Employees are encouraged to learn things even if they are not directly related to the job.
21. It's hard to get people to do their work.
22. New approaches to things are rarely tried.
23. The work is usually very interesting.
24. Things tend to stay just about the same.
25. Supervisors meet with employees regularly to discuss their future work goals.
26. Things always seem to be changing.
27. Employees function fairly independently of supervisors.

Scoring

This awareness exercise consists of three dimensions: involvement, independence, and innovation (I^3). A high I^3 score means high empowerment. The lower the I^3 score, the greater the likelihood that you're not experiencing much, if any, empowerment at work.

Give yourself one point if you've marked these statements as follows: $1 = T; 4 = F; 8 = F; 11 = T; 13 = T; 17 = F; 19 = T; 21 = F;$ and $23 = T.$ Your score for involvement is _____.

Give yourself one point if you've marked these statements as follows: $2 = F; 6 = T; 10 = T; 12 = T; 16 = T; 18 = F; 20 = T; 25 = T;$ and $27 = T.$ Your score for independence is _____.

Give yourself one point if you've marked these statements as follows: 3 = T; 5 = T; 7 = T; 9 = T; 14 = F; 15 = F; 22 = F; 24 = F; and 26 = T. Your score for innovation is _____.

If your score is 0 to 3, that particular dimension is very low; 4 to 5 is below average; 6 is average; 7 is above average; 8 is well above average; and 9 is very high.

An understanding of your job environment can help you deal with both the positive and the negative aspects of your work. This information may help you in improving the various aspects of empowerment.

DELEGATION

Delegation of responsibility has been a central topic in supervisory and management texts for decades. But today's demands on police employees to initiate far-reaching actions and to think creatively propel the issue toward the top of the list.

Delegation frees up the police organization to work faster and with less traditional hierarchy (e.g., strict adherence to chain of command, rules and regulations for everything, established routines). Much more delegation is required now than ever before in meeting the changing challenges of police work.

Yes, But . . .

A very bright trainer once commented, "When you delegate you are always delegating one thing for certain—uncertainty!" In other words, will the person who now possesses the responsibility come through? Will the empowered individual perform the task, and if so, will it be done correctly?

The media are quick to expose police corruption. It makes exciting news. In many instances, a newspaper article will implicitly point out that someone or a group of officers failed to execute their duties correctly or faithfully. The officers may have been delegated certain responsibilities and either accidentally or willfully violated the trust placed in them.

Is it any wonder that many police supervisors are fearful of delegating? After all, when something goes wrong, they're accountable. They must answer for their decision to delegate. At the same time, how would police work ever get done if delegation did not occur? The "yes, but . . . " syndrome is often voiced like this: "Yes, but if I delegate this task, it may not get done, or it may not be done to my satisfaction." This causes us to not really let go.

Really Letting Go

The plain fact is that nine out of ten police supervisors are not delegating enough. They think they are. They hand over tasks and pass out assignments routinely. But rarely does the officer really become empowered with true ownership—and its parallel, the sense of being 100 percent responsible.

FIGURE 8–1   Officer effort and results.

What goes wrong? First of all, there is a distinction between "letting go" and "really letting go." However, does really letting go mean chaos, confusion, and substandard performance? Perhaps, but not necessarily. Steps can be taken to avoid the pitfalls of delegation, all the while ensuring that its advantages are secured for the police agency. Before I review these steps, it's important that we consider the benefits of delegation.

Who Benefits

Many police organizations would cease to function, or at minimum would be highly dysfunctional, if delegation did not occur. After all, the chief or the sheriff cannot effectively both administer the department and conduct criminal investigations. Watch commanders cannot effectively supervise their crew if they're responding to police radio calls. The key word here is *effectively.*

   Assuming no loss of efficiency, a police officer can generate one hour of effort and produce one unit of police services (Figure 8–1). A leader, however, can invest one hour of energy and create ten or fifty or one hundred units of services through effective delegation (Figure 8–2). Police supervision, after all, is shifting the fulcrum over to achieve 1:10 or 1:50 or 1:100. Effective supervision is effective delegation.

   Four parties benefit from appropriate delegation. First, there is the community. Empowered police employees are typically more skillful and dedicated. Hence we the community gets better, less costly services. In turn, the community is more likely to respect and support its police department.

   Second, the organization itself harvests the wealth of brainpower that exists within its ranks. Everyone says, "I'm 100 percent responsible!" Everyone sets his or her sights on excellence.

   Third, you benefit as a supervisor because you're

- Building motivation for getting the job done

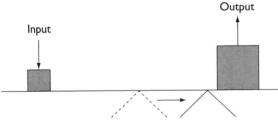

FIGURE 8–2   Supervisor effort and results.

- Increasing mutual trust between yourself and your officers
- Enhancing the officers' job skills and knowledge
- Encouraging a feeling of ownership
- Leveraging your power to provide quality police services (most important)

Fourth, your staff benefits by becoming more

- Motivated to do their work
- Trusting and trustworthy
- Professional
- Competent
- Self-confident
- Capable of producing top-notch police work (most important)

Obviously, everyone stands to benefit from really letting go, but far too many of us are unwilling to take the risk. We resort to the "yes, but . . . " tactic. The "yes, but . . . " game that some of us play today cannot be tolerated any longer. Empowerment is the game, and being 100 percent responsible is the price you pay to play it.

Setting the Context

Eight forces must be at work when you delegate. Without them, you're taking a big risk. With them in place and functioning, you are apt to achieve superb performance:

- Those being delegated to must be well trained in doing their job, and it must be ongoing, reliable, and pertinent training.
- You should project high standards, which demand of everyone uniformly—including yourself.
- You should understand the values and needs of each employee.
- From the preceding, establish and maintain a conduit for open and candid communications.
- Known anticipations should exist for those who fulfill their duties—rewards.
- Known anticipations should exist for those who do not fulfill their duties—reprimands.
- There should be feedback systems. New employees should receive feedback more often because they are earning your trust. Established officers should receive feedback less frequently because they have gained your faith.
- You must trust the person.

Four Types of Delegation

Delegation does not come in one style or shape. There are four ways to delegate: (1) stewardship; (2) gofer delegation; (3) delegation dump; and (4) microdelegation. Only stewardship promotes empowerment. The last three either inhibit or prevent empowering employees.

Stewardship. Stewardship delegation concentrates on results instead of methods. It affords police personnel a choice of method, but more important, it makes them 100 percent responsible for results. Stewardship delegation means no nagging on your part. Within the guidelines and standards you set, the other person becomes the boss. Admittedly, it takes more time in the beginning, but it's time wisely invested. Stewardship delegation moves the production fulcrum way over, thereby increasing your empowerment leverage. This holds for both growth and routine activities.

Stewardship delegation involves commitment regarding expectations in five areas:

- *Desired results.* Generate a mutual understanding of what needs to be accomplished, focusing on what, not how, and on results, not methods. Spend time. Visualize the needed outcome. Have the officer describe for you how the results will look and when they will be achieved.
- *Guidelines.* Carefully identify the boundaries within which the person must function. These should be as flexible as possible. If you know of any land mines, be certain to reveal them. In other words, instruct the officer in what not to do, but don't tell him or her what to do. Keep the responsibility for the officer's performance with the officer—to do whatever is essential, but within the guidelines.
- *Resources.* Identify the various resources that the officer can use to obtain the preferred outcomes.
- *Accountability.* Establish minimum standards that will be applied in evaluating the officer's work effort and determining whether violations have occurred.
- *Consequences.* Indicate what will happen, both positive (rewards) and negative (reprimands) as an outcome of the evaluation.

Stewardship delegation on occasion includes some highly routine processes. Writing crime reports can become monotonous after a while. Routine work is unavoidable. It happens to all of us. The saving grace is that at least it's our routine and not someone else's. We own it and can even change it within the guidelines.

Gofer Delegation. Gofer delegation is highly routine assigned work wherein you go for this, go for that. You're not encouraged to think of the task as being part of your job. Indeed, you're probably not encouraged to think at all.

Gofer delegation is a turnoff for police employees. Ask them, and they'll tell you it is. Some even respond, "Why don't you just do the job yourself? I'm merely an errand boy. I'm not learning anything. I'm not growing."

Delegation Dump . Delegation dump occurs when you give one of your staff all of your work. Or you assign your work out over all of your team. Those who engage in the dumping of their work on others are viewed as lazy and incompetent. The delegation dumper rationalizes that he or she is doing a great career service to others. They're learning to do advanced types of tasks. In reality, they are being victimized by a clueless boss who is assigning them excessive work.

STRUCTURED EXERCISE 8–5

Make a list of responsibilities you could delegate, and identify the police personnel you could delegate to or train to be responsible in these areas. Determine what is needed to start the process of delegation or training.

Microdelegation.   Microdelegation is microsupervising. The microdelegators are afraid that if they do not direct you each and every moment, the work won't be done right. They look over your shoulder and constantly meddle in your work. How much does microdelegation really accomplish? How many people is it possible to supervise when you microdelegate? The answers are, respectively, "not much" and "very few." Employees subjected to microdelegation are often angry, frustrated, and seeking another work team. In an environment where we must have every good idea from every man and woman in the police organization, we cannot afford management or supervisory styles that suppress and intimidate.

Assessing Your Delegation Style

Are you delegating appropriately? These questions will help you determine whether you are or not:

1. Have you transmitted the overarching vision with clarity? Does the officer, through demonstrated behavior, clearly "buy in"?
2. Is the officer aware of the level of performance standards?
3. Do you trust the officer, and have you conveyed your trust?
4. Are you known for butting in at the last minute to handle a problem that someone is experiencing with his or her assignment?
5. Do you hold your tongue when asking questions about someone's work efforts?
6. Have you avoided excessive reporting?
7. When the officer stops by, do you avoid giving direct orders or implying that such and such may be a better approach?

PARTICIPATION

I have seen on the desks of a couple of police supervisors the epigram "When I want your opinion, I'll give it to you." Unfortunately, I discovered that they weren't kidding. A few years ago a police chief told me, "I'm a great believer in participative management. I'm going to manage, and you'd damn well better participate." How would you feel about working for this type of supervisor? (Are *you* this type of supervisor?)

Misconceptions about Participation

> Allowing others to have an opportunity to express their ideas, needs, and hopes about an issue or a pending decision that affects them—that's what *participation* means.

Some police supervisors voice irritation with, and resistance to, participation. "We're not running a democracy here," they say. "I make the decision, and they're expected to get with it." In part, I agree. A police organization cannot be effective if the majority rules. Can you imagine a police sergeant, during roll call briefing, asking his officers to vote on whether they want to patrol or stay in the station? The sergeant is being paid to make such decisions.

> Do you wonder why people reject an idea, general order, or new policy? Often it is because they had no input— "No one asked me!"

The truth is that letting others participate in decisions that may affect them does not surrender your authority or responsibility for the ultimate decision. It's yours; you got it when you decided to become a supervisor. You can give it away, but no one can take it away from you. Through the participation of others, you listen, you learn, and then you're highly likely to make a much more reliable decision.

Why Allow Others to Participate?

Should you allow—or encourage—others to participate in decisions that might affect their ability to do their job? Here are some reasons why you should:

- The best means for getting a good idea is to generate a lot of ideas.
- Participation makes others believe that you really care about their welfare and work.
- Inclusion in a decision-making process usually increases participants' commitment to the eventual implementation of the decision.
- Increased commitment often causes increased productivity.
- Participation fosters a sense of teamwork.
- Teamwork leads to synergy, wherein the mental energy of a few people multiplies into what hundreds are capable of contributing.

Let's now examine some reasons not to encourage your staff to get involved in the decision-making process:

- Participation takes time. You'll have to listen to others (eight, nine, or more people at one time).
- You may experience a sense of frustration or insecurity when confronted with ideas that refute yours.

- You may be convinced of the correctness of their approach—the easy route—and thus opt for group consensus.
- Some may accuse you of manipulating or conning them. "The sergeant asked me for my opinion. She then proceeded to do the exact opposite of what I suggested." (This can be corrected by simply providing feedback on the reasons for your decision. It may be as candid as "My gut told me so.")

These lists of reasons for and against participation are starter lists. Add to them as you deem appropriate. But if you've decided to empower yourself and those who work for you, then participation is nonnegotiable.

Why Is Participation So Effective?

In today's employer-employee relations, few practices have been as successful in developing consensus and attaining common goals as the development of participation by the police supervisor.

- Participation is an amazingly simple way to inspire police employees. And its simplicity lies in the definition of *participation*: "to share in common with others."
- Sharing, then, is the secret. You must share knowledge and information with others to gain their cooperation. You must share your own experience so that officers will gain from it. You must share the decision-making process itself so that personnel can have impact. And you must share credit for achievement.

Once you've learned how to share, participation is self-perpetuating. Leadership becomes easier when police employees begin to share responsibility with you. No longer do you alone have to watch for every problem. Employees won't wait for you to say what to do in an emergency. You'll find the officers using their own initiative to keep crime down. So sharing pays off as employees share your decision and their work accomplishments with you.

Three Rules

There are three fundamental rules to abide by. First, recognize that without group support your chance of achievement is reduced. Second, your best chance for winning group support is by allowing the forces within the group to comment on a decision that you're going to make. But you must not stand by while your "team strikes off in the wrong direction. You can offer sound coaching by providing facts that might be overlooked and by asking the group to weigh pros and cons of various options. Again, the decision remains yours to make. Third, be honest with yourself. Are you using participation to motivate or to manipulate? If it is the former, congratulations. If it is the latter, eventually the officers will discover that they are being conned. When this happens, kiss both your supervisory power and leadership goodbye.

Police supervisors must strive for the antithesis of blind obedience. They need people who have the self-confidence to express opposing views, get all the facts on the table, and respect differing opinions. It's a preferred mode of learning; it's how we form balanced judgments.

ENTITLEMENT IS EMPOWERMENT IN EXCESS

All the recent attention to empowerment has reinforced, unintentionally, our zeal for entitlement (you-owe-it-to-me). Believing that, now empowered, we can do exactly what we want, and get all that we ask for, is simply trying to win at the new game. Doing our own thing is a self-serving act. Line employees can use empowerment as a weapon. In the name of empowerment, people have asked for

- More pay
- A larger budget
- More people, more empire
- Freedom to pursue strictly personal projects
- Greater recognition and privilege
- Immunity from disappointment from those above
- A risk-free environment

Just because we have been encouraged to find our voice and stand up without getting mistreated does not mean that we are going to get all we ask for. Empowerment is a commitment to a dialogue, not an act of concession. It is based on reciprocal commitments. When coming out of a high-control management system, there is a tendency to take advantage of the choice handed us. The following are three ways police employees can exploit their freedom:

- If a decision is made that we don't agree with, we begin to undermine that decision, either actively or passively.
- We do not take responsibility for promises others in our unit have made. The belief that no one else can represent my viewpoint is a subtle form of disobedience.
- In expressing our opinion, we expect immunity from our coworkers' rejection or resentment.

> A sense of being entitled is based on the "you owe it to me" syndrome. It is a warped sense of duty to one's self. When we think of looking out for our own interests as a duty, it legitimizes a self-absorbed viewpoint that puts personal desires on equal footing with our ethical responsibilities to others, both within and outside the workplace.

Entitlement also rests on the belief that something is owed us because of sacrifices we have made. What is hard to accept, though, is that, whatever we think we sacrificed, it was a choice that we made. In fact, the more the police department gives us that we may not have earned, the more entitled we feel.

Choosing Empowerment

The decision to pursue the principles and practice of empowerment is an issue of leadership strategy, but at its core, it is foremost a matter of individual choice. Police chiefs can create the social architecture and practices to support empowerment, but individuals have to make the decision to accept it. Finally, training people to be empowered requires team training, which is Responsibility 9.

KEY POINTS

- Supervisors are responsible for motivating their staff to accomplish the mission for the department.
- The reasons for having motivated police workers are improved job performance and high job satisfaction.
- Motivating others must start with you.
- Motivation and performance are not identical.
- Motivators can be intrinsic or extrinsic.
- Individual job satisfaction determines group morale.
- No longer can supervisors avoid the power and practicality of recognizing and rewarding their staff.
- The first and most critical requirement when praising people is sincerity.
- Retaining police employees depends on the ability of the police leader to motivate them to stay with the agency.
- While everyone is capable of benefiting from being motivated to achieve the department's mission, there are usually a few who resist doing so.
- Delegation and participation lead to empowerment of personnel.
- A lot is known about the benefits of empowerment, but few supervisors actually practice it.
- When it comes to delegation, there is a significant difference between "letting go" and "*really* letting go."
- Four parties benefit from proper delegation: the community, the department, the supervisor, and the staff.
- There are four ways to delegate: stewardship, gofer delegation, delegation dump, and microdelegation.
- Building a workplace context requires training, high standards, values and needs, communication, rewards, reprimands, feedback, and—most of all—trust.
- Letting others participate in decisions that are going to affect them does not surrender a leader's authority or responsibility for the final decision.
- Teamwork is participative supervision.
- The key to participation is sharing.
- Uncontrolled empowerment, results in an "entitlement mentality."

EXTENDED LEARNING

1. Why might a police officer with a very high level of motivation perform poorly?
2. Why might an employee with a very low level of motivation be a top performer?
3. How do motivation and job satisfaction relate to each other?
4. Add to the list of causes of job satisfaction.
5. Also, add to the list of consequences of poor job satisfaction.
6. What is meant by "really letting go" when one delegates? What are the advantages in doing so? Are any risks involved?
7. There are eight forces that must be functioning when a leader delegates. Rank the eight forces in terms of their importance.
8. When is a police supervisor justified in using gofer delegation or microdelegation? Explain.
9. Why should others participate in decisions that are going to affect them? Why shouldn't they?
10. What is the key or secret of participation? Why is it effective?
11. What should the leader do to avoid or combat entitlement thinking within the work team?

RESPONSIBILITY 9

Team Training

> The police supervisor is responsible for training a group of independently minded employees with all of their vast diversity and forging them into an interdependent team—one that is united, but not uniform.

> All of the prior responsibilities are now fused with mutual trust and team training in order to deliver team-based decision making.

Team spirit means you are willing to sacrifice personal considerations for the welfare of all. That defines a team player.

—John Wooden

One of a baby's earliest words is *mine*. We enter the world totally dependent on others for our survival. Most of us are encouraged as we grow up to be independent—to be self-sufficient, to be competitive. We place a high value on being independent. But being interdependent is of higher value than being independent.

As we grow and mature, we become increasingly aware that all of nature is interdependent. We realize that an ecological system governs nature, including society and the organizations within it. We further discover that human life also is interdependent.

Let us look at maturity as a continuum:

- Dependence is seeing the world in terms of *you*—you take care of me; you help me; you're responsible for me.
- Independence is seeing the world in terms of *I*—I can do it; I am responsible; I can choose.
- Interdependence is the model of *we*—we can do it; we can cooperate; we are responsible.

> Dependent employees need others to get what they want. Independent employees can get what they want through their own effort. Interdependent employees combine their efforts—form a work team—to achieve their goals.

It is the successful supervisor who realizes the need for the best thinking, a coordinated effort, and mutual support to be truly effective. Independent supervisors who do not have the maturity to think and act interdependently may be good individual producers, but they won't be good leaders or team players.

Teamwork depends on people who are willing to function as interdependent contributors. For this to occur, they must first trust one another and then be trained to operate as a team. This chapter focuses on the need for interdependence rather than independence or dependence. In the sections that follow, we'll cover the important advantages of team performance. We deal with trust and training, which are the two essential underpinnings for team building. Finally, we will look at a major hurdle confronted by any endeavor to foster teamwork: cultural diversity and core cracking. This team approach will be the hallmark of the great police departments of the twenty-first century.

WHY ESTABLISH TEAMS?

Although establishing teams frequently involves a lot of training, the effort provides three things important to group effectiveness:

- Synergy
- Interdependence
- A support base

Synergy

What energy is to the individual, synergy is to groups. The synergy of a group is always potentially greater than the sum of the energies of its members. Most often a group effort results in a better performance than that achieved by the group's most competent member. If you doubt it, have three people independently make a bed. Then have them make three beds jointly. Successful police supervisors create synergy in their work unit.

Interdependence

Effective teams are made up of highly independent individuals who must combine their separate efforts to produce an organizational result. The focus of the team effort is on combining rather than on coordinating resources. Interdependence in today's organizations is a simple reality. Police services are too complex and the respective technologies too specialized for any one individual to master alone. Successful police supervisors create interdependence in their work unit.

A Support Base

The police team constructed for alignment has the potential to provide social and emotional support for its members, producing a more satisfying and work-productive environment. It is important to note that, for a group truly to function as a support base, the group norms that emerge for any specific team must originate from within the team itself and not represent a set of "shoulds" from the behavioral sciences or other social institutions. It is more fun (or it should be) to work with someone else than to work alone! Successful police supervisors create a supportive work climate for their crew.

TRAINING

It is a paradox that while everyone seems to be in favor of teamwork, there isn't a lot of it around. Trust building and team building are connected. You push for one, and the other responds as well. Hence if you start training police employees as a team, they are likely to trust one another more and function as a team.

Regretfully, the majority of police training is individually based. One person heads for a problem-oriented policing seminar and another for an ethics course. The majority of police training today at all levels in a department constrains team building. The more team training, the better the morale and the better the quality of services.

As a trainer (or developer of human resources), you influence an officer's values, attitudes, perceptions, learning, motivation, job satisfaction, stress, and wellness. As a trainer, you sway group dynamics, communications, and followership (your leadership). Likewise, you affect goal setting, planning, managing by objectives, performance appraisal, discipline, conflict resolution, community relations, labor relations, and your professional success. Pointedly, then, much of your success or failure as a supervisor hinges on your ability to train—especially teamwork.

The Police Supervisor as Trainer

The police supervisor is in a most advantageous position to influence personal and organizational development in a law enforcement agency. Hence the basic premise: The police supervisor has a responsibility to improve the human resources within his or her purview, in line with attaining the goals of the agency.

Many police agencies have established a field training officer (FTO) position. This officer is usually provided with some form of incentive to "coach" a newer officer in the performance of his or her duties while on the job (on-the-job training, or OJT). Agency after agency has found the FTO program most helpful in assisting a new police officer to quickly build proper job attitudes and behavior. Briefly, an FTO program provides close coaching and monitoring of a new officer's demeanor by a senior officer who has received special training. Untrained FTOs can create as much damage as benefit to a department. An FTO program should be used by a police supervisor as one of many training methods for ensuring the agency that their assigned staff are peak performers. An FTO program does not eliminate or reduce the supervisor's responsibility for training.

Training Goals

Training has two fundamental goals: to make lasting improvements in the performance of the officer's job and to develop his or her capacity for handling higher levels of responsibility. Consequently, training means a change—that is, a change on the part of the individual and the organization. Both are interdependent partners in any process of change.

Six key attitudes underscore police training goals today:

- Motivations attached to skills lead to action. Skills are acquired through practice.
- Learning is a result of the motivation and capacity of the individual, the norms of the training group, the training methods and the behavior of the trainers, and the general climate of the police organization.
- Improvement on the job is caused by individual learning, the norms of the working group, and the general climate of the organization. Individual learning, unused, leads to frustration.
- Training is the responsibility of three partners: the organization, the trainee, and the trainer. It has preparatory, pretraining, and posttraining phases.
- Training is a continuous process and a vehicle for consistently updating the skills of individual officers.
- Training is also a continuous process and a vehicle for consistently improving the capacity of individual officers to behave as a team.

STRUCTURED EXERCISE 9–1

LEARNING NEEDS QUESTIONNAIRE

Circle the number that you feel best represents your experience.

I am not well prepared for my job.	1	2	3	4	5	I am fully prepared for my job.
I lack essential skills for my job.	1	2	3	4	5	I have all the essential skills for my job.
I was not carefully introduced to my job.	1	2	3	4	5	I was carefully introduced to my job.
I found it difficult to learn my job.	1	2	3	4	5	I learned my job with minimal difficulty.
I have no opportunities for development.	1	2	3	4	5	I have good opportunities for development.
I have far too little proper training.	1	2	3	4	5	I have sufficient training.
My boss is not concerned about training needs.	1	2	3	4	5	My boss is concerned about training needs.

Establishing Training Objectives.   Since any training objective is based on the vision of the police department, the main question is whether the department's objectives are realistic. Furthermore, is the training input of the program realistic? Or is training in danger of being misused? For example, is it too little and too late?

> The training objectives must support organizational activities, and the training objectives must be realistic.

To accomplish these two foundational training principles, the following four questions must be answered:

1. *Is the training needed?* Be certain that a needed change calls for training. What the police organization needs may not be training, at least not immediately, but lots of detailed operational planning and implementation of plans. Training at this stage would be a disservice if it deprived the organization of skilled people currently needed for action.
2. *Where does it fit?* Define the part that police training can play in the change. What new competencies does the department require, and which of these can be acquired through systematic training? Training strategy determines which goals can reasonably be achieved through a training program and which cannot. And vice versa: The goals determine which training strategy is most appropriate.
3. *How much, and who?* The third step is more taxing and worthy of the most careful consideration; it concerns questions of quantities and levels of police personnel to be trained, and of timing and training as well.
4. *The team?* The final question involves training for teamwork. People who work together must be trained together. The truly effective police work units are trained like any successful sports team. All members know what their job consists of, what they should provide to others, and what they can expect of others.

Selecting Training Strategies.   Any attempt to train—that is, to change—an individual automatically means a freezing-up of relations between people. The freezing-up of relations involves three stages: unfreezing, moving, and refreezing.

Unfreezing is necessary because the police officer (and his or her organization, family, and locality) comes with habits, values, and practices—the very opposite of a clean slate. To affect the officer through training, normal habits first have to be questioned and disturbed, or unfrozen.

Training can do this by focusing on needs that new police officers cannot develop by habitual behavior. The supervisor then introduces other events that allow officers to try new ways of behaving, that is, changing. If the police officers find the new behavior more useful in meeting the "new" needs, they can then be helped to make it habitual. Each officer thus gains a new set of behavioral patterns, which he or she then freezes.

Delivering Training.   As a police supervisor, you are responsible for the delivery of needed training to your personnel. While the style may vary from a stand-up, roll-call lecture to ride-along coaching, train you must.

It is not sufficient to make police training supplemental to work; police work must be organized to facilitate training and development. Three factors support this conclusion:

- First, training by a police agency is critical because the training demands are ever expanding in local law enforcement.
- Second, we live in an age of revolution in the processes, in the systems, and in the products of public and private organizations.
- Third, in some instances you and the agency may be legally vulnerable if personnel are not trained in certain critical skills.

The training duties are great. Increasingly, training must be part and parcel of the work itself, and it should be increasingly supplied and directly monitored by the immediate supervisor.

> If your department managers are astute, they are rating your performance as a police supervisor, to a major extent, on your ability to deliver timely and useful training to others. Trainers and supervisors are one and the same. Effective trainers and effective supervisors build teams.

Evaluating Your Accomplishments.   The evaluation of training frequently becomes a popularity contest or merely an instance of selective feedback. The key questions should be

- What, precisely, did you learn?
- Why is it important to you and your agency?
- How do you plan to use your new knowledge or skills?

These questions demand follow-up and feedback on your part. A final critical and, at times, risky question is, "How can I, your supervisor, improve as a trainer?"

TEAM TRAINING

By its very nature, teamwork depends on the effectiveness of the interaction among team members. The concepts of contact, role, and values are elements of effective team interaction. Good contact is based on authenticity among team members. It implies that each individual is aware of his or her individuality and is willing to state views and ideas clearly and to support the principles of openness and conscious choice. An environment that encourages the open expression of disagreement, as well as agreement, accepts the reality that an individual may like some coworkers more than others. This is legitimate as long as openly stated preferences do not result in discriminatory, unfair, or task-destructive behavior.

All decisions, whether made by individuals or by groups, are based on work ethics. Three work ethics identify good working police teams: (1) task effectiveness, (2) dealing in the present, and (3) viewing conflict as an asset.

- *Task effectiveness.* The well-functioning group of police officers places a high value on task effectiveness, with greater emphasis on doing the right things than on doing things right. This ethic holds that the team also focuses on the objective, or end result, rather than only on the team's ongoing activity.

- *Dealing in the present.* The effective team focuses on "right here, right now," an emphasis that allows a flexible response to changing conditions within the team itself and within the larger organization. The team can make more appropriate decisions when it is concentrating on what is happening rather than on why it is happening.

- *Viewing conflict as an asset.* Conflict provides two very necessary elements to the effective work group. First, it is the prime source of energy in systems, and second, it is the major source of creativity. Because conflict is absolutely unavoidable in any case, an effective team's approach to dealing with it is to use it, rather than to try to resolve, avoid, or suppress it. More potential for ineffectiveness and marginal performance exists in avoiding conflict than in conflict itself. When conflict is seen as an opportunity, the preferred approach is to deal with it through collaboration (although competition is not precluded, when needed).

STRUCTURED EXERCISE 9–2

WORK GROUP EFFECTIVENESS INVENTORY

Work Group: _____

Date: _____

Complete this questionnaire and share the results. Circle one number for each statement (1 is low and 5 is high).

1. I have been speaking frankly here about the things that have been uppermost in my mind.	1 2 3 4 5			
2. The other members of this team have been speaking frankly about the things that have been uppermost in their minds.	1 2 3 4 5			
3. I have been speaking directly and to the point.	1 2 3 4 5			
4. The other members of this team have been speaking directly and to the point.	1 2 3 4 5			
5. I have been listening carefully to the other members of this team, and I have been paying special attention to strongly expressed views.	1 2 3 4 5			
6. The other members of this team have been listening carefully to me and to one another, and they have been paying special attention to strongly expressed views.	1 2 3 4 5			

(continued)

STRUCTURED EXERCISE 9–2 *(continued)*

7. I have been asking for and receiving constructive feedback regarding my influence on the team.   1 2 3 4 5

8. I have been providing constructive feedback to those who have requested it—to help them keep track of their influence on me and the other team members.   1 2 3 4 5

9. Our team's operating procedures and organization have changed rapidly whenever more useful structures or procedures have been discovered.   1 2 3 4 5

10. Everyone on the team has been helping the team keep track of its effectiveness.   1 2 3 4 5

Members of this team have been listening carefully to one another, and we have been paying special attention to strongly expressed values.   1 2 3 4 5

We have been speaking frankly to each other about the things that have been uppermost in our minds.   1 2 3 4 5

We have been speaking directly and to the point.   1 2 3 4 5

We have been helping our team keep track of its own effectiveness.   1 2 3 4 5

Our team's internal organization and procedures have been adjusted when necessary to keep pace with changing conditions or new requirements.   1 2 3 4 5

11. All members of this team understand the team's goals.   1 2 3 4 5

12. Each member of our team understands how they can contribute to the team's effectiveness in reaching its goals.   1 2 3 4 5

13. Each of us is aware of the potential contributions of the other team members.   1 2 3 4 5

14. We recognize each other's problems and help each other make a maximum contribution.   1 2 3 4 5

15. As a team, we pay attention to our own decision-making and problem-solving processes.   1 2 3 4 5

Calculate your score, and compare it to those of others. Where are the similarities and differences? What should be done to improve the scores?

ADVANTAGES OF TEAMS

The term *team* means

> Together
> Everyone
> Achieves
> Much

Despite the potential advantages of creating a shared-responsibility team, many supervisors express strongly negative sentiments about teams, groups, committees, and meetings. They associate teams with delays, endless talk (or false, constrained politeness), avoidance of responsibility, and other useless outcomes.

Suppose, however, that your staff could function as a team with the following characteristics:

1. Everyone knows their own and others' tasks well enough so that nothing falls through the cracks; everyone knows who is, and who should be, doing what.

2. Trust is so high that the officers do not need to meet on every issue. Each member is confident that no one, including the boss, would act without consultation unless there was a good reason, such as prior general agreement, special expertise, legitimate time pressures, or the unavailability of the affected parties. And the person who does act would know that others would back any action.

3. Such a group is not very clingy and does not waste time meeting about trivial issues or limiting those who have taken individual initiative.

4. Members who are clearly more expert than the others in certain areas are given great latitude to make the decisions on those matters.

5. Nevertheless, if issues cross several areas or affect the department as a whole, members seriously address the issues together, fight hard and openly for their beliefs, and insist that their concerns be addressed, while still paying attention to the needs of the department as a whole. Everyone is comfortable wearing at least two hats, one for their area and one for the department.

6. Although skilled at persuasion and willing to fight hard over important differences, members feel no obligation to automatically oppose initiatives from other members or the manager. There is no competition for competition's sake. Members enthusiastically support the positions or ideas of others when they happen to agree.

7. Despite members' willingness to fight when necessary, the climate is pervasively supportive, encouraging members to ask one another for help, acknowledge their mistakes, share resources (people, information, or equipment), and generally further everybody's performance and learning.

8. The group pays attention to successful task achievement and to individual members' learning. Members are not restricted to areas where they have total competence and hence can't acquire new expertise; neither are they so overloaded with learning experiences that group performance seriously suffers.

9. The group has self-correcting mechanisms; when things aren't going well, all members are ready to examine the group's processes, discuss what is wrong, and take corrective action. Whatever the problems—overly lengthy meetings, inappropriate agenda items, unclear responsibilities, lack of team effort, overly parochial participation, or even poor leadership practices—the group takes time out to assess its way of operating and to make midcourse corrections. Individual members as well as the manager feel free to raise questions of team performance.

Does this team profile sound too ideal? Is a well-developed team a fantasy that will remain frustratingly out of reach in the real world of petty politics, indirection, waffling, and hushed-corridor cabals? It could be, but not necessarily. I've seen police teams achieve this level of alignment. If you want a team effort, develop one. Trust and training are a two-edged tool for shaping teamwork.

STRUCTURED EXERCISE 9–3

Reread the nine characteristics of a well-functioning team. Think carefully about each characteristic as it pertains to your work group. Circle the proper number, and then compare your ratings with your fellow employees. How do you look as a team? Where are your strengths, and where are your deficiencies?

1. No One Knows / Everyone Knows

| 1 | 2 | 3 | 4 | 5 | 6 | 7 |

2. Low Trust / High Trust

| 1 | 2 | 3 | 4 | 5 | 6 | 7 |

3. Groupthink / Individual Initiative

| 1 | 2 | 3 | 4 | 5 | 6 | 7 |

4. Little Expertise / A Lot of Expertise

| 1 | 2 | 3 | 4 | 5 | 6 | 7 |

5. Issues Are Buried / Issues Are Addressed

| 1 | 2 | 3 | 4 | 5 | 6 | 7 |

6. Dysfunctional Competition / Functional Competition

| 1 | 2 | 3 | 4 | 5 | 6 | 7 |

7. No Support / Great Support

| 1 | 2 | 3 | 4 | 5 | 6 | 7 |

8. No Attention to Task Achievement / High Attention to Task Acheivement

| 1 | 2 | 3 | 4 | 5 | 6 | 7 |

9. External Correcting Mechanisms / Self-Correcting Mechanisms

| 1 | 2 | 3 | 4 | 5 | 6 | 7 |

TRUST

In Responsibility 5, we saw trust as forming "trust bank accounts" (TBAs). Return to that section now to refresh your memory, if necessary. What was stated there applies here.

There is no foolproof formula for establishing and maintaining trust in a work group. Nonetheless, there are steps that have proven valid in "funding" TBAs:

Believing

Police leaders must have an enduring belief that most people want to do a good job and that it is important for them to enjoy their work. Closely coupled with this is a strong belief that all individuals should be treated with consideration and respect and that their achievements should be recognized. This belief should encourage a work culture in which each person in the department counts and every job (from dispatcher to chief) counts.

Personality

One should not base one's work relationship on another person's personality, chemistry, or enjoyment. He or she may be a fun person, clever, bright, and more. But this doesn't mean you can trust that person. Supervisors who rely only on similar tastes, on personalities that mesh, or on the right chemistry and who ignore character and values, are setting themselves up for great disappointment.

Their Values

Find out what the other person's values are. Have a dialogue with the person, and probe his or her values. How important are goodness, honesty, and unselfishness to the person? What, if anything, is more important to the person than personal happiness? Not only are the person's answers to these questions important, but also it is revealing if the person gets annoyed when such issues are raised.

Finally, ask yourself, "If I had to prove to someone who never met my coworker how decent a person he or she is, what concrete evidence could I submit?"

Behavior

Pay at least as much attention to how the person treats others—especially people from whom they need nothing—as to how the person treats you. Watch, for example, how your staff members treat citizens and coworkers.

People generally treat decently those from whom they want something—a better assignment, help, approval, or a special favor. That someone treats you well may, therefore, reveal nothing about character (and may, therefore, not indicate how that individual will treat you later).

Your Values

Know your own values (Responsibility 2). If you don't have strong values yourself, or if you do but cannot clearly articulate them, the previous suggestions may be useless. How can you inquire or talk about values that you yourself either don't hold or can't identify? Thus the stronger and more focused your values become, the less likely you are to trust people with poor values.

Having the right values serves a professional purpose. Those who live by solid, proven values tend to bring such people into teams. And such employees are a great deal less likely to disappoint us as teammates.

In summary, you can best determine whom to trust (or not trust) by following these rules:

- Do not trust coworkers based on personality, chemistry, or congeniality alone.
- Find out what the other person's values are. While values are not enough to ensure a good working relationship, they can guide you in terms of whom to trust.
- Pay careful attention to how the coworker treats others, especially others from whom he or she needs nothing, and how the coworker treats you.
- Know your own values. If you do not have firmly held values and cannot clearly articulate them, the above rules are useless.

TEAM-BASED DECISION MAKING

Team training cultivates team-based decision making.

Team-based decision making is not a democratic process. (This is the crux of empowerment, as examined in Responsibility 8.) There isn't any vote among your crew on whether you should patrol tonight or stay in the station. Rather, team-based decision making is a process wherein everyone is expected to think out and voice their opinions on a subject or an issue. The supervisor retains full accountability for the ultimate decision.

Why consider using a team-based approach for making decisions? First, you get more and better ideas. Second, individual commitment to implementing the decision is significantly enhanced. Third, it makes for fast and accurate decision making when teams are under duress but must act.

Team training is neither simple nor easy. It is complex and time-consuming. It depends on your galvanizing a group of independently minded police officers into a mutually supportive crew that is dedicated to getting results. Any rewards or accolades go to the team, not to an individual. A supervisor's ability to lead a team is now a function of the team members' capacity to participate in its leadership.

TRAINING A DIVERSE WORKFORCE

Until the 1950s, American law enforcement primarily consisted of white, male employees representing two to three generations. The few female employees were relegated to clerical and technical jobs. Hence police departments were largely homogeneous in appearance. Obviously, the employees did differ due to their own unique individuality. As compared with today, training diverse workers was relatively simple. That's not the case now.

Training a diverse workforce means creating and maintaining a work environment in which all employees are respected because of their differences and all can contribute and be rewarded on the basis of their results.

"Respected because of their differences" means that we need to understand two things. First, "different" does not mean "less than." Second, different approaches and different opinions can be beneficial to making decisions and delivering services to a diverse customer base.

"Rewarded on the basis of their results" means that people should be rewarded because of what they do and how they produce, not because of who they know or because of their race, gender, age, religion, or any other characteristic.

There are four harmful misconceptions about diversity:

- *Training a diverse workforce is a disguise for affirmative action programs.* Often, in an organization in which perceptions and behaviors are not explored carefully, some people express the opinion that the oranization's goals for training are simply an attempt to meet affirmative action goals and quotas.

- *Training a diverse workforce is cultural diversity training.* Some may think that training is simply teaching appropriate behaviors to use when interacting with people of diverse races, national origins, mental or physical abilities, sexual orientations, or lifestyles.

    Team training for diversity goes beyond learning to act out a prescribed behavior. For some organizations or work teams, it will mean a basic change in the way people communicate, interact, process information, make decisions, and serve citizens. It is not a quick-fix recipe!

- *Training a diverse workforce is sensitivity training.* Team training is not some touchy-feely training session. Supervising and training are a way for us to understand and appreciate ourselves better so we can understand the factors and situations that motivate our personal beliefs, values, and behaviors. This allows us to accept, then respect, others who may have different beliefs, values, lifestyles, and ways of doing things at work.

- *Training a diverse workforce is an effort to mirror our citizen base.* Some, managers and organization leaders feel it is important that we mirror, or look like, the citizens we serve. While it may give us some initial comfort, merely having work teams that look like those we serve cannot represent the ultimate goal for achieving success.

    When we train effectively, we discover that added personal differences or personal similarities cannot be attributed necessarily to race, gender, or lifestyle. We get better at recognizing the differences, respecting the differences, and expecting the differences to enrich our relationships and contribute to better-quality performance and behavior results.

Everyone Belongs to a Minority Group

> The all-male workforce is history. Sameness of sex and ethnicity is out, and diversity is in.

In terms of sheer numbers, women dominate the "information age." Ninety percent of working women are part of the information service sector. Of the people whose job titles fall under the category of "professional"—versus clerical, technical, or laborer—the majority are women. Forty-four percent of adult working women (ages 25 to 64) are college-educated, compared with 20 percent in 1965. Further, six out of ten people joining the workforce right now are female.

Today, white men are already less than half of the labor force. By 2010, married couples will no longer be a majority of households. Asians will outnumber Jews by a margin of two-to-one, and Hispanics will lead blacks as the nation's largest minority.

By 2020, immigration will become more important to U.S. population growth than natural increase (the growth that occurs because births outnumber deaths). The population will diversify even more rapidly.

Dangerous Delusions

No other nation is as challenged as the United States in bringing large numbers of highly diverse people together in organizational settings and then expecting supervisors to build cooperative and happy work teams. Unfortunately, some of us have been deluded by these false hopes or assumptions:

Laws and Policies.   Legislating and policy making are not the answers to worker diversity! Granted, we need laws and policies concerning hate crimes, discrimination based on age, sexual harassment, and other such illegal behaviors. But these laws do not ensure antiracist, antisexist, or antisectarian thoughts. The ideal we seek is best approached by encouraging individuals to share and resolve their differences. Team training works!

Political Correctness.   Being politically correct (PC) means suppressing "hate speech," which is loosely defined as anything that any recognized minority group chooses to find offensive. Hence there is considerable latitude in determining what is or is not PC. In my opinion, political correctness is insincere, deceitful, and dysfunctional.

A more honest alternative for building solid working relationships is being professionally correct (PRO-C). If you are PRO-C, then you are automatically behaving in accordance with ethical standards and common decency. You are being truthful to yourself and others while simultaneously being sensitive to human feelings. Team training helps!

"Give Me the List."   Some of us are deluded by assuming that you can get a laundry list of do's and don'ts and that following that list will help you be PC and avoid blunders. In matters of humor or just ordinary topics of discussion, you have to shed knee-jerk assumptions. Not every African-American plays basketball. Not everyone with a Latino surname speaks Spanish. Not all Asians are Chinese. For that matter, not all whites come from the ruling class. As a consequence, assume nothing about a person except that he or she has values and that you must understand them to be successful in your job as supervisor and leader.

Diversity for Profit.   There are consultants, lecturers, tests, and films: an entire industry has been born to fuel and feed off of the privilege of a lifetime—being who you are.

> American society, long founded on the notion of "from many, one,"—*e pluribus unum*—is being deluded into a poisonous floodtide of negation, sectarianism, self-pity, confrontation, vulgarity, and flat-out old-fashioned hatred.

Almost a hundred years after the last great immigration wave changed the face of American society, vast numbers of Americans—including, sadly, the best educated—are again being taught to identify themselves with the qualifying adjectives of race, religion, generation, and gender. Our self-identity is shaped not by will, choice, reason, intelligence, and desire but by membership in groups. We are not individuals but components of categories.

What Can a Police Leader Do?

Here is a list of things that you, as a leader, can do to team-train a diverse workforce:

- Remember that each one of us is diverse—we're individuals with unique value systems. Appreciate the differences.
- When your values are being assaulted, remember that conflict will ensue.
- Remember that in many cases, what may be referred to as a "diversity problem" (e.g., male versus female) is in reality a supervisory problem, such as one caused by status differences (e.g., sworn officers demeaning the work of civilian dispatchers). A work issue cleverly masked as a diversity issue will be made worse if you use the wrong approach to resolve it.
- Remember that the three core values for either avoiding or solving employee diversity problems are caring, trusting, and communications/understanding.
- You will have to be especially adroit in team-training a more diverse workforce. Be sure to recognize the enormous power that is unleashed by a diverse workforce. It is one of this nation's paramount strengths, and this should hold true for its police agencies.
- Finally, remember that team-training a diverse workforce demands a lot of intelligence—emotional intelligence.

KEY POINTS

- Teamwork requires interdependent thinking and effort.
- The main purpose for teamwork is, through alignment, to produce synergy within the work group.

- An FTO program does not diminish or detract from a supervisor's training function.
- Your delivery of training should be subjected to constant evaluation by your boss, yourself, and the trainees.
- Teamwork can occur only if there is mutual trust and training as a team.
- Trust should be based on knowing the other person's values, as well as your own.
- Team training is a key responsibility of a police supervisor.
- The most difficult of all training goals for the supervisor is that of building and maintaining a work team.
- Team training is the basis of team-based decision making.
- Team training is one of the better ways to solve diversity problems.
- Emotional intelligence is the cornerstone for team training in a diverse workforce.

EXTENDED LEARNING

1. Why is an interdependent work group so important? How can an interdependent group avoid the pitfall of groupthink?
2. Review the steps mentioned for building trust. Are there steps that should be added? If so, what are they? Can you like someone but not trust that person? What about the reverse—trust but not like someone?
3. In your opinion, what are the major training needs of a police officer today? Rank them in terms of importance.
4. What is being done in your department or work unit to respect diversity (individuality) while forging a team effort? What else should be done?
5. Who has the primary responsibility when making a team-based decision—the team leader or the team members?
6. When an individual speaks out against the group consensus in your police organization, what is the probable outcome? Will the individual be rewarded or censured?
7. What is emotional intelligence, and how does it relate to team training?
8. How do you rate your own EI? Explain.

RESPONSIBILITY 10

Vitality

The police supervisor is responsible for understanding and effectively promoting individual and organizational vitality within the workforce.

All of the preceding responsibilities, as well as those that follow, encompass change, and change is stress-laden. We can either convert stress into human vitality or allow it to wear us down.

The height of human wisdom is to bring our tempers down to our circumstances, and to make a calm within, under the weight of the greatest storm without.

—Daniel Defoe

Victor Frankl was a Jewish psychiatrist imprisoned in the death camps of Nazi Germany, where he experienced the living hell of the Holocaust. Except for his sister, his entire family died. He suffered torture and the daily uncertainty of being sent to the gas ovens.

One day, naked and alone in a small room, he became aware that his Nazi captors could not take away his freedom or his power to choose, within himself, how all of the threats, punishments, and injustices were going to affect him.

Using his disciplined mind and applying mainly his memory and imagination, he exercised his freedom of choice until he actually had more freedom than his captors. He survived the death camps, and he wrote and lectured about his experiences for many years thereafter.

Every day we have many choices facing us. One choice is to use stress or incoming demands for change as a positive force for vitality. Another choice is to allow it to unnecessarily beat us up.

179

As a police supervisor, you are responsible for preventing stress from attacking your vitality and the vitality of your staff.

STRESS AND VITALITY

Stress is an everyday fact of life. You can't avoid it! Stress is any change that you must adapt to, ranging from the negative extreme of actual physical danger to the exhilaration of falling in love or achieving some long-desired success. And in between, even the most well-managed life encounters a continuous stream of potentially stressful experiences. All stress is not bad. In fact, stress is not only desirable but also essential to life. Whether the stress you experience is the result of major life changes or the cumulative effect of minor everyday worries, it is how you respond to these experiences that determines the impact stress will have on you.

A recent poll reported that adults experience stress in their daily lives: frequently—42%; sometimes—38%; rarely—18%; never—2%.

Stress is a given; the only way to eliminate it is to die. If mismanaged or ignored, stress can cause us a great deal of harm. It can become distress. But if recognized and managed, stress can produce wellness. Like Victor Frankl, you have a choice. When a change occurs, will you handle it as something distressful or as an opportunity for wellness?

We will first cover some general information about stress. Next, you'll explore your stress level. Finally, we will consider personal mastery, your wellness, and vitality as a supervisor. Keep these two points in mind as you proceed:

- Stress is a demand on us to change.
- How we handle stress determines whether it is harmful (distress) or helpful (vitality).

THE FIGHT-OR-FLIGHT RESPONSE

The groundwork for the modern meaning of *stress* was laid by Walter B. Cannon, a physiologist at Harvard around the turn of the last century. He was the first to describe the "fight-or-flight response" as a series of biochemical changes that prepares us to deal with threats or danger. Primitive man needed quick bursts of energy to fight or flee such predators as a saber-toothed tiger. These days, when social custom prevents you from fighting or running away, this "emergency response" is rarely useful.

What Happens to Our Body

Hans Selye, the first major researcher on stress, was able to trace exactly what happens in the body during the fight-or-flight response. He found that any problem, imagined or real, can cause the cerebral cortex (the thinking part of the brain) to send an alarm to the hypothalamus (the main switch for the stress response, located in the midbrain). The hypothalamus then stimulates the sympathetic nervous system to make a series of changes in your body. Your heart rate, breathing rate, muscle tension, metabolism, and blood pressure all increase. Your hands and feet get cold as blood is directed away from your extremities and digestive system into the larger muscles that can help you fight or run. You experience butterflies in your stomach. Your diaphragm and anus lock. Your pupils dilate to sharpen your vision, and your hearing becomes more acute.

While all of this is going on, something else happens that can have long-term negative effects if left unchecked. Your adrenal glands start to secrete corticoids (adrenaline, epinephrine, and norepinephrine), which inhibit digestion, reproduction, growth, tissue repair, and the responses of your immune and inflammatory systems. In other words, some very important functions that keep your body healthy begin to shut down.

The Relaxation Response

The same mechanism that turned the stress response on can turn it off. This is called the "relaxation response." As soon as you decide that a situation is no longer dangerous, your brain stops sending emergency signals to your brain stem, which in turn ceases to send panic messages to your nervous system. Three minutes after you shut off the danger signals, the fight-or-flight response burns out. Your metabolism, heart rate, breathing rate, muscle tension, and blood pressure all return to their normal levels. You can use your mind to change your physiology for the better, improving your health and perhaps reducing your need for medication. This is the relaxation response, which refers to a natural restorative process.

A Threefold Process

The response to stress involves a threefold process consisting of (1) the direct effect of the stressor on the body, (2) internal responses that stimulate tissue defense or help to destroy damaging substances, and (3) internal responses that cause tissue surrender by inhibiting unnecessary or excessive defense. Resistance and adaptation depend on a proper balance of these three factors. Specific steps to protect yourself and your personnel are covered later. But for now, realize that most standard medical textbooks attribute anywhere from 50 to 80 percent of all disease to psychosomatic or stress-related origins. And stress-related psychological and physiological disorders have become a major social and health problem in the last decade. Stress-induced disorders have long since replaced epidemics of infectious disease as the major medical problem of twenty-first-century infotech nations.

VITALITY AND INTEGRITY

Vitality is as much a question of integrity as it is a matter of time pressure and fear of failure.

STRUCTURED EXERCISE 10–1

When faced with a potential compromise of your integrity, try using the Three-Minute Temptation Buster. Find a quiet and private spot, take off your watch, and sit down. Focus on your integrity and what you stand for. In less than three minutes, you'll find that the temptation has vanished.

When we are tempted to compromise our values, we are tampering with our integrity. When we succumb to such temptation and do something we really don't believe in doing to attain a goal, one of two very stressful things occurs: Either we gain the prize and realize it wasn't worth it, or we end up with neither the prize nor our integrity. One person put it this way: Even if you end up winning the rat race, you're still a rat. And this is highly stressful.

Your vitality and wellness depend on maintaining your integrity. Integrity means being whole, unbroken, undivided. It describes a person who has successfully united the different parts of his or her character. A person with integrity has no difficulty solving ongoing internal battles. This person is at peace with themselves. Stressful events are easily and quickly dispatched because of a character that is centered in integrity. Character counts, but it only counts when based on integrity. Vitality and values are positive teammates; we need them in our quest for the person and supervisor we want to be. Conversely, moral compromise and its partner—debilitating distress—are cleverly programmed to attack our character and destroy our number one value: integrity.

No matter how competent, a supervisor without integrity is doomed to failure.

THE RESPONSIBILITY OF THE POLICE SUPERVISOR

The responsibility of the police supervisor is to understand and effectively promote individual and organizational vitality within the workforce.

Individual Implications

There is a "stress fad," or syndrome, in police organizations today. Granted, police work is a stressful occupation. But so are many others. I can assure you that the business supervisor, fire captain, supervising nurse, construction foreman, and so on experience stress in their daily activities. What is important is (1) knowing when stress has become too much or too little and (2) maintaining a stress-reduction or wellness program. This applies to both the supervisor and their assigned personnel.

Police supervision is largely a constant process of adaptation to the "spice of life" that is change. The prescription for health and happiness is (1) to successfully adapt to ever-changing circumstances and (2) to remember that the penalties for failure to adjust to change are illness (physical and mental) and unhappiness. Interestingly, the very same stressful event or level of stress that may make one person ill may be a motivating experience for someone else. It is through the general adaptation syndrome that the various internal organs, especially the endocrine glands and the nervous system, help us adapt to the constant changes that occur in and around us and navigate a reasonably steady course toward whatever we consider a meaningful purpose.

As a supervisor, remember that your vitality and the vitality of your staff depend on how well you cope with stress:

- Stress in daily life is natural, pervasive, and unavoidable and thus is to be expected.
- Depending on how you choose to cope with stressful events, the experience of stress can be positive (healthy and vital) or negative (sickening and exhausting).
- Because people differ in a variety of ways, their means of and success in coping with stressful incidents will vary.
- A mental-physiological mechanism known as the "general adaptation syndrome" helps us adjust to demands for change.
- By definition, stress is the nonspecific response of the body to any demand for change. The demand can be from within or from the environment.
- Police supervisors are subjected to megachanges. As a result, they typically experience high levels of stress.
- Supervisors are in a key position to help their staff deal with stressful events and, in turn, preserve their vitality.

STRUCTURED EXERCISE 10–2

The way to reduce physical stress is relatively simple. The principle underlying physical stress control is that it is impossible for anyone to exist in two contradictory states simultaneously. You cannot be short and tall at the same time. You cannot be pregnant and not pregnant concurrently. Vigor and fatigue cannot coexist. Similarly, it is impossible to be stressed and physically relaxed at the same time. If you know how to find a state of physical relaxation and how to sustain it, you will be better able to prevent the occurrence of physical stress overload, and you will be able to control excessive tension once it has occurred.

A stress-control formula is useful here. You need to learn how to focus on physically relaxed states, how to rehearse physical relaxation responses until they can be achieved quickly and with ease, and how to implement the physical relaxation response before or during a stressful event.

Focusing on a physically relaxed state is achieved in three steps. First, use diaphragmatic breathing in slow, four-second "in" and four-second "out" excursions to assist the relaxation process. Lie down on a flat surface, facing up, and place your hand on your stomach. When you breathe in, your stomach should slowly rise because the diaphragm, acting like a piston, moves out of the chest cavity to suck air into your lungs. At the same time, the diaphragm descends into the abdominal cavity, pushing your intestines down and forward—the cause of your rising stomach. Exhale slowly, and your stomach falls. Your rib cage should be quite still. It is needed

(continued)

STRUCTURED EXERCISE 10–2 (*continued*)

only during extreme exertion. Counting to four on each inhalation and exhalation is a restful breathing pattern.

Second, you must learn to relax your muscles and blood vessels. When your blood vessels are relaxed, your hands feel warm. When the blood vessels in your body are tense, your hands feel cold and clammy. You can increase the warmth of your hands by focusing on the sensations in your hand as it rests on the arm of the chair beside you. You can feel the texture of the arm of the chair on which your hand rests. Whatever the room temperature may be, your hands can feel the sensations of airy coolness, as well as of warmth. If you wish to intensify the warmth, simply keep "warmth" in a relaxed focus in your mind. Imagine lying on a sunny beach with the sun beating down on your hand. Imagine your body filling up with warmth from the toes on up.

To relax your muscles, you can take the hand that is gently resting on the arm of the chair beside you and tense all your fingers without pressing them into the chair. Your hand will feel like it is hovering just above the arm of the chair. Tense muscles make your limbs feel light. Now relax your arm, wrist, and fingers. The limb will feel heavy as it slouches on the arm on the chair.

Third, starting from the top of your head and proceeding through every muscle and joint in your body down to your toes, contract each muscle to feel the sensation of tension—the lightness—and then the weight and heaviness associated with muscular relaxation.

You must now learn to rehearse warming your hands, relaxing your muscles and joints, and breathing slowly with your diaphragm. Take about twenty minutes to do so. Do not watch the clock—just guess at a time span of roughly twenty minutes, and rehearse the relaxation of your breathing, blood vessels, and muscles.

While relaxing your body, you may wish to simultaneously relax your mind by using a mind-focusing exercise. When I practice relaxation, I breathe in cycles of three breaths, repeating in my mind the following:

Breath 1. Give up caring

Breath 2. Heavy and warm

Breath 3. Breathe and relax

As distractions enter my consciousness, I do not let them trouble me, even if they temporarily throw me off my pattern. I simply resume my slow, three-breath cycle.

When you have rehearsed these relaxation exercises for a period of several days, you can then begin to implement them in your daily life.

Organizational Implications

A major issue for the police supervisor is how stress affects job performance. At low stress levels, individuals maintain their current level of performance. Under these conditions, individuals are not activated, do not experience any stress-related physical strain, and probably see no reason to change their performance level. If not supervised well, these employees could become bored, lazy, and poor performers.

On the other hand studies indicate that under conditions of moderate stress, people are activated sufficiently to motivate them to increase performance. Stress, in modest amounts, acts as a stimulus for individual vitality. The toughness of a problem often pushes the supervisor to his or her performance limits. Similarly, mild stress can be responsible for creative activities as police personnel try to solve challenging problems.

Finally, under conditions of excessive stress, both individual vitality and performance drop markedly. Here the severity of the stress escalates into a consuming distraction, thus causing employees to waste valuable energy.

STRESSORS

Stressors come from one of three sources: personal, environmental, and organizational/social. The first source is within the individual; the latter two are external. Most often they present their demands for change in combination with one another. Let's explore the sources in more detail and then focus our attention on the four types of stress they produce for all employees in a police organization. (While doing so, remember that your decision on how to handle stress determines whether it is a plus or minus to your vitality and the vitality of your staff.)

Three Sources of Stress

Personal.   A review of all the possible personal or inner stressors would be impossible here. They can range from sexual disorders to grief due to the loss of a loved one to a fear of flying. We will focus on those that are potentially job-related. Roughly, they can be assigned to one of two categories: our emotions and our power base.

Emotions.   The majority of us have received little training in how to deal with our own emotions. (The section on "Emotional Intelligence" in Responsibility 9 covered this subject.) At best, we have probably been given some advice on what to do during emotional periods; for example, being told that "there is nothing to fear but fear itself" when we are feeling frightened. Such advice is rarely ever truly helpful in overcoming the effects of the emotion. There are five very potent negative emotions that you should be able to recognize and deal with: depression, anxiety, guilt, failure, and disapproval.

Power.   The position of supervisor involves both the right to supervise and the opportunity to lead others. In the introduction, you learned that the right to supervise is centered in the position of police supervisor, while the opportunity to lead is centered in one's personal ability to do so. Since supervision and power are closely allied, they both involve stress and responsibility. Police supervisors who feel the pangs of stress are usually responding to the use of supervisory power (by themselves or others) to cause change. For some, the term *power* suggests a negative action. It can be, but it also can be a positive action.

Environmental.   The environmental stressors can be labeled as technological, economic, or political. Frequently, an environmental stressor can be assigned to all three. For example, the computer is causing numerous and profound technological changes for the police supervisor. Economically, computers require capital outlay and maintenance.

And politically, they imply power. Pollution in the work setting can be stressful, too. Insufficient work space often elevates tension. I could continue, but I believe you know what these stressors are because you're probably experiencing some of them right now.

Organizational or Social.   Here the stressors are too much, too little, uncertain conditions, and problem personalities. (Although posed in a job sense, many demands for change will occur via the family and other nondepartmental relationships.)

Too much.   There are two types of input overload, or hyperstress: quantitative and qualitative. Quantitative input overload is a result of simple demands, but too many of them for the time allotted—for example, too many phone calls to make, memos to read, or meetings to run in the time allowed. Increases in blood pressure, pulse rate, and cholesterol are associated with quantitative input overload. Qualitative input overload is a result of complexity and limited time. There are not as many tasks, but the time allotted to do these tasks is less than is needed to do them up to standard, or the tasks are so complex that they overwhelm (intimidate) the worker.

Too little.   Low levels of mental and physical activity can cause hypostress—that is, hypostress is caused by quantitative and qualitative input underloads. Naturally, certain forms of hypostress (such as recreation and self-reflection) are eustressful (desirable); but if a protracted period of nothingness is experienced, one may be confronted with hypostress, which is distressful (undesirable). Similar to hyperstress, hypostress can be either good or bad, depending on how one adjusts to its demands.

Uncertain conditions.   The police supervisor is responsible for making decisions (often high-risk ones) under above-average conditions of uncertainty. Herbert A. Simon alluded to this situation when he described programmable decisions in comparison with nonprogrammable decisions. (The police supervisor frequently experiences nonroutine, nonprogrammable, high-risk decision making.) Clearly, the bureaucratic, decision-making, operational turf of a police supervisor is filled with ambiguity and confusion, which may be stress-inducing.

Problem personalities.   Certain types of personalities commonly act as stressors. A supervisor cannot evade them. Typically, there are one or more problem employees in every work group. It only takes one malcontent to make the supervisor's job very frustrating. One negative individual can drain the vitality and lower the morale of an entire work team unless that person's behavior is confronted and corrected.

Four Dimensions of Stress

There are four major dimensions to stress or change:

- Hyperstress: Change overload.
- Hypostress: Change underload.
- Eustress: Favorable or positive changes.
- Distress: Unfavorable or negative changes.

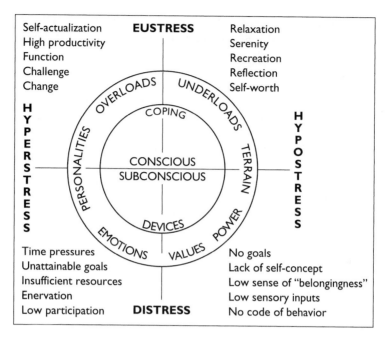

FIGURE 10–1   Coping with stress.

The main sources of stress are implicit in each section of Figure 10–1.

Our coping mechanisms are divided into two basic categories: the subconscious and the conscious. Space does not permit adequate treatment of the subconscious mechanisms, but essentially, the subconscious coping techniques are developed through our formative years, and we have learned to rely on one or more, much like a reflexive action. The conscious coping techniques are those that we can practice and use to reduce stress and perhaps even to convert distress into eustress.

> The police supervisor must develop a capability for detecting signs and symptoms of distress within himself and members of his team.

MEASURING YOUR STRESS LEVEL

You now have an opportunity to assess your own and others' existing stress levels. The four questionnaires that follow should be self-admininstered (1) once a year; (2) at a time of frequent or major changes in your life, and (3) when you notice certain telltale signs of mounting tension or uneasiness in yourself or in members of your department. The scales probe for hyperstress (eustress and distress). Hypostress cannot be effectively dealt with in the pages allotted for this subject. (The majority of police supervisors rarely experience this form of stress anyway.)

STRUCTURED EXERCISE 10–3

EPISODIC, WORK-RELATED STRESS EVALUATION

Listed in this exercise are many episodic work-related events that have been found to stimulate stress reactions in employees. The numerical value of each event reflects the degree of disruption it causes in the average person's life. Generally, the higher the score, the greater the probability of a significant health change in the near future. (Note: Because individuals vary in their tolerance for stress, the total score should be taken as a rough guide only.)

For each of the events listed here that you have experienced during the past twelve months, place its value in the My Score column. If you have experienced an event more than once within the past twelve months, you may record its value for up to four episodes. Then add all the numbers in the My Score column to obtain your total episodic, work-related stress score.

Event	Value	My Score
Being transferred against my will to a new assignment	81	_____
Being assigned to a less important job	79	_____
Experiencing a decrease in status	68	_____
Being disciplined or reprimanded by my boss	67	_____
Having my request to transfer to a better job rejected	65	_____
Sustaining an abrupt and major change in the nature of my work	60	_____
Learning of the cancellation of an important project in which I was involved	60	_____
Encountering major and/or frequent changes in policies or procedures	59	_____
Being promoted or advanced at a slower rate than planned	58	_____
Being voluntarily transferred to a new position or assignment (not a promotion)	52	_____
Facing my forthcoming retirement	47	_____
Experiencing a major reorganization in my unit	46	_____
Experiencing a sudden reduction in the number of positive strokes for my work accomplishments	46	_____
Encountering a major change (increase or decrease) in the technology affecting my job (computers, techniques)	46	_____
Giving a major briefing (not roll call) or formal presentation	46	_____

Event	Value	My Score
Encountering a significant deterioration in environmental conditions, such as lighting, noise, temperature, space, or filth	45	_____
Acquiring a new boss	45	_____
Sustaining an immediate, significant decrease in the pace of my work	43	_____
Sustaining an immediate, significant increase in the pace of my work	43	_____
Undergoing a major physical relocation of my workplace	31	_____
Acquiring an increase in status	30	_____
Being compelled to work more hours per week than usual	29	_____
Experiencing the transfer, resignation, termination, or retirement of a close coworker	24	_____
Being promoted or advanced at a faster rate than expected	24	_____
Acquiring new subordinates	23	_____
Receiving a major work schedule change	23	_____
Acquiring new coworkers (peers)	21	_____
Experiencing an increase in the number of positive strokes for my accomplishments	20	_____
Encountering a significant improvement in environmental conditions, such as lighting, noise, temperature, or space	17	_____
Undergoing a minor physical relocation of my workplace	5	_____
Total episodic, work-related stress score:		_____

STRUCTURED EXERCISE 10–4

EPISODIC, NON-WORK-RELATED STRESS EVALUATION

Listed in this exercise are many episodic non-work-related events that have been found to produce stress. The numerical value of each event reflects the degree of disruption it causes in the average person's life. Generally, the higher the score, the greater the probability of a significant health change in the near future. The severity of health change also tends to increase with higher scores. (Again, since individuals vary in their tolerance of stress, the total episodic, non-work-related stress score should be taken as a rough guide only.)

(continued)

STRUCTURED EXERCISE 10–4 *(continued)*

The same rules apply here as in Structured Exercise 10–3. The event must have occured within the past twelve months. If the event occurred more than once, then multiply the number of times (up to four episodes) against the stress value.

Event	Value	My Score
Death of spouse/partner	100	_____
Divorce/permanent separation	73	_____
Marital separation	65	_____
Jail term	63	_____
Death of close family member	63	_____
Personal injury or illness	53	_____
Marriage	50	_____
Fired from work	47	_____
Marital reconciliation	45	_____
Retirement	45	_____
Change in family member's health	44	_____
Pregnancy	40	_____
Sexual difficulties	39	_____
Addition to family	39	_____
Business readjustment	39	_____
Change in financial status	38	_____
Death of close friend	37	_____
Change to different line of work	36	_____
Change in number of marital arguments	35	_____
Mortgage or loan over $10,000	31	_____
Foreclosure of mortgage or loan	30	_____
Change in work responsibilities	29	_____
Son or daughter leaving home	29	_____
Trouble with in-laws	29	_____
Outstanding personal achievement	28	_____
Spouse begins or stops work	26	_____
Starting or finishing school	26	_____
Change in living conditions	25	_____
Revision of personal habits	24	_____
Trouble with boss	23	_____
Change in work hours or conditions	20	_____
Change in residence	20	_____
Change in schools	20	_____
Change in recreational habits	19	_____

Event	Value	My Score
Change in church activities	19	_____
Change in social activities	18	_____
Mortgage or loan under $10,000	17	_____
Change in sleeping habits	16	_____
Change in number of family gatherings	15	_____
Change in eating habits	15	_____
Vacation	13	_____
Christmas season	12	_____
Minor violation of the law	11	_____
Total episodic, non-work-related stress score:		_____

STRUCTURED EXERCISE 10–5

LONG-TERM WORK-RELATED STRESS EVALUATION

Stressful day-to-day, long-term work conditions are listed in this exercise. Indicate the relative frequency with which you experience each of the following sources of stress by assigning each a number from the frequency scale.

Frequency Scale

> 1 = never
>
> 2 = infrequently
>
> 3 = occasionally
>
> 4 = frequently
>
> 5 = always

Condition	Frequency
I am uncertain about what is expected of me.	_____
My peers appear unclear about what my role is.	_____
I have differences of opinion with my superiors.	_____
The demands of others for my time are in conflict.	_____
I lack confidence in top management.	_____
My boss expects me to interrupt my assigned work for new priorities.	_____
Conflict exists between my unit and others it must work with.	_____

(continued)

STRUCTURED EXERCISE 10–5 (*continued*)

Condition	Frequency
I get feedback only when my work is unsatisfactory.	_____
Decisions or changes that affect me are made without my knowledge or involvement.	_____
I am expected to endorse the decisions of management without being informed of their rationale.	_____
I must attend meetings to get my work done.	_____
I am cautious about what I say in meetings.	_____
I have too much to do and too little time in which to do it.	_____
I do not have enough work to do.	_____
I feel overqualified for the job I have.	_____
I feel underqualified for the job I have.	_____
The personnel I supervise are trained in a field that is different from mine.	_____
I must go to other units (bureaus) to get my job done.	_____
I have unsettled conflicts with my peers.	_____
I get no personal support from my peers.	_____
I spend my time "fighting fires" rather than working according to a plan.	_____
I do not have the right amount of interaction (too much or too little) with others (bosses, peers, staff).	_____
I do not receive the right amount of supervision (too much or too little).	_____
I do not have the opportunity to use my knowledge and skills.	_____
I do not receive meaningful work assignments.	_____
Total long-term work-related stress score:	_____

List here any ongoing sources of stress you experience at work that are not included in the evaluation form.

_____

_____

_____

_____

_____

_____

Long-term stress, even after we become accustomed to it, causes presures that induce illness, lower our feelings of satisfaction, and inhibit growth and work effectiveness. When many episodes involving work-related change occur in an organization in which people are already working in long-term, highly stressful conditions, the use of sick leave and the seriousness of illnesses, accidents, and inattention to work can increase rapidly.

STRUCTURED EXERCISE 10–6

LONG-TERM NON-WORK-RELATED STRESS EVALUATION

Listed in this exercise are several potentially stressful long-term, non-work-related conditions. Indicate how stressful each is for you personally by assigning each a number from the severity scale.

Severity Scale

1 = not stressful
2 = somewhat stressful
3 = moderately stressful
4 = very stressful
5 = extremely stressful

Condition	Severity
Noise (traffic, airplanes, neighbors, etc.)	_____
Pollution (air, water, toxic waste, etc.)	_____
Personal standard of living and ability to make ends meet financially	_____
Crime and vandalism in immediate neighborhood	_____
Law and order in society	_____
Personal long-term ill health	_____
Long-term ill health of family member or close friend	_____
Racial tensions	_____
Regular drug or alcohol abuse of family member or close friend	_____
Concern over future of my own career	_____
Concern over values or behaviors of family members	_____
Political situation in this country	_____
Possibility or existence of war	_____
Concern over financing my own retirement, my children's education, and so on	_____
Economic situation in this country	_____
Changing morals in our society (regarding family life, sexuality, and so on)	_____
Total long-term non-work-related stress score:	_____

List here any ongoing non-work-related sources of stress you experience that are not included in the evaluation form.

_____
_____
_____
_____

Reliable Data

The four instruments that you've completed are awareness scales. Many people have discovered that they accurately forecast degrees of our human vitality (or lack of same). The first scale, in particular, is exceptionally well known and accepted; more than sixty years of hard data demonstrate its ability to detect distress.

The first step in any stress-management and vitality program is to secure reliable data. The bottom-line scores are indicants (not guarantees) of vitality. The following scores should cause you reflective concern:

- Episodic, work-related stress   300 points or more
- Episodic, non-work-related stress   150 points or more
- Long-term, work-related stress   64 points or more
- Long-term, non-work-related stress   33 points or more

If I self-administer the scales (and I do so annually) and discover my score on one or more of the scales to be above the level cited above, I immediately check for signs of distress and simultaneously implement a program of wellness and enhanced vitality.

Prevention

If practical, compare your scores with those of other people who have completed the scales. Focus on common and dissimilar results and particular stressors. Also, share your thoughts and feelings about the levels and types of stress you are now experiencing.

Here are some additional ways that you can use the four evaluation instruments to maintain your health and prevent illness:

- See if you can find a pattern in the four sets of results.
- Determine whether one type or source of stress is more prevalent than the others.
- Discuss your scores with a friend or police colleague to provide additional insights.
- Remind yourself of the amount of change that you have experienced by posting the four evaluation sheets where you and your family can easily see them.
- Think about the meaning of each change for you, and try to identify some of the feelings you experience.
- Think about ways that you can best adjust to each change.
- Be compassionate and patient with yourself. It is not uncommon for people to become overwhelmed by all the stresses in their life. It takes a while to put into effect coping strategies to increase your vitality.
- Acknowledge what you can control and what you cannot control, and when possible, choose which changes you take on.
- Try out the wellness management and relaxation techniques presented in this chapter, and incorporate the ones that work best for you into your own personalized vitality program.

TRANSFORMING STRESS INTO VITALITY

Now that we have learned about the sources and effects of stress and our own stress levels, we can consider wellness management and our need for vitality. Keep in mind that a healthy police supervisor is in much better shape to be an effective one. Obviously, this holds true for all police employees.

> Although many people associate vitality only with fitness, nutrition, or stress reduction, vitality is really much more. Vitality confronts us with self-discipline and empowering others.

The transformation of stress into vitality is the personal responsibility of each supervisor. Be accountable not just for your own vitality but for that of your work group. If you are unwilling to commit to this goal through the use of one or more of the strategies that follow, then stop reading at this point and move on to the next chapter.

SIX STRATEGIES FOR MAINTAINING VITALITY

It seems that everyone has a particular vitality-enhancement program that he or she wants others to use. What works for one person may not work for the other. Jogging, for example, may be helpful stress therapy for one public employee, while another may find it harmful to the knees. Hence a vitality program must be custom-designed to meet the specific requirements of the individual.

Six vitality strategies follow. The astute police supervisor will select components from one or more of these strategies and *act on them* in order to maintain vitality while combating the harmful consequences of distress, discouragement, and disorder.

Strategy 1: Supportive Relationships

Supportive Structures.   Build supportive structures in your home, including times for family rituals and protected settings for recuperation. Build supportive structures within yourself, which are associated with your own attitude toward discomfort, work, personal needs, and the like.

Helpful People.   No person is an island. This statement has proved helpful in terms of mental health and coping with stressors. Everyone needs people, especially helpful people, who will give support when you are depressed, anxious, unhappy, angry, or simply distressed. (To whom do you turn when you are experiencing a strong sense of confusion or impending failure?)

Give and Take.   In establishing a supportive relationship, remember two things. First, a supportive relationship requires cultivation; if it is unattended, it may dissolve. Second, the relationship must be reciprocal—that is, there must be both giving and taking.

Positive Strokes.   It takes positive strokes to develop emotionally healthy people with a sense of "okayness." Without supportive relationships, this would be impossible.

Stay-Away-from Folks.   Avoid negative, pessimistic doomsayers. Hang out with the "go-to people," and avoid "stay-away-from folks."

Strategy 2: Mental Discipline

Keep It Simple.   Learning to reduce the complexity and the number of tasks that confront you will help you reduce stress. You will cope more effectively when problems are handled one by one, on a priority system, and in manageable installments.

Time Management.   Learning to reduce the time pressures on yourself will help you reduce stress. Nature has been good enough to give us a natural reflex for reducing time pressures when faced with overwhelming stress, but many of us fight nature's automatic mental stress-control mechanism. The old adage "Who's going to know the difference in a hundred years?" seems proper here.

Mind Focusing.   Mind-focusing exercises are very helpful for reducing mental stress. Various meditative methods have been developed and promoted to help people unload tensions by focusing their minds on neutral thoughts, such as a mantra, a number, or deep breathing. In effect, meditation allows you to put down your mental burdens several times a day, to rest your mind for twenty minutes, and then to pick up your burdens once again with more mental energy. People who practice mind focusing or spiritual meditation respond better to stress and seem to recover much more rapidly from the effects of stress than do people who don't meditate.

Comfort Zone.   All of us need a comfort zone, which causes us to feel good, to feel secure. Indeed, a comfort zone allows us to feel our feelings. A "safe and happy place" should be a place of your own choosing, but you must find one if you have not already done so. Your place may be a particular room, a camper van, a fishing stream, an athletic club, a mountain trail, a book—anything, anyplace. Moments of self-renewal, relaxation, introspection, and serenity can and frequently do occur there.

Avoid the 90-10 Trap.   Most of us tend to focus our attention, thinking, and conversations on the worst 10 percent of our lives. The 90 stands for the 90 percent that happens during our day that is usually pretty good. We seem to dwell on what's wrong with life instead of what's right or okay with it. I'm not suggesting that we bury the bad stuff. I'm suggesting that the other 90 percent is also worthy of attention. In other words, accentuate the positive. Problems steal too much of our time. It's easier to deal with the stress and hassles of your life when you're also aware of what's right with your life. Consider for a moment the people you know who evidence a lot of vitality. I bet you they frequently point out what is great, good, right, and positive. Avoid the 90-10 trap; your vitality depends on it.

Strategy 3: Helping Others

While it is hard to know what to say to a person who has been struck by a distressful event, it is easier to know what not to say. Anything critical of the distressed person ("Don't take it so hard" or "Try to hold back your tears—you're upsetting people") is wrong. Anything that tries to minimize the person's pain ("It's probably for the best" or "It could be a lot worse" or "She's better off now") is likely to be unappreciated. Anything that asks the individual to disguise or reject their feelings ("We have no right to question God" or "God must love you to have selected you for this burden") is wrong as well.

People under enormous adverse conditions need sympathy more than advice, even good and correct advice. There will be a time and a place for that later. They need compassion, the sense that others feel their pain with them. They need physical comforting, people sharing their strength with them, holding them rather than scolding them.

The phrase "Job's comforters" has come to describe people who want to help but who are more concerned with their own needs and feelings than they are with those of the distressed person, and this makes things worse. As a supervisor, you should anticipate and address three things in a person suffering from a distressful circumstance:

- Anger
- Guilt
- Jealousy

Be There.   Seeking out the unfortunate person is the first and most important step you can take in your responsibility to help a coworker through a bad situation. It is not pleasant to see a grieving coworker, and most of us would rather avoid the experience. However, your mere presence will be significantly comforting and encouraging to them.

Listen Carefully.   Empathetic listening is best. Do not lose your self-control by, for example, interjecting, "I understand what you're experiencing." Listen! Once you're certain that the person has finished speaking, then you are in a position to say (if you really mean it), "I'm sorry about what has happened to you. How can I help?" Remember, by being there and listening, you have already helped a lot.

Being Angry Is Okay.   Typically, the injured person is angry about their misfortune. They need to know that it's okay to be angry. "Cheer up, my friend, it's not that bad" only adds to the person's misery. If angry, hopefully the person is able to focus on the issue and not turn the anger inward. Anger turned inward instead of discharged outward causes depression. Distress is bad enough without depression casting its intensifying gloom on the situation.

Who's Responsible for All This Mess?   The distressed person will usually engage in the blame game, asking, "Who caused this horrible situation?" The answers can be (1) I did it to myself, (2) you did it to me, (3) God caused this, and (4) stuff happens. Like anger, the blame game is okay if you're willing to work your way through it. The first response is "I'm sorry. I forgive myself." The second response is "I forgive you." The third is a response that if not appropriately addressed, can erect a barrier between us and all the sustaining, comforting resources of religion. The fourth answer is in reality a response—distress is distributed very widely; everyone gets his share. "It's unfair, rotten, totally undeserved, but it's my turn, and I'm going to work my way through it."

Jealousy: Why Not You?   For us to suffer distress is bad enough. But for us to suffer it while those around us don't is even worse. "Everyone except me on the police lieutenant's list will be promoted." "Everyone except me who asked for a transfer got one." "Everyone except me has a happy marriage." We know that we hurt ourselves more than anyone else by feeling jealous. But we still feel it.

Perhaps the only cure for jealousy is to realize that the people we resent for not being in our miserable condition probably have emotional wounds and physical scars of their own. They may even be envying us. "You think you've got problems? Let me tell you my problems, and you'll realize how well off you are." This won't help the affected person. As mentioned above, the "Why me?" is best answered by "Why not you?" Apparently, it is your turn.

Chronic Distress Syndrome.   If the above remedies do not lessen the burden, the frustration, and the depression associated with the problem, then the supervisor should recommend that the person seek professional counseling. Remember, this recommendation applies equally to you, the supervisor.

Strategy 4: The Three Rs

- Reading for fun and enjoyment
- Relaxation as a voluntary control of stress
- Recreation as a release and as a revitalization

Strategy 5: Altruistic Egoism

Hans Selye coined the expression and advanced the practice of "altruistic egoism," which basically is looking out for yourself but in an altogether different frame of reference than you might initially suspect. Selye went on to reveal that this egoism is to be developed in and around being necessary to others. Eliciting the support and goodwill of others is a key ingredient in the practice of altruistic egoism.

Earning Benevolence.   Earn thy neighbor's love. This motto, unlike love on command, is an enduring part of our human nature. Who would blame anyone who wants to ensure his or her own self-worth and happiness by accumulating the treasure of other people's benevolence? Avoid remaining alone in the midst of the overcrowded society that surrounds you. Trust people, despite their apparent untrustworthiness, or you will have no friends, no support. If you have earned your neighbor's love, you will never be alone.

Strategy 6: Don't Worry, Be Happy

A merry heart makes a cheerful countenance.

—Proverbs 15:113

Several years ago, there was a popular song with the chorus, "Don't worry, be happy." How happy are you? Complete Structured Exercise 10–7 to find out.

How did you do? The good news is that your happiness can be increased and expanded. The bad news is that, likewise, it can be decreased and curtailed. Even the happiest of people feel unhappy at times.

Happiness attacks our negative emotions, such as worry. The word *worry* is derived from the Greek word meaning "to choke." Our quest to be vibrant, well, and optimistic as a police supervisor is frequently derailed by worry. To worry is not difficult; anyone can do it. Worse yet, it can become a habit, and it is contagious. Don't we all know some people who actually seem to enjoy worrying? Of course, worrying about an event can actually be worse than experiencing the event.

> Police organizations need happy, not worried, supervisors.

STRUCTURED EXERCISE 10–7

HOW HAPPY AM I?

Read the following five statements. Then use a scale of 1 to 7 to rate your level of agreement, 1 meaning "not at all true" and 7 meaning "absolutely true."

In most ways, my life is close to my ideal.   _____

The conditions of my life are excellent.   _____

I am satisfied with my life.   _____

So far, I have gotten the important things I want in life.   _____

If I could live my life over, I would change almost nothing.   _____

Total score: _____

Scoring Range

31–35: Extremely satisfied with your life
26–30: Very satisfied
21–25: Slightly satisfied
    20: Neutral point
15–19: Slightly dissatisfied
10–14: Dissatisfied
  5–9: Extremely dissatisfied

Since the late 1990s, there has been a great deal of scientific research on the subject of happiness, positive emotions, and healthy mental characteristics. Basically, what makes us happy or unhappy can be divided into three interrelated components: (1) pleasure, (2) relationships, and (3) purpose. In all three components, there exists the element of human choice. "Should I take the time to take pleasure in this sunset?" "Should I include this individual in my close personal relationships?" "Should I devote myself to a more intense exercise program or to community service?" It's clear that we can change our level of happiness widely, either up or down.

> The art of living a happy life lies not in having more of what you want, but in getting better at enjoying what you have!

Here are seven steps toward a more satisfying life at work and elsewhere. If you practice these steps daily, you will be a happier, more vital, and healthier supervisor.

We either make ourselves happy or miserable. The amount of work
is the same.

—Carlos Castaneda

1. *Count your blessings.* Keep a gratitude journal, and record in it the things for which you are grateful. Pick a specific time in your day or week for making entries in your journal.
2. *Practice "random acts of kindness."* Being kind to others is a gift to you, one that multiplies the more you give it away. Ralph Waldo Emerson said, "You cannot do a kindness too soon because you never know how soon it will be too late."
3. *Pause for pleasure.* Pay close attention to momentary pleasures, savor them, and save their memories to "replay" in less happy circumstances.
4. *Express thanks.* Think carefully about the people to whom you owe gratitude—for example, those who guided you at important times in your life—and thank them. A letter or e-mail may do it, but best of all is the old-fashioned method of talking to them in person.
5. *Forgive.* Harboring ill will is fatiguing, wastes time, and detracts from your pursuit of success. Let anger and resentment go, and move on. Resentment merely adds unnecessary weight to your burden. Get rid of it!
6. *Devote prime time to relationships with your friends and your family.* Research has demonstrated that where you live, how much money you have, and even your success in your job have only small effects on your satisfaction level. The biggest addition to your happiness quotient is through strong and positive relationships with family members and friends.
7. *Invest in your own well-being.* Hans Selye, the scientist whose most important body of work dealt with stress, called this principle "altruistic egoism." Take good care of yourself. It will strengthen your ability to take good care of others.

STRUCTURED EXERCISE 10–8

Drawing from the six strategies for vitality and wellness, and adding your own unique steps, custom-design a one-page action plan for yourself.

YOUR TURN

There are some tabloids that report on events such as "Mother Gives Birth to Eighty-Year-Old Twins." You'll find them at newsstands and markets. Recently, I spotted a front-page headline, "The Ultimate Secret to Stress Reduction." For fifty cents, how could I go wrong? Here is what I learned.

A fellow in Canton, Ohio, buys an enormous amount of Jell-O. When distressed, he puts it into his bathtub, gets in, and lies there until it congeals. He assured readers that it works. His worries, troubles, and aches and pains disappear.

Well, I didn't try it. It made for amusing reading, though. It probably helped him, but what works for one person may not work for another.

Now, here is what I learned. Wellness programs must be custom-designed. What works for me may not help you. You must identify and apply those techniques that avoid the barriers of distress and provide the carriers of success. Now complete Structured Exercise 10–8.

Life is a grindstone. Whether it grinds us down or polishes us up depends on us.

—L. Thomas Holdcroft

KEY POINTS

- Supervisors are responsible for preventing stress from damaging their vitality and that of their work team.
- Stress is unavoidable in everyday life.
- Stress is created by any change, either positive or negative.
- When stress is mismanaged, it is damaging. However, when stress is managed well, it can promote vitality in the work group.
- One of the most negative of stressors is an attack on one's integrity.
- There are three sources of stress: (1) personal, (2) environmental, and (3) organizational or social.
- Supervisors can convert stress into a positive experience by demonstrating self-discipline and empowering others to do the same.
- Police supervisors must be alert for general and specific symptoms of stress in themselves and their staff.

- There are six strategies for promoting vitality and avoiding the negative effects of stress: (1) supportive relationships, (2) mental discipline, (3) helping others, (4) the three Rs, (5) altruistic egoism, and (6) being happy.
- Every supervisor needs a custom-designed plan, one that he or she creates to ensure wellness and vitality.
- A supervisor's vitality, or lack of it, is directly related to his or her effectiveness.

EXTENDED LEARNING

1. How are vitality and integrity connected?
2. As a group, identify five major changes affecting you or your work group.
3. Of the four organizational or social stressors, which one seems to dominate in your organization?
4. Identify the three episodic, work-related stress events that you personally feel are the most stressful. Discuss them as a group. Be alert for similarities and differences.
5. Which of the six strategies for maintaining vitality makes the most sense to you? Explain.
6. What do supervisors worry about? Make a list, and prioritize it. Now, what can you do about each item on the list?

Teamwork

RESPONSIBILITY 11

Organizing

The police supervisor is responsible for designing a work structure that facilitates all employees' making a maximum contribution to accomplishing the mission of the department.

With all prior responsibilities attended to, the supervisor is now faced with organizing the staff into a cohesive, focused, and dynamic work unit that is capable of implementing a community-oriented policing program.

And Moses chose able men out of Israel, and made them heads over the people, rulers of thousands, rulers of hundreds, rulers of fifties, and rulers of tens.

And they judged the people at all seasons: The hard causes they brought unto Moses, but every small matter they judged themselves.

—Exodus 18:25–26

Organizations have existed for tens of thousands of years. More than forty thousand years ago, hunters and gatherers were organized into small clans and probably led by the strongest male.

Around 8000 B.C., humans entered the farming age, and our organizational structure was centered on villages comprised of several clans. In this age, the wealthiest landowner was likely to be the leader.

Then came the industrial age, which commenced in the late eighteenth century. During the industrial age, productivity increased fifty times over what was possible on the family farm. Today, only 3 percent of Americans are farmers. It was the industrial age that gave birth to bureaucratic organizations capable of managing thousands of workers.

A transition around 1947 led to the knowledge worker age. It was a dramatic shift in our economy as well as in the type of organization needed to support it. The knowledge worker age calls for an agile organization—the very opposite of bureaucratic organization. Here's the rub . . .

> Eighty-seven percent of us are knowledge age workers. However, many organizations continue to operate with an industrial age mentality that absolutely represses the release of human potential.

The mind-set of the industrial age and its bureaucratic organizations still dominates much of today's workplace. Unfortunately, this applies to many police organizations, which continue to be restricted by bureaucratic operating principles. This chapter deals with two types of governance—top down (bureaucratic) and bottom up (agile). Here, you will find a strong case for the agile organization.

The industrial age model of governance promoted these ideas:

- Workers are an easily replaced commodity.
- Workers must be strictly controlled.
- People are an expense, and machinery is an asset.
- It is imperative to "achieve the numbers" at all costs.

When treated like a commodity, police officers are insulted, alienated, distrustful, and essentially turned off. Feeling uninspired, constrained, and undervalued, they often turn to their police unions for strength. In contrast, the agile organization (and more and more police agencies fall into this category) seeks to correct the conditions described above by treating employees with dignity and by empowering them to encourage and harvest their creativity.

Nothing is as powerful as an idea whose time has come.

—Victor Hugo

GOVERNANCE

So far we have concentrated on supervision and leadership. The concept of governance recognizes the political nature of our lives and workplace and serves as an umbrella for both. A leader must cope with decisions on how to govern an organization. Governance encompasses questions about service, community, power, commitment, purpose, and achievement.

If those who govern answer the above questions based on a top-down, bureaucratic, hierarchical point of view, you'll get one set of answers. Those who answer with a bottom-up, agile form of governance in mind give us a totally opposite approach. Top down or bottom up—which is best? We'll explore both types of governance, recognizing that they exist in various combinations in all organizational settings.

Top-Down Governance

On paper, the top-down organization paper looks like a rigid pyramid. It consists of many layers of managers and supervisors; it thrives on written policies and rules; it emphasizes complexity. The manager and supervisor are the bosses, and authority flows from the top. This is a bureaucratic organization.

- *Service.* The police managers and supervisors decide on what types and quality of services are best for the community.
- *Community.* The people served are seen and served as one, as if they share a sameness.
- *Power.* Power is viewed as having clearly defined boundaries. It is centralized at the top of the department.
- *Commitment.* There is bottom-up commitment to the bosses and elite work groups.
- *Purpose.* The purpose of the department and its divisions is defined by top management.
- *Achievements/advancements.* Opportunities to achieve and be rewarded for it (e.g., promotion, a better job) are limited to those who demonstrate every day a commitment to the top managers.

> Top-down governance relies on a bureaucratic organization to get the mission accomplished. Management is primary and leadership secondary in this governance system.

Bottom-Up Governance

The bottom-up organization looks like a fluid Frisbee. It consists of a few layers of leaders with little attention to official emblems of rank; it thrives on flexibility and action; it emphasizes simplicity. The leader is the senior partner, and authority flows from the bottom. We refer to this as the "agile organization."

- *Service.* The leader, in concert with his or her work team, communicates with the community to decide what is best for the citizens.
- *Community.* The people served are seen and served as unique individuals.
- *Power.* Power is understood as being infinite. It is dispersed throughout the agency. Every employee is empowered.
- *Commitment.* Similar to power, there is an equal commitment by the department to the welfare of all employees.
- *Purpose.* The purpose of the department and its divisions is determined by people representing all levels and job assignments within the agency.
- *Achievements/advancements.* The chances for career growth and job accomplishments are unlimited and not tied to a particular manager or preferred supervisory style.

STRUCTURED EXERCISE 11-1

Visualize an organization—one that you currently work for or one that you worked for in the past. Respond to the following questions about the organization by circling the most appropriate number.

1. Service mix is decided at the top.   Service mix is decided by everyone.

    1   2   3   4   5   6   7

2. Community is seen as a whole.   Community is seen as made up of individuals.

    1   2   3   4   5   6   7

3. Power is centralized.   Power is dispersed.

    1   2   3   4   5   6   7

4. Commitment is to top management.   Commitment is to all employees.

    1   2   3   4   5   6   7

5. Purpose is defined by   Purpose is defined by all levels
   top management.   in the department.

    1   2   3   4   5   6   7

6. Achievement is judged by   Achievement is judged by individual
   management standards.   contributions.

    1   2   3   4   5   6   7

Add up the numbers you circled. The higher the sum is (36 or more), the more likely it is that the organization is agile and in need of leader-managers. The lower the score is (24 or less), the more likely it is that the organization is highly structured and in need of manager-leaders.

> Bottom-up governance depends on an agile organization for mission fulfillment. Leadership is primary and management/supervision secondary in this governance system.

Which One Is Best?

All things considered, and all things being equal, the bottom-up, or agile, organization is the most beneficial of the two for the delivery of high-quality police services. However, in the real world of police work, not all things are considered, and all things are not equal. Thus before a decision is made on what form of a governance system is best for an agency, the following questions or issues must be explored:

- How much tolerance is there for making mistakes—for taking risks?
- What is the nature of the community, and what do its residents expect from their police?
- What is the skill level of the personnel?

- Do the employees support the mission of the department?
- How motivated is the staff?
- How ethical is the staff?
- How much trust is there among the personnel and among the work units?

Once these questions have been answered and evaluated, those in power can decide on the type of governance system.

The type of governance system selected determines which organizational design should be used. If "supervisor and manager," then the bureaucratic, or top-down, organization is required. If "leader," then the agile, or bottom-up, organization is called for. A revolt will occur if the wrong organizational system is applied. Managers and supervisors will struggle, if not fail, within an agile organizational setting. And leaders will struggle in a bureaucratic environment.

Structured Exercise 11–2 is a keystone for the final part of this section. Review it carefully.

STRUCTURED EXERCISE 11–2

I remember a particular roll call that took place when I was a police officer. A newly appointed sergeant appeared and introduced himself to the twelve of us. He went on to say, "This isn't a democracy. I believe in participative supervision. I'm going to supervise, and you're going to participate. I run a benign dictatorship."

Later that evening while on patrol, my partner remarked, "It appears that this sergeant is the same as the last. Clearly, he is not interested in our ideas or opinions. He's big into control. And if we want to get along okay with him, then we best comply with his orders."

Several years afterward I recalled this episode. I saw a gross paradox in our daily lives as compared with our organizational lives. First of all, we live with political institutions that celebrate the rights of individuals to express themselves, to assemble, to pursue happiness and individual purposes, to pick their own political leaders. We pay enormous attention to the rights and procedures of due process. At times, we seem to be on the edge of anarchy, and yet we cling tenaciously to our political beliefs. Conversely, when we shift into our occupational life, those beliefs are best ignored. Consistency, control, and compliance become the dominant values.

For many years, I faced the frustrating dilemma of how to most effectively govern an organization. I was convinced that democracy would not work. Can you imagine voting on whether we should wear uniforms, who will work the night shift, or whether to evaluate employee performance? I was equally convinced that while a top-down autocracy could work, it was filled with pitfalls like transparent loyalty, weak commitment, low trust, poor communications, and zero risk taking.

If neither one of these governance systems is relevant, it raises these questions: What might prove successful? What is the most reliable alternative?

Before reading further, think about these questions. What are your answers? Discuss them with your coworkers.

ORGANIZATIONS

Organizations are social units (human groupings) deliberately constructed and reconstructed to seek specific goals. Business corporations, military units, schools, churches, and police departments are all types of organizations; ethnic groups, friendship groups, and family groups are not. An organization is characterized by (1) goals; (2) a division of labor, authority, power, and communication responsibilities in a rationally planned—rather than a random or traditionally patterned—manner; (3) a set of rules and norms; and (4) the presence of one or more authority centers that control the efforts of the organization and direct them toward its goals.

The Bureaucratic Organization

> *It is only through enforced standardization of methods, enforced cooperation that this faster work can be assured. And the duty of enforcing the adaptation of standards and of enforcing this cooperation rests with the management alone.*

> —Frederick W. Taylor

Most police organizations are bureaucratic in nature and foster top-down governance systems. This is changing, and we now see pockets of agile thinking, where leaders are in charge.

Bureaucracies are among the most important institutions in the world because they not only provide employment for a very significant fraction of the world's 6.3 billion people, but they also make critical decisions that shape the economic, educational, political, social, moral, and even religious lives of nearly everyone on earth. Figure 11–1 depicts a bureaucratic system.

The Four Cornerstones of Bureaucracy.

The bureaucratic organization developed over a number of centuries and finally matured in the 1930s. It is exemplified in Luther Gulick's essay "Notes on the Theory of Organization,"[1] in James Mooney and Alan Reiley's *Principles of Organization,*[2] and in Max Weber's writing on bureaucracy.[3] All these theorists were strongly oriented toward economy, efficiency, and executive control. These values, when combined, create a bureaucratic organization that has four cornerstones: division of labor, hierarchy of authority, structure, and span of control.

Of the four, division of labor is the most important; in fact, the other three are dependent on it for their very existence. The hierarchy of authority is the legitimate vertical network for gaining compliance. Essentially, it includes the chain of command, the sharing of authority and responsibility, the unity of command, and the obligation to report. Structure is the logical relationship of positions and functions in an organization, arranged to accomplish the objectives of the organization. Classical organization theory usually works with two basic structures, the line and the staff. Both structures can be arranged four ways: purpose, process, people (clientele), and place where services are rendered. The span of control concept deals with the number of

Bureaucracy

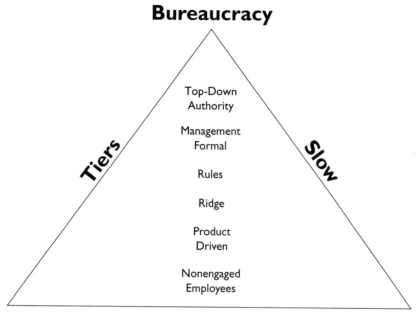

Top-Down
Authority

Management
Formal

Rules

Ridge

Product
Driven

Nonengaged
Employees

Tiers

Slow

Independent Work Units

FIGURE 11–1   Bureaucracy, the science of hierarchy.

subordinates a superior can effectively supervise. It has significance, in part, for the shape of the organization. A wide span yields a flat structure; a narrow span results in a tall structure.

The contemporary bureaucratic organization evolved from the thinking and practice of

- Max Weber, who emphasized the need for rationality
- Frederick W. Taylor, who concentrated on its scientific aspects
- Luther Gulick and Lyndall Urwick, who formulated principles

Weber: Rationality.   Max Weber was a founder of modern sociology as well as a pioneer in administrative thought. Weber probed bureaucracy, here essentially synonymous with "large organization," to uncover the rational relationship of bureaucratic structure to its goals. His analysis led him to conclude that there are three types of organizational power centers: (1) traditional—subjects accept the orders of a supervisor as justified on the grounds that it is the way things have always been done; (2) charismatic—subjects accept a superior's orders as justified because of the influence of his or her personality; and (3) rational-legal—subjects accept a superior's orders as justified because these orders agree with more abstract rules that are considered legitimate.

Power and authority.   The type of power employed determines the degree of alienation on the part of the subject. If the subject perceives the power as legitimate, he or she is more willing to comply. And if power is considered legitimate, then, according to Weber, it becomes authority. Hence Weber's three power centers can be translated into authority centers. Of the three types of authority, Weber recommended that rational structural relationships be obtained through the rational-legal form.

Six safeguards.   In each principle of bureaucracy described below, Weber's constant concern about the frailness of a rational-legal bureaucracy is apparent. His primary motive, therefore, was to build into the bureaucratic structure safeguards against external and internal pressures so that the bureaucracy could at all times sustain its autonomy. According to Weber, a bureaucratic system, to be rational, must contain these elements:

- *Rulification and routinization.* A bureaucracy is a continuous organization of official functions bound by rules. Rational organization is the opposite of temporary, unstable relations—thus the stress on continuity. Rules save effort by eliminating the need for deriving a new solution for every situation. They also facilitate standard and equal treatment of similar situations.
- *Division of labor.* Each person has a specific sphere of competence. This involves a sphere of obligation to perform functions that have been marked off as part of a systematic division of labor. It provides the incumbent with the necessary means of compulsion clearly defined, and their use is subject to definite conditions.
- *Hierarchy of authority.* The organization of offices follows the principle of hierarchy; that is, each lower office is under the control and supervision of a higher one.
- *Expertise.* The rules that regulate the conduct of an office may be technical rules or norms. If their application is to be fully rational, special training is necessary. Only a person who has demonstrated an adequate technical training is qualified to be a member of the administrative staff—an expert.
- *Written rules.* Administrative acts, decisions, and rules are formulated and recorded in writing.
- *Separation of ownership.* It is a matter of principle that the members of the administrative staff should be completely separated from ownership of the means of production or administration. There exists, furthermore, in principle, complete separation of the property belonging to the organization, which is controlled within the spheres of the office, and the personal property of the official.

Weber did not expect any bureaucracy to have all the safeguards he listed. The greater the number and intensity of those an organization possessed, however, the more rational and, therefore, the more efficient the organization would be.

Taylor: Scientific Management.   Frederick W. Taylor, production specialist, business executive, and consultant, applied the scientific method to the solution of factory problems, and from these analyses he established principles that could be substituted for the trial-and-error methods then in use. The advent of Taylor's thinking in the early 1900s opened a new era: that of scientific management.

Contributions.   Taylor's enormous contributions lay, first, in his large-scale application of the analytic, scientific approach to improving production methods. Second, while he did not feel that management could ever become an exact science in the same sense as physics and chemistry, he believed strongly that management could be an organized body of knowledge and that it could be taught and learned. Third, he originated the term and concept of *functional supervision.* Taylor felt that the job of supervision was too complicated to be handled effectively by one supervisor and should therefore be delegated to as many as eight specialized foremen. Finally, Taylor believed that his major contribution lay in a new philosophy of motivating workers and management.

Enforced cooperation.   Taylor consistently maintained—and successfully demonstrated—that through the use of his techniques it would be possible to obtain appreciable increases in a worker's efficiency. Furthermore, he firmly believed that management, and management alone, should be responsible for putting these techniques into effect. Although it is important to obtain the cooperation of the workers, it must be "enforced cooperation."

Five methods.   Taylor prescribed five methods for "scientifically" managing an organization. First, management must carefully study the worker's body movements to discover the one best method for accomplishing work in the shortest possible time. Second, management must standardize its tools based on the requirements of specific jobs. Third, management must select and train each worker for the job for which he or she is best suited. Fourth, management must abandon the traditional unity-of-command principle and substitute functional supervision. As already mentioned, Taylor advocated that a worker receive his or her orders from as many as eight supervisors. Four of these supervisors were to serve on the shop floor (inspector, repair foreman, speed boss, and gang boss) and the other four in the planning room (routing, instruction, time and costs, and discipline). Fifth, management must pay the workers in accordance with their individual output.

Impact.   Taylor's general approach to management is widely accepted today in production-oriented business organizations. Scientific management became a movement, and it still has a tremendous influence on industrial practice. More specifically, it had a major effect on the reform and economy movements in public administration and thus also influenced police administration. Its impact on public organizations is readily apparent at the present time; one can find numerous managers and supervisors (private and public alike) who firmly believe that if material rewards are directly related to work efforts, the worker consistently responds with maximum performance.

Gulick and Urwick: Principles.   While the followers of Taylor developed more scientific techniques of management and work, others were conceptualizing broad principles for the most effective design of organizational structure. Luther Gulick and Lyndall Urwick were leaders in formulating principles of formal organization.

The first and main principle.   Gulick and Urwick proposed eight principles, the first of which underlies and influences the seven others: division of labor. Their approach rests firmly on the assumption that the more a specific function can be divided into its simplest parts, the more specialized and therefore the more skilled a worker can become in carrying out his or her part of the job. They emphasized that any division of labor must be in strict accordance with one of the following four rationales:

- The major purpose the worker is serving, such as designing microprocessors, controlling crime, or teaching
- The process the worker is using, such as engineering, medicine, carpentry, programming, or accounting
- The person or things dealt with or served, such as immigrants, victims, minorities, mines, parks, farmers, automobiles, or the poor
- The place where the worker renders his service, such as Hawaii, Washington, Rocky Mountains, beach resorts, college campuses, or sports arenas

Seven additional principles.   Gulick and Urwick went on to underscore seven more principles for organizing:

Unity of command. A man cannot serve two masters. This principle is offered as a balance to the division of labor and conflicts with Taylor's "functional supervision."

Fitting people to the structure. People should be assigned to their organizational positions "in a cold-blooded, detached spirit," like the preparation of an engineering design, regardless of the needs of that particular individual or of those individuals who may now be in the organization.

One top executive (manager). Gulick and Urwick both strongly supported the principle of one-person administrative responsibility in an organization. Hence they warned against the use of committees and would have choked on the words *teamwork* and *partners*.

Staff: general and special. The classical writers' concern about staff assistance to top management deserves special attention. When management expressed a need for help from larger and larger numbers of experts and specialists, this need immediately raised the question of the relation of these specialists to the regular line supervisors and employees. In this instance, Gulick recommended that the staff specialist obtain results from the line through influence and persuasion and that the staff not be given authority over the line. The next question to be answered was that of coordination. Top management would have more people to supervise, since they would be responsible for not only the line, but also the special staff. The Gulick-Urwick answer to this problem was to provide help through "general staff" as distinguished from "special staff" assistance. Significantly, general staff are not limited to the proffering of advice. They may draw up and transmit orders, check on operations, and iron out difficulties. In doing so, they act not on their own, but as representatives of their superior and within the confines of decisions made by them. Thus they allow their superior to exercise a broader span of control.

Delegation. They emphasized that "lack of the courage to delegate properly and of knowledge how to do it is one of the most general causes of failure in organization." In larger organizations, we must even delegate the right to delegate.

Matching authority and responsibility. They dealt with both sides of the authority-responsibility relationship. It is wrong to hold people accountable for certain activities if the necessary authority to discharge that responsibility is not granted. On the other side, the responsibilities of everyone exercising authority should be absolute within the defined terms of that authority. Managers should be personally accountable for all actions taken by subordinates. They set forth the widely quoted axiom that "at all levels authority and responsibility should be continuous and coequal."

Span of control. Gulick and Urwick asserted that no supervisor can supervise directly the work of more than five or, at the most, six subordinates whose work interlocks. When the number of subordinates increases arithmetically, there is a geometric increase in all the possible combinations of relationships that may demand the attention of the supervisor.

POSDCORB. Gulick took the concept of management and defined it as consisting of seven activities—which can be abbreviated POSDCORB.

Planning: The working out in broad outline of what needs to be done and the methods for doing it to accomplish the purpose set for the enterprise

Organizing: The establishment of a formal structure of authority through which work subdivisions are arranged, defined, and coordinated for the defined objective

Staffing: The whole personnel function of bringing in and training the staff and maintaining favorable conditions of work

Directing: The continuous task of making decisions, embodying them in specific and general orders and instructions, and serving as the leader of the enterprise

Coordinating: The all-important duty of interrelating the various parts of the organization

Reporting: Keeping those to whom the executive is responsible informed as to what is going on, which includes keeping themselves and subordinates informed through records, research, and inspection

Budgeting: All that goes with budgeting in the form of fiscal planning, accounting, and control

Bureaucracy in Review. The words *bureaucracy* and *bureaucrat* have negative connotations. If we do not like an organization, we can label it a bureaucracy. If we do not like a government worker, we can call him or her a bureaucrat. This is an injustice to both the organization and the person. To use these terms belies the fact that all organizations of a few or more people are bureaucracies and all workers are to some degree bureaucrats—even the agile ones with their leader-managers and partnerships.

The underpinnings of bureaucracy are three interlocking cornerstones: rationality of structure, scientific management, and principles of organization. One way of classifying these three concepts is as follows: First, Weber's writing was primarily descriptive; however, it did indicate that a particular form of organizational structure was preferable.

Second, the theories of both Taylor and the Gulick-Urwick team were prescriptive; that is, they expressed the one right way to manage and organize a body of people. It is the "one right way" thinking that gets bureaucracies into trouble. The agile organization rejects such thinking with its motto "there are many right ways."

The Agile Organization

An organizational structure, once created, should be flexible and responsive to the developing needs of the organization and changes.

—David Packard

Success today and in the future depends on police organizations that can create new knowledge that results in value-added services. Success now and in the future will depend on police employees who have a passion for the profession, who generate new ideas—ways of doing things that result in new knowledge, which in turn results in innovative and unique services. With these current and future demands, do we want to place our bet on consistency, control, and compliance?

> The agile organization and its teamwork style of governance are not an idle, idealistic dream. They exist. Most of them are in the private sector, but they are beginning to emerge in government.

Continuity and Change. The governance system of an agile organization is constantly reconfiguring in order to balance continuity (its core values) and change (internal and external cultural and technological demands). The agile organization and its seven primary components are shown in Figure 11–2. The subsections that follow briefly describe each of the seven components.

Speed

- Today's environment, with its virtually real-time information exchanges, demands that an institution embrace speed.
- Faster, in almost every case, is better! From decision making to performance making to communications to services, speed, more often than not, ends up being the success differentiator.
- If it's worth doing, it's worth doing poorly.

Boundarylessness

- Those in a boundaryless organization have an obsession for finding a better way—a better idea—be it a source, a colleague, another organizational unit, or a neighboring organization or one on the other side of the globe that will share its ideas and practices.
- Aligned with not boundaryless behavior is a rewards system that recognizes the adapter or implementer of an idea as much as the originator.

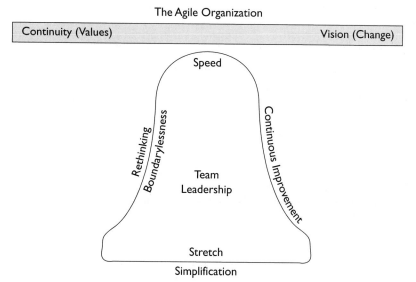

The Agile Organization

| Continuity (Values) | Vision (Change) |

Speed

Rethinking Boundarylessness

Continuous Improvement

Team Leadership

Stretch

Simplification

FIGURE 11–2 The agile organization.

- Creating this open, sharing element magnifies the enormous and unique strength of an organization—an endless stream of new ideas and best practices.
- Deploy "seam teams." These are work teams that link up and integrate two or more operations, for example, traffic units that work as a common unit to combat a drug-infested area.
- Bureaucracy-bashing is ensuring that written rules, memorandums, and the like do not hamper operational efficiency. The larger the operations manual, the more it will burden the agency.
- Tier-trashing is keeping the number of horizontal levels to a minimum. The more tiers, the more inefficiency. Remember: Keep it simple, keep it lean.

Stretch

- In an organization where boundarylessness, openness, informality, and the use of ideas from anywhere—and speed, with its bias for action—are increasingly a way of life, an overarching operating principle—stretch—is a natural outgrowth.
- Stretch, in its simplest form, says "nothing is impossible," and the setting of stretch targets inspires people and captures their imaginations.
- Stretch does not mean "commitments are out." Stretch can occur only in an environment where everyone is totally committed to maintaining a rigid set of core values—integrity, trust, quality, boundaryless behavior—and to outperforming every one of their global competitors in every market environment.
- Stretch does mean we are not fixated on a meaningless, internally derived, annual budget number that does nothing but make bureaucrats comfortable.
- A stretch atmosphere replaces a grim, heads-down determination to be as good as you have to be and asks instead, "How good can you be?"

Simplification

- The overlay for speed, boundarylessness, stretch, and everything else you do is simplification!
- Simplify everything you do.
- Use straightforward communication with one another and even simpler communication with your customers.
- The efficacy of statistics, budget data, and the like will be measured by their simplicity, and that simplicity will improve their quality, their cost, and their speed in reaching the intended consumer.

Rethinking

- At least annually, compare the performance of an operation or an agency with the performance of all others (benchmarking), with the best becoming the standard to be met by all the following year.
- Conventional policy making ranks programs and activities according to their good intentions; rethinking ranks them according to their results.
- On a routine basis, reinventions should be expected and not celebrated as unique.
- Downsizing per se is not rethinking; it may cause "amputation before diagnosis." It can be a casualty, rather than a cure.
- Rethinking is identifying the activities that are productive—those that should be strengthened, promoted, and expanded.
- Rethinking does not give us answers but forces us to ask the right questions.
- Place particular focus on
  - Performance objectives
  - Quality objectives
  - Cost objectives

Continuous Improvement

- Continually evaluate everything that you do.
- Place particular focus on
  - Performance objectives
  - Quality objectives
  - Cost objectives
- Link the improvements to some form of incentive or recognition.
- Make incremental improvements before the service reaches a peak or goal.

Team Leadership

- Team leadership equals a swarm of people acting as one—folks who have left behind their self-interest. They supervise things and lead people. With people, fast is slow and slow is fast—it takes time.

- There is no place for halfhearted interest or halfhearted effort.
- Even the most capable supervisors have trouble transitioning from an emphasis on command-and-control supervising (micromanaging) to team leadership. The cause is simple human nature—reclaiming the sandbox for themselves, reverting to old habits. "Corecracking of a team is like having a baby tiger given to you; it does a wonderful job of keeping the mice away for about twelve months, and then it starts to eat the kids."
- Transitional tips: (1) Don't be afraid to admit ignorance; (2) think about what you take on, not what you give up; (3) learn when and where to intervene; (4) get used to learning on the job; and (5) learn to really share (let go of) power.

Agility in Review.   Many of the elements of agile organizations are now a part of police agencies. We frequently see innovative personnel rating systems, self-managing teams, total quality efforts, teamwork, community attentiveness, and flattened pyramids. They are rarely, however, put together in a pervasive governance strategy. As a result, we end up too often working against ourselves. We share control with the left hand and take it back with the right. One moment we are on the fast track toward agility, and the next moment we are instituting more bureaucratic controls.

Figure 11–2 depicts the pivotal role that the team leader has in striking a balance between continuity (core values) and vision (change). The demand for change is constant.

A CASE FOR AGILE ORGANIZATIONS

The way a police department is organized affects employee motivation and performance. There are bureaucratic organizations in which the person at the top issues an order and it is passed on down the line until the person at the bottom does as he or she is told without question or reason. This is precisely the type of police organization I am arguing against. I am convinced that the objectives of community-oriented policing can best be achieved by people who understand and support them and who are allowed flexibility in working toward common goals in ways that they help determine are best for their operation and their department.

Some of the basic ideas we hold about how to run police agencies and organize work aren't working. We have been burdened with a belief that control, consistency, and predictability are essential. Even our efforts to implement empowerment and team leadership are curtailed by our innate need for control, consistency, and predictability.

A common management paradigm is that changing the organizational structure will change the values and behavior of personnel. Changing structure alone is never enough. If you make structural changes (e.g., move the internal affairs unit from investigations to the chief's office), but the value of maintaining central consistency and predictability remains untouched, nothing really changes.

We have been swinging between centralization and decentralization for decades in police work. Decentralization usually means that instead of one chief at the top, we now have several deputy chiefs running decentralized divisions. Yes, decentralization presents a change in structure, but it does not automatically foster a different pattern or style of supervising and leading.

The notion of the supervisor as "boss" in a professionally led police organization is nonsense. Supervisors no longer plan, organize, delegate, and control; they act as coaches, trainers, resources, and advisers. But they are not distinct and separate from their teams. They are player-coaches. They're in the game and not observing from the bench.

Organization = Interdependence

Organization is another word for "interdependence." We need each other for a thousand reasons, both emotional and practical. That is why most of us live in communities. When you fly across our nation or any nation, note the open space with people gathered in small villages, medium-sized cities, and large metropolises. The problem we face is that the organizational forms that we have inherited and use do not fulfill our need for security, freedom, and service. Police supervisors are attempting to meet these needs by answering these questions:

1. What will it take for me to claim my leadership and create a work unit of my choosing? (In turn, they are resisting the yoke of bureaucratic control.)
2. What is it I uniquely have to offer? What do I wish to leave behind here? (Clearly, they are wanting to make a difference.)
3. When will I finally choose adventure and accept the reality that there is no safe path? (These supervisors accept that their security comes from within themselves.)

Democracy has as its essence a widely distributed sense of ownership and responsibility. Creating interdependence or "teamwork in police work" is a way of affirming the democratic experience. This experience inside police organizations ensures broader forms of participation in the community. And this broader participation translates into community-oriented policing.

> We have swallowed the belief that police organizations, and even communities, can survive only with the strict enforcement of consistency and control. If we believe this is true, a police-community partnership will never happen. What we do within the police workplace makes an enormous difference. The supervisor's work unit must become the crucible from which the partnership is forged and community policing rediscovered.

KEY POINTS

- Governance includes leadership and supervision plus the political nature of our organizational lives.
- Top-down governance is found in bureaucratic organizations.
- Bottom-up governance is found in agile organizations.
- A bottom-up or supervisor-as-leader style of governance is not a democracy.
- It is imperative that there be a fit between the type of governance and the type of organizational structure.

- Organizations are social units deliberately constructed to attain goals.
- Of all the cornerstones and principles of bureaucracy, division of labor is the most important.
- The agile organization maintains a balance between consistency (value) and change (vision).
- Organizations and the interdependence of work units and police employees are synonymous.
- Community-oriented policing either starts or stops in the supervisors' work unit.

EXTENDED LEARNING

1. What does *governance* mean in an organizational context?
2. What are the differences between top-down and bottom-up types of governance?
3. What are the main features of a bureaucracy?
4. What are the key aspects of an agile organization?
5. Thinking about your organization, how bureaucratic is it? How agile is it?
6. Why isn't the agile organization more prevalent among police departments?
7. How can you reconcile continuity and change being the twin pillars of an agile organization?
8. Build an argument for creating an agile police department rather than a bureaucratic one.

NOTES

1. Luther Gulick, "Notes on the Theory of Organization," in *Papers on the Science of Administration,* ed. Luther Gulick and Lyndall Urwick (New York: Institute of Public Administration, 1937), pp. 1–45.
2. James D. Mooney and Alan C. Reiley, *Principles of Organization* (New York: Harper and Row, 1939).
3. The best-known translation of Max Weber's writing on bureaucracy is H. H. Gerth and C. Wright Mills, trans., from *Max Weber: Essays in Sociology* (New York: Oxford University Press, 1946).

RESPONSIBILITY 12

Performance

The supervisor's responsibility for an employee's job performance encompasses planning for it, setting specific objectives, and measuring their attainment.

Team leadership (Responsibilities 2 through 6), team building (Responsibilities 7 through 10), and organizing (Responsibility 11) have set the stage for developing a system for measuring change in performance over time.

I am a great believer in luck, and I find the harder I work, the more I have of it.

—Thomas Jefferson

There were two fellows hard at work next to a road. One carefully dug holes while the other waited a moment and then filled them up. It all appeared rather foolish, and finally a supervisor confronted the workers and demanded an explanation. The fellow who dug the holes said he had been doing the same job for more than ten years; his cohort quickly chimed in that he had been filling the holes for the same period.

Upon further questioning they confessed it made more sense in the past when a third person worked with them. His job had been to put a new tree into the hole. But when he retired, he was never replaced, so the two just kept on working as before. "Why didn't you tell somebody?" the supervisor sputtered. "Hey," they said, "you signed Jim's retirement letter. We figured you knew."

The kinds of unproductive, inefficient, and even counterproductive job performance that go on in most workplaces defy logic and reveal a great deal about the work ethic. After all, the ethical principle of responsibility includes a moral duty to improve things, to pursue excellence, and to produce and demand quality performance. Yet basically good employees in virtually every workplace regularly engage in or witness some process or practice that is unhelpful, wasteful, or even harmful to the ultimate goals of the organization.

> Although top management is ultimately responsible, people of character shouldn't passively demean the value of their work by becoming part of anything second-rate or stupid. It may take tact and timing, maybe even some courage, but it's the supervisor's duty to be a force for excellence. The bottom-line benefit is that the quality of our lives improves dramatically when we take pride in our job performance.

A SPIRIT OF PERFORMANCE

The biggest room in the world is the room for improvement.

—Anonymous

The bottom line test of a police organization is the spirit of performance. All fifteen of the responsibilities covered in this book are intended to resonate a spirit of excellence. This spirit cannot be evoked by mere exhortations, lofty sermons, or well-meaning intentions. It *must be e*videnced in five baseline conditions or practices.

Baseline 1: Nonnegotiable High Standards

The focus of a police agency must always be on performance. The first practice is setting nonnegotiable high performance standards for the group as well as for each officer. The department must establish a habit of achievement. However, performance does not mean success every time. Rather, performance is a "batting average." It will—indeed, it must—have room for mistakes and even for failures. What performance has no room for is complacency and low standards.

Baseline 2: Opportunities

Everyone must have the opportunity to grow career-wise, experience rewards for good work, enjoy their job, and sense being a valued part of their work team. Here the practice is converting obstacles into opportunities and problems into solutions. The workforce seizes opportunities to get the best results for its community.

Baseline 3: Character

Here the quest for high performance turns to the character of the organization. In doing so, we again reflect on three important responsibilities: values, ethics, and vision. Together they formulate and articulate a supervisor's character. Moreover, if enthusiastically pursued and clearly demonstrated, they enlarge the supervisor's character to include leadership as well.

Baseline 4: Emotional Intelligence

The leader sets the emotional standard. (Emotional intelligence was examined in Responsibility 9.) No matter what you set out to do, your success depends on how you do it. Understanding the powerful role of emotions in the workplace separates the leaders from the supervisors.

> The leader knows that he or she has maximal power to sway everyone's emotions. The leader knows that when people feel good, they do their best work. The leader knows that more than anyone else, he or she creates the conditions that directly determine a police officer's ability to work well. The leader possesses, in essence, above-average emotional intelligence. Without a healthy dose of heart, a supervisor may supervise, but he or she does not lead.

Baseline 5: Teamwork

High performance depends on teamwork. Groups of people working together are both smarter and achieve much more than they could individually. It is the leader who balances a team's focus on the task at hand with attention to the relationships among the team members. The glue that holds people together in a team and that commits people to an organization is the emotions they feel. Officers take their emotional cues from their boss. Hence the leader sets the emotional standard. Optimistic, enthusiastic leaders get the best out of their staff.

With the five conditions being fulfilled, we can proceed on the path of attaining high job performance. The path actually commenced in Responsibility 4, Vision, and its coverage of strategic thinking. We pick up on our journey now by taking four significant steps:

- Supervising by objectives
- Setting objectives
- Evaluating performance
- Designing and implementing a personnel-evaluation system

SUPERVISING BY OBJECTIVES

The only place you find success before work is in the dictionary.

—Mary V. Smith

Supervising by objectives is essentially a threefold process that

- Sets a course of desired direction—the objective
- Motivates the person to proceed in that direction—the result
- Ensures self-control via feedback—managing/supervising

Supervising by objectives (SBO) necessitates setting goals that are tangible, verifiable, and measurable. Rather than using goals to control, SBO seeks to use them to motivate. The remainder of this section concentrates on the development and use of SBO in police organizations. The practice of SBO by police supervisors has yielded enormous positive payoffs for the overall organization.

SBO operationalizes the concept of objectives by devising a process by which objectives cascade down through the organization. As depicted in Figure 12–1, the organization's overall goals are translated into specific objectives for each successive level (i.e., division, bureau) in the police department. This linking ensures that the objectives for each unit are compatible with and support those of the unit just above it. At the individual level, SBO provides specific personal performance objectives. All police personnel, therefore, have an identified specific contribution to make to their unit's performance. If all the individuals achieve their objectives, then their unit's objectives will be attained, and the organization's basic goals—crime control, crime prevention, order maintenance, and human services—are pursued.

Goals and Objectives

Once the overarching goals and the more specific objectives have been decided, the supervisor can "supervise" by them. While the literature on SBO is extensive and covers both public and private organizations, the term still remains subject to varying

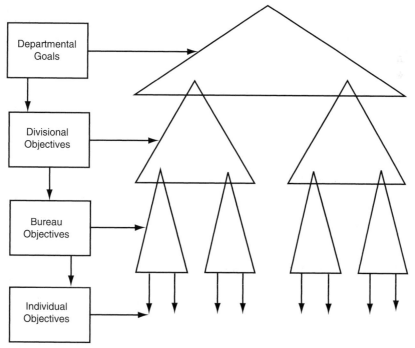

FIGURE 12–1 From goals to objectives.

definitions. Peter Drucker first coined the term *managing by objectives* in 1954, and describing it as a mutual understanding between the manager and his or her subordinates of what their contribution will be for the organization over a given period of time. It thus establishes parameters of self-control and common direction. Moreover, it establishes parameters that target the individual and the agency, both in the direction of accomplishing the much-to-be-desired goals.

Who Sets Objectives?

Objectives should be established supervisors in light of (1) their expected contribution to the agency, (2) the expectation of their subordinates, and (3) the expectation of their manager. The supervisor's boss makes the ultimate decision for approval or rejection.

To accomplish all three, a sizable amount of information exchange must occur. Thus managing supervisors, or supervising police employees, requires special efforts to establish common direction. Mutual understanding can never be attained by "communication down." It can result only from "communication down, up, and across." It requires the supervisor to really listen to the staff.

SETTING OBJECTIVES

> *It's not enough to be busy; so are the ants. The question is: What are we busy about?*
>
> —Henry David Thoreau

The objective-setting process consists of seven interrelated steps:

1. Identification of the issue
2. Definition of the issue in a specific statement
3. Development of alternative strategies to deal with the issue
4. Selection of the appropriate alternative
5. Implementation
6. Evaluation
7. Feedback

Step 1: Identification of the Issue

At first glance, this might appear to be an oversimplification, but experience has shown that this step is often the most difficult part of the entire process. For example, let us assume that a sergeant in a medium-sized police department has the responsibility for supervising a team of fourteen police officers. In addition to this overall responsibility, he is also responsible for the division's in-service training program and supply requisitioning. He is actively pursuing his own formal education and will soon be awarded his associate of arts degree from the local college. The chief of police is interested in converting the traditional patrol patterns and assignments to a community-oriented policing (COP) program. The agency has never experienced such an ambitious undertaking and, in fact, is understrength by approximately four people. Because the department uses a formal hierarchy, the sergeant's immediate supervisor is a lieutenant (the agency has four). The chief has selected the sergeant to research, develop, and present to him a position paper exploring the team-policing concept for their agency.

Various techniques can help here. These include thinking reflectively, analyzing available data, generating new data about the problem, brainstorming, using paper slip techniques (index cards), making personal observation, and asking someone internal or external to the agency who may have had more experience with such issues. The critical part, however, remains thinking clearly about the issue and then writing it down in the most specific terms possible. This might require several attempts; it is important to keep at the task until satisfied that what has been written is an accurate statement about the issue—and that it is the real issue.

Step 2: Specific Statement

This step of the process is somewhat similar to the identification step; however, it is separated due to its importance. In addition to the advice and cautions offered previously, the supervisor should concentrate on the "objective statement." It is often productive to use colleagues and a work group as a sounding board to modify, correct, or reinforce the objective statement and to ensure the supervisor that what has been written is, in fact, a specific issue statement amenable to solution and measurement.

Step 3: Alternative Strategies

In this step, here the supervisor is to develop as many alternatives as possible to solve the issue. In the first phase of the exercise, the supervisor should not disregard any possible alternative. The same techniques indicated before can be used to do this—ranging from individual thinking to group thinking. After all the possible alternatives have been identified, the supervisor can then proceed to reduce the list to the handful that hold the most promise.

Factors that affect the decision to leave an alternative on the list or remove it are almost limitless. They include

- Values
- Time
- Money
- Personnel
- Political ramifications
- Tradition and custom
- Attitudes
- Skill of the participants

Step 4: Selection of an Alternative

This step is what the supervisor has been aiming for from the start of the process. After following the preceding steps, the supervisor is finally ready to select the best alternative and implement it. One caution deserves to be reinforced here: The best alternative is not always the most feasible. The supervisor should be aware of this and should not become disillusioned if the number one alternative cannot be implemented. This is caused by a variety of reasons, ranging from money to politics to personal bias.

Step 5: Implementation

In preparing to implement the selected alternative, the supervisor should have thought through the alternative to the point where he or she knows which individuals are going to be affected, how they will be affected, and where the alternative will be exercised. In effect, the supervisor must have a "battle plan" for following through with the selected alternative.

Step 6: Evaluation

Performance evaluation is highlighted later in this chapter.

Step 7: Feedback

The term *feedback* means communicating the results of the objective-setting process back to those above and below us in the hierarchy. Whether the results are favorable or unfavorable, it is imperative that we communicate the results back into the system. This is done for the following reasons:

- It keeps people informed of results.
- It leads to refined objectives, one building on the results of the last.
- It continues the process of constantly refining our ability to affect issues in our work group.
- It builds a database on which to build future objectives and decisions.

To sum up, the objective-setting process is critical in the supervisor's ability to lead. The following questions should be addressed for each objective:

1. Is the objective a guide to action?
2. Is it explicit enough to suggest certain types of action (alternatives)?
3. Does it suggest tools to measure and control effectiveness?
4. Is it challenging?
5. Does it reflect the reality of internal and external constraints?

Roadblocks

Much like the "I've got good news and bad news for you; which do you want first?" jokes, I have revealed but one side of SBO—the good news. Now for some bad news. SBO is

STRUCTURED EXERCISE 12-1

This exercise is intended to build your skill in the use of SBO. Based on the agency for which you work, select one of the following subjects, or generate one of your own. Write a goal (objective) statement related to the subject, using no more than 250 words. Be certain that the goal statement is clear, specific, and attainable.

- Pursuit policy
- Residential burglary rate
- Commercial burglary rate
- Commercial robbery rate
- Officer-involved traffic accidents
- Citizen complaints
- Response times
- Shooting policy
- Use-of-force policy

If possible, divide your group into teams of five to seven individuals. Each person should read aloud his or her goal statement. Then collaborate to refine the statement into a highly practical objective worthy of implementation in a police department. Repeat the process at least once or twice. Practice ensures your successful use of this powerful supervisor's tool.

not without roadblocks. As expressed thus far, the advantages are that police managers and supervisors are encouraged to think seriously about their objectives and to try to get them into meaningful and also measurable terms; also, it encourages forecasting, planning, and dialogues between all administrative levels. The disadvantage is that the system is new to police work and should be approached with patience and persistence.

EVALUATING PERFORMANCE

The highest reward for a man's toil is not what he gets for it, but what he becomes by it.

—John Ruskin

Performance evaluation encompasses three key purposes: (1) behavioral motivation, (2) control, and (3) feedback. To a large extent, your success as a supervisor is directly related to your ability to appraise the performance of your assigned personnel.

Performance evaluation (or performance appraisal or rating) is both a process and a method by which a police agency obtains feedback on and provides guidelines for the effectiveness of its personnel—feedback, in the sense that past work effort is evaluated, and guidelines, to the extent that performance objectives are specified for the immediate future. Traditionally, the evaluation process and methods were designed with feedback as an end in mind; having guidelines as part of the evaluation system is more recent. (An evaluation system that uses both feedback and guidelines is referred to as SBO.)

Performance evaluation is very challenging for several reasons. First, it must serve many purposes (see below), including evaluating the success of selection decisions, assessing the effectiveness of a leader, evaluating training efforts, and determining the quantity and quality of individual work effort. Second, the assessment of performance itself is a difficult measurement task because so many factors influence performance, including environmental, organizational, and individual factors. Finally, a great number of ethical and emotionally charged issues arise when performance is evaluated. The results of the process can have profound influences on the job, career, attitude, personal self-concept, and general sense of well-being of a police employee.

> Personnel decisions can be made without performance evaluation systems. They can be made by drawing random numbers, by choosing whomever you like best, by choosing the person you owe a favor to, by choosing someone who wears the best-smelling aftershave lotion or perfume, and so on. Clearly, a successful police organization requires a proven process and an accurate method for assessing the current performance and the future potential of its most valuable asset: its people.

Performance evaluation serves at least the following purposes:

- Promotion, separation, and transfer decisions
- Feedback for each employee regarding how the organization views his or her performance
- Evaluations of relative contributions made by individuals and entire departments in achieving higher-level organizational goals
- Reward decisions, including merit increases and promotions
- Criteria for evaluating the effectiveness of selection and placement decisions, including the relevance of the information used in those decisions
- Ascertaining and diagnosing training and developmental needs for individual employees and entire divisions within the organization
- Criteria for evaluating the success of training and development decisions
- Information on which work-scheduling plans, budgeting, and human resources planning can be based
- Specification of new performance objectives (SBO) for the future

Performance Evaluation Must Be Job-Related

All the frustrations to which police supervisors and employees point when performance is reviewed can be summarized by two terms: *reliability* and *validity*. Both terms are qualities of the evaluation process and refer to the adequacy of the information that is generated and employed in subsequent decisions about employees.

> The prime means for a police agency to ensure the job relatedness (reliability and validity) of a performance-evaluation system is job analysis.

A job is a cluster of similar work tasks carried out to achieve some essential and enduring purpose in an organization; job analysis consists of defining the job and discovering what the job calls for in employee behaviors. Job analysis, then, is a procedure for gathering the judgments of people who are knowledgeable about the organization, the positions within it, and the specific content of a job. Furthermore, the content of the job is defined to be specific work activities or tasks. In effect, job analysis is a broad term describing an entire series of judgments that are made in the design of an organization.

Selecting a Performance-Evaluation System

There are several critical factors to assess when designing or selecting a performance-evaluation system:

- Specific organizational and environmental properties, such as technology and the design of the agency
- Unique individual characteristics that influence police performance, including specific skills and abilities and motivation levels
- The mix of specific work behaviors that are appropriate, given departmental and individual officer considerations
- The mix of relevant performance dimensions, given the agency and personnel involved
- The specific set of goals to be achieved at divisional and unit levels

Rater and Rating Errors

Errors in the performance-evaluation process mainly occur in the rater or in the process itself. There are four common types of errors to guard against: halo errors, strictness errors, leniency errors, and central tendency errors.

Halo Errors. These occur when an evaluator incorrectly treats two or more dimensions of performance as if they were identical or highly correlated. For example, if a police employee's work performance in report writing is observed as "superior," the evaluator accidentally assigns the same high mark to "personal appearance."

Strictness Errors. This type of error occurs when an evaluator rates all employees as very poor performers. Ratings given by this type of evaluator tend to cluster closely toward the low end of the rating scale.

STRUCTURED EXERCISE 12–2

Imagine yourself in this scenario. As a new police supervisor, you take your job most seriously, especially performance rating. During your recent two-week Supervisor's Training Course, eight hours were devoted to the do's and don'ts of rating.

Your agency uses a rating scale, which it applies every March. Your lieutenant instructed you and the other field sergeant to administer the scales. He went on to add, "In the next few months, a number of critical personnel decisions will be made. Your ratings are likely to determine the outcome of some of these pending decisions."

You have a fairly good feel for the police personnel in your unit as compared with the other sergeant's. If anything, your group is a slight cut above the other crew. Nonetheless, you recognize that your staff is not perfect. The results of your first rating are (1) two "improvement needed," (2) four "competent," and (3) one "outstanding." All seven officers read, discussed with you, and signed the form. No problem!

Three days later it was revealed that your colleague sergeant rated all seven of his personnel "outstanding." Rumors and complaints quickly surfaced among your team of officers. The lieutenant has asked to see you and the other sergeant about this situation. What is on your mind? What are you planning to say? What is your position on this matter? How might it be resolved?

Leniency Errors.   These are the opposite of strictness errors; with leniency errors, the evaluator mistakenly gives all employees uniformly high ratings. Ratings given by this type of evaluator cluster at the high end of the scale.

Central Tendency Errors.   These errors are similar to leniency and strictness errors, except that in this case the ratings made by the evaluator cluster artificially at the middle of the scale.

THE PERFORMANCE DOMAIN RATING SCALE

Police agencies have recognized the urgent need for making their evaluation method more relevant to the performance of a police officer. To this end, some agencies have succeeded in designing highly valid and reliable rating scales. These scales are produced in conjunction with the performance domain; that is, what the officer should be doing in his or her work assignment is what is appraised. This can be referred to as a performance domain rating scale (PDRS). A PDRS is job-related and thus does not fall prey to the inadequacies of a global rating scale. Figure 12–2 presents a PDRS that (with necessary modifications) may improve the effectiveness of your overall rating system. (Keep in mind that this particular PDRS does not apply to other performance domains, such as civilian personnel.) Depending on the unique characteristics of each agency, three to six PDRSs may be required to ensure and maintain job-related personnel evaluations. One final comment: A key feature of a PDRS that is often overlooked is that it depends on narrative comments.

City of Arvada

POLICE DEPARTMENT
OPERATIONS BUREAU POLICE OFFICER

EVALUATION OF PERFORMANCE

Employee Name: •   Employment Date: •

Position: •   Div./Dept.:   Patrol/Public Safety

Appraisal Period from: •   Time in Position: •

Appraised By: •   Title: •

PART I. EVALUATION OF PAST YEAR'S PERFORMANCE:

A. Accomplishment of Objectives

> During the past year, what were results of the employee's work? The purpose is to compare the objectives agreed upon in the previous evaluation with actual performance.

OBJECTIVES	COMMENTS ON ACCOMPLISHMENTS
•	

FIGURE 12–2   Police department evaluation of performance. *(Courtesy Arvada Police Department, Arvada, Colorado.)*

PART II. PERFORMANCE STANDARDS

Evaluators are to review each and every item of performance under each of the Standards. The degree to which an employee is <u>capable</u> of engaging in a specific item may vary with the shift or assignment.

When evaluating the employee, the evaluator is to check off the appropriate rating for each element of an evaluation category. Each rating is given a value as follows:

Unsatisfactory	= 1
Below Expectations	= 2
Meets Expectations	= 3
Exceeds Expectations	= 4
Distinguished Performance	= 5

After completing the evaluation of each element of a category (i.e., Customer Service - Community Problem Solving), the evaluator is to total the rating scores in that category and multiply by the <u>Weight</u> for that category. This provides a score for that category. At the conclusion of the evaluation, all category scores are totalled to yield a final evaluation <u>total</u> which is divided by the possible total score of 935 to give the percentage score which can be used (as can the point score) to determine the overall performance rating of the employee.

The supervisor must be able to articulate, in detail, the justification for a specific performance category (element) score. "Description of Performance Guidelines" as found in the <u>Supervisor's Guide to Performance Evaluations</u> is to be used when assigning one of the 5 performance levels to a given Standard of performance. A narrative explanation <u>must</u> accompany any score which is either a "Distinguished" or below the "Meets Expectations" level. This narrative must detail the reasons for the score and, in the case of "Below Expectations" and "Unsatisfactory", there must be a plan explaining what is necessary to improve performance to a "Meets Expectations" level. These comments are to be done by listing the letter (a, b, c, etc.) of the corresponding element in the "Comments" section of the page, followed by the brief explanation.

When a general category (i.e., Customer Service) contains a series of "4" (Exceeds Expectations) ratings, the evaluator must justify that rating, but may provide that justification in the "Comments" area with detailing each sub-section (i.e., a, b, f, i).

FIGURE 12–2 *(continued)*

1. CUSTOMER SERVICE/COMMUNITY PROBLEM SOLVING - WEIGHT 3	1	2	3	4	5
a. Responsive to service requests	•				
b. Displays helpful, cooperative attitude					
c. Sensitive to citizen needs					
d. Participates in community programs including Neighborhood Watch Meetings, D.A.R.E. classes/graduations, community meetings					
e. Actively identifies and recognizes the origins of community problems, evaluates issues and develops possible solutions to problems					
f. Awareness of and use of community/citizen/city government resources					
g. Appropriate use of citizen contacts					
h. Achieves a positive community image					
i. Effective initiation of and follow-up on Police Service Requests					
TOTAL (Element Score)					

Weight 3 x Total of All Element Scores ____•____ = Performance Standard Score ___•___

COMMENTS:

•

2. TEAMWORK/INTERPERSONAL ACTIONS - WEIGHT 2	1	2	3	4	5
a. Takes steps to eliminate bias in the department when observed	•				
b. Cooperates with others in establishing reasonable objectives and achieving desired results					
c. Displays behavior which builds trust and mutual respect and cooperation among fellow workers					
d. Has a positive approach when participating in routine activities, assignments, and problem solving					
e. Avoids unnecessary confrontation and adequately resolves conflicts when necessary					
f. Shares information with other members of the organization					
g. Respectful when interacting with co-workers and supervisors					
h. Actively seeks the opportunity to assist peers with their work performance					
i. Displays an awareness of shift/department workload and makes himself/herself available to assist fellow workers					
j. Makes comments and takes action to constructively enhance a team environment					
TOTAL (Element Score)					

Weight 2 x Total of All Element Scores ____•____ = Performance Standard Score ___•___

COMMENTS:

•

FIGURE 12–2 *(continued)*

3. COMMUNICATIONS - WEIGHT 3	1	2	3	4	5
a. Radio transmissions are clear, concise and follow procedures	•				
b. Expresses thoughts in writing and orally in a clear, concise, and well organized manner					
c. Displays good penmanship, grammar, and spelling in written reports					
d. Courtroom testimony is clear, accurate, and prepared					
e. Demonstrates ability and willingness to listen					
f. Understands and properly carries out instructions and orders					
g. Able to give and receive constructive feedback					
h. Ability to adjust communicative style for differing groups and situations					
i. Follows chain of command					
j. Comments, suggestions, and criticisms are presented in a constructive manner					
k. Written reports are grammatically correct and clearly understandable					
TOTAL (Element Score)					

Weight 3 x Total of All Element Scores _____•_____ = Performance Standard Score ___•___

COMMENTS:

•

4. INITIATIVE - WEIGHT 3	1	2	3	4	5
a. Accepts direct responsibility for District/assignment	•				
b. Shows initiative in everyday work activity - identifies and addresses community problems - initiates PSR's based upon knowledge of problems					
c. Ability to adapt to change					
d. Strives to improve the work product					
e. Serves as a role model for peers					
f. Ability to work constructively with a minimum of supervision					
g. Volunteers to direct or manage tough assignments					
h. Demonstrates ability to organize and coordinate various activities/operations					
i. Generates ideas and approaches to improve Police Department/City performance and the operation of the organization					
j. Maintains activity and productivity levels consistent with shift averages and expectations of supervisors and the community					
k. Looks for, and engages in, non-assigned productive activities which try to fulfill the community's needs.					
l. Looks for opportunities to conduct follow-up investigation on own initiative					
TOTAL (Element Score)					

Weight 3 x Total of All Element Scores _____•_____ = Performance Standard Score ___•___

COMMENTS:

•

FIGURE 12–2   *(continued)*

5. PROFESSIONAL JUDGEMENT - WEIGHT 3	1	2	3	4	5
a. Demonstrated awareness of impacts of decisions	•				
b. Ability and willingness to make sound decisions based on available information without the assistance of supervisors					
c. Willing to take acceptable risks, but not recklessly					
d. Accepts responsibility for decisions and the subsequent results					
e. Proper use of police discretion					
f. Sensitive to needs of community or individuals					
g. Alert to surroundings and able to understand and react quickly and appropriately					
h. Has full understanding and application of the laws, rules and procedures governing the use of force, pursuit policy, search and seizure, arrest, and domestic violence					
i. Exercises proper degree of assertiveness when needed					
TOTAL (Element Score)					

Weight 3 x Total of All Element Scores ____•____ = Performance Standard Score ___•___

COMMENTS:

•

6. WORK PERFORMANCE/QUALITY - WEIGHT 3	1	2	3	4	5
a. Keeps current with legal changes and changes in Rules and Procedures Manual	•				
b. Proper recognition, collection and preservation of evidence					
c. Demonstrated understanding and application of State/Federal Laws, Municipal Ordinances, Departmental Rules and Procedures, Rules of Criminal Procedure, legal decisions, and directives					
d. Knowledge of and proper use of equipment and investigative techniques: Radar, Intoxilyzer, camera equipment, crime scene equipment (fingerprinting), computers Nystagmus, firearms, to include follow-up activities when appropriate					
e. Assignments/investigative reports are properly carried out and completed in a timely manner					
f. Knowledge of police patrol districts					
g. Continuous adherence to the RPM and other procedural guidelines					
h. Work product is consistently completed in a professional, thorough manner					
i. Documentation is an accurate reflection of a thorough investigation to include the elements of the crime, proper classification, correct report formatting, complete witness information, MO, and suspect information					
TOTAL (Element Score)					

Weight 3 x Total of All Element Scores ____•____ = Performance Standard Score ___•___

COMMENTS:

FIGURE 12–2   (*continued*)

7. PERSONAL APPEARANCE, GENERAL SAFETY PRACTICES AND PRIDE IN WORKING ENVIRONMENT - WEIGHT 1	1	2	3	4	5
a. Cares for uniform, equipment, police facility, vehicle, and weapons as required	•				
b. Cognizant of personal health and keeps physically fit					
c. Maintains positive image in appearance and demeanor at all times among peers and members of the public					
d. Exercises proper field survival practices					
e. Operates motor vehicles in a safe and prudent manner - obeys traffic laws					
TOTAL (Element Score)					

Weight 1 x Total of All Element Scores ____•____ = Performance Standard Score ___•___

COMMENTS:

•

8. PROFESSIONAL AND ORGANIZATIONAL COMMITMENT - WEIGHT 2	1	2	3	4	5
a. Is a positive role model for others to emulate	•				
b. Demonstrates loyalty and commitment to department and profession					
c. Continually strives to improve the image of the Arvada Police Department in the eyes of the public					
d. Demonstrates pride in the performance of others as well as self					
e. Demonstrates understanding of and commitment to Accreditation Standards					
f. Takes overt steps to overcome and combat bias in the community					
TOTAL (Element Score)					

Weight 2 x Total of All Element Scores ____•____ = Performance Standard Score ___•___

COMMENTS:

•

FIGURE 12–2 *(continued)*

PART III. Overall Rating

1. Customer Service/Community Problem Solving   _____

2. Teamwork/Interpersonal Actions   _____

3. Communications   _____

4. Initiative   _____

5. Professional Judgement   _____

6. Work Performance/Quality   _____

7. Personal Appearance, General Safety Practices, and Pride in Work
    Environment   _____

8. Professional and Organizational Commitment   _____

                         TOTAL POINT SCORE   _____

    Total __Point Score__   = _•_ %
          935 Points

                    OVERALL RATING SCORE = ___•___

	Below	Meets	Exceeds	Distinguished
Unsatisfactory [__]	Expectations [__]	Expectations [__]	Expectations [__]	Performance [__]
(20-34)	(35-54)	(55-71)	(72-91)	(92-100)

Relative to this employee's overall work record during this evaluation period, I recommend:
(Include status and salary recommendations within the parameters listed in the "City of Arvada
Supervisor's Guide to Performance Evaluations")

    •

PART IV. EMPLOYEE ASSESSMENT

Based upon current performance, what are the current employee strengths and development
needs?

A. Employee Strengths:

    •

B. Development Needs:

    •

FIGURE 12-2   *(continued)*

C.   Enter other comments relevant to the employee's performance.

*

PART V.   ESTABLISHMENT OF OBJECTIVES FROM *   TO *

This section establishes the objectives to be accomplished during the next evaluation period.
Objectives should be as specific as possible, including where appropriate, completion date.
The supervisor's objectives for the employee <u>and</u> the employee's objectives for her/himself
are to be included.

OBJECTIVES	PLANS TO MEET THE OBJECTIVE	PROPOSED COMPLETION DATE
*		

FIGURE 12–2   *(continued)*

PART VI.

Comments:

_____	_____	_____
Supervisor's Signature	Title	Date

Comments:

_____	_____	_____
Lieutenant's Signature	Title	Date

Comments:

_____	_____	_____
Bureau Commander's Signature	Title	Date

Comments:

_____	_____	_____
Chief of Police's Signature	Title	Date

Comments:

_____	_____	_____
Admin. Ass't. Signature	Title	Date

Comments:

_____	_____	_____
Personnel Signature	Title	Date

FIGURE 12–2   _(continued)_

PART VII.

Any comments which the employee would like to make, or modifications of performance evaluation by the Supervisor due to the discussion of this evaluation, should be noted here.

My Supervisor reviewed and discussed the contents of the Performance Evaluation with me. My signature below does not indicate whether I agree or disagree with this evaluation.

_____   _____

Employee's Signature   Date

Employee Comments Reviewed By:

_____   _____   _____   _____   _____
Supv. Init.   Div.Hd. (Lt.)   Bur.Cmdr.   C.O.P.   Admin.
                        Init.   Init.   Init.   Asst. Init.

_____
Personnel
Init.

FIGURE 12–2   *(continued)*

Police Officer Performance

935 Possible Points

	Percentage Spread	Point Spread	Salary Adj.-*Scale
Distinguished	97-100	906-935	10%
	92-96	860-905	9%
Exceeds	87-91	813-859	8.5%
	82-86	766-812	8%
	77-81	720-765	7.5%
	72-76	673-719	7%
Meets	67-71	626-672	6%
	60-66	561-625	5%
	55-59	514-560	4%
Below	50-54	467-513	2%
	40-49	374-466	0
	35-39	327-373	-2%
Unsatisfactory	30-34	280-326	-3%
	25-29	233-279	-4%
	20-24	187-232	-5%

*Non-top step employees - Increases are only possible up to the maximum top step.

FIGURE 12–2 *(continued)*

Of the many available examples of a PDRS, I chose to include here the Arvada (Colorado) Police Department's. On behalf of Chief Ahlstrom, Commander Scott wrote a letter of explanation as follows. (His letter is one of the reasons that I decided to present their PDRS.)

In order for you to better understand these evaluations, I would like to provide you with some background information on the process used to arrive at the content and format of these evaluations. Since time immemorial, supervisors and officers within the department have complained about a variety of concerns with the previous evaluation formats. Supervisors expressed the desire to have a check-off type of evaluation form. At the same time, officers and supervisors were concerned with the fact that a generic evaluation for a given rank did not address the specifics found within particular job assignments, i.e., the difference between detective, patrol officer, traffic officer, narcotics officer, etc.

In the interim, the city Personnel Department and the City Manager's Office came down with a mandate that the various city departments would develop evaluations which would have weighted values for various performance categories and would also be utilized, based upon overall score, to determine salary increases or decreases. When the original mandate came down from the City Manager and Personnel Department, performance categories were examined for content and revised to a greater or lesser degree to more accurately reflect the expectations of various assignments within the department. Nevertheless, the final forms were still somewhat generic and really did not address the specific expectations of particular assignments.

. . . I began the revision process for the performance evaluations within the Operations Bureau. I took the previous evaluation format which, in essence, consisted of a series of performance categories which were then explained by a paragraph of narrative detail. These performance categories were then broken down by myself into particular elements within a category with a point rating of 1 to 5 for the level of performance for each of those particular elements within a category. The category was then weighted based upon input from supervisors and the personnel to be evaluated. This weight value was then multiplied times the raw score to give an overall score for that performance category. At the end of the evaluation, the supervisors are to tabulate all of the calculated scores (raw score times weight value) to calculate a final raw score. This raw score is then divided by the total possible points for that particular evaluation to determine a percentage score, which is then used to determine the overall quality of performance and which can then be correlated with the City's breakdowns for salary increase or decrease.

I have instructed each of the elements and units within the Operations Bureau to critically evaluate and review the performance evaluation for each of their units. They are then authorized as a unit to revise the performance evaluation . . . based upon what they perceive as those elements which specifically address the performance and expectations in their particular unit. For example, the undercover officers, while they are still police officers, have very specific performance criteria that are much different than the detectives (police officers) and street officers (police officers). In this way, each unit can develop a customized evaluation for the members of that unit. They are free to add, delete, and revise the elements within the performance criteria for that unit, based upon their specific expectations and job duties. This will allow for the customization of evaluation forms for specific ranks and assignments within the Operations Bureau. This allows the evaluation process to be dynamic and changeable through the years as programs and priorities change with time. In the end, the total possible points will vary, depending upon the degree of customization for that particular form, but the percentage utilized by personnel for determination of salary increase or decrease will still be available by dividing the total possible points into the performance points totaled at the end of the form.

While this all may seem fairly complex and confusing, it is being done in a systematic manner in an attempt to reduce the amount of confusion felt by the supervisors and employees. I would like to call your attention to page 2 of each of the performance evaluations, making special note of the areas which state that documentation must be provided to varying degrees depending upon the evaluation score for each of the elements within an evaluation category. This is to insure that supervisors are, in fact, able to justify the scores given to their personnel and . . . to provide feedback, and in the case of the low expectations performance, a program for improvement, to both the employee being evaluated and the individuals reviewing all performance evaluations.

DESIGNING AND IMPLEMENTING A PERSONNEL-EVALUATION SYSTEM

Work joyfully and peacefully, knowing that right thoughts and right efforts will inevitably bring about right results.

—James Allen

Time to summarize. Remember the common precept of this entire book: that there is no one best way to do anything, organizationally speaking. However, there are better ways of doing things. The thirteen steps described here are a better (not perfect) way to assess police personnel.

1. *Job analysis: what is to be evaluated?* The first step to be taken in building a reliable and valid evaluation process is to conduct a comprehensive, in-depth job analysis.

2. *Multiple raters.* It is recommended that multiple raters be used in completing the form—for example, the current supervisor, the most recent past supervisor, and a supervisor who is on the same work shift. The present supervisor would be responsible for coordinating efforts and conducting the one-on-one interview with the officer. There are many advantages to the use of more than one rater, such as enhanced objectivity, improved clarity, more information, and greater acceptance on the part of the ratee.

3. *The raters.* There are five possible sources of performance appraisal: (1) supervisors, (2) peers, (3) the person being evaluated, (4) subordinates of the person to be appraised, and (5) people outside the immediate organization, such as citizens. Who the best person is to make the appraisal depends on the purpose of the appraisal and the level of the criteria being evaluated (immediate behavior versus intermediate and ultimate outcomes). Most performance appraisals are made by

an officer's immediate superior. This is particularly true when the major purpose of the appraisal is evaluation, rather than employee development.

A few police agencies have tried to introduce evaluation by peers or self-evaluation. These two methods work best under conditions of high interpersonal trust, highly specialized skills, and high visibility among peers and when development rather than evaluation is the major purpose to be served by the appraisal.

4. *Trained raters.* I have frequently asked police supervisors and managers if they are required to assess the performance of their subordinates' work activities, and the majority say yes. However, when I ask the same group of people if they received any training on rating, the most common answer is no! Those responsible for rating should be trained as raters.

5. *Rating the raters.* Although rating is acknowledged to be a fundamental and critical task of a police supervisor, in many cases the raters are not rated on their own willingness or ability to rate. In other words, a paramount dimension is being missed in terms of assessing a supervisor or manager's performance, which would be analogous to expecting patrol officers to behave with proper attitudes toward the public, but not rating them on their citizen contacts. Raters should be evaluated on their rating skills.

6. *A rating manual.* All performance-evaluation systems need a guide or a manual. Without a set of common definitions (such as the meaning of "community and human relations"), instructions, and procedures, the entire process is apt to suffer severe problems of ambiguity and integrity. A pertinent rating manual should address the obligations and concerns of the police agency, the police rater, and those to be assessed. A manual is a must.

7. *Significant (critical) incidents: a database.* We are prone to have a better recall of the immediate past, which is human nature. Thus when rating, a rater normally has a clearer memory of those events that occurred over the preceding few weeks than of those that occurred months ago. Indeed, by being "Officer Perfect" shortly before evaluation, an officer can often receive a fairly high evaluation.

This phenomenon cannot be totally eliminated, but it can be guarded against through the use of the significant incident technique (SIT). (The critical incident technique was first introduced in a business setting as a single method for evaluating a person's performance. I prefer to substitute the term *significant* for *critical* to avoid the negative connotations of the latter term.)

The SIT involves the recording of what can be termed significant or highly important behavior on the part of a police officer, which can be of either a positive or a negative nature. Over the course of the evaluation period, the rater documents the significant behavior of his or her ratees. Typically, two to three are generated per week. When rating, the supervisor uses this database to complete the rating form and the interpersonal interview. The SIT is most useful in fulfilling the activity that follows next.

8. *Feedback.* Employee-supervisor feedback is a clear-cut must. It can be event feedback, time-triggered feedback, or preferably both. In event feedback, as favorable conduct is observed it should be positively reinforced. ("Good job, officer. Let's discuss it for a few minutes.") As misconduct is witnessed, it should be corrected. ("Hey,

officer, you really fouled up! Let's discuss it for a few minutes.") Most of us want to know when we are doing right or wrong—not once every six to twelve months, but at that moment in time so that we can continue or abandon a particular behavior. Such events are best made a part of a SIT. Feedback is the breakfast of champions!

9. *Supervision by objectives.* While you as a supervisor should initiate the SBO process, it is best structured as a two-way channel. As a type of a contract, both parties ought to be included in drafting and approving the agreement. Because an SBO statement acts as a basis for both past and future performance ratings, it should encompass the thinking of both the rater and the ratee. All police supervisors should separately produce tentative SBO contracts for employees. Concurrently, employees should be requested to independently generate their own contracts. Once both contracts have been finished, the two should confer and negotiate a final form.

   Both event feedback and time-triggered feedback are necessary. Monitoring an employee's performance assists in determining when each type should be applied. Time-triggered feedback is especially relevant for SBO in that set time periods or milestones should be reviewed according to schedule on a one-to-one basis (supervisor-subordinate). This is where SITs and counseling merge to act as a reinforcer or corrective motivator for getting the needed performance. (Figure 12–2 incorporates SBO.)

10. *Making mission statements happen.* In Responsibility 4, I underscored the importance of a leader's projecting a vision of where the department is headed and why. Some agencies have put muscle into their mission statements by expanding them into performance-rating systems. In other words, the values and standards comprising the department's mission are being looked for in an employee's daily work effort. Connecting performance appraisal to a mission statement increases the likelihood that it will be practiced and not just preached.

11. *Avoiding failure.* Here are some reasons why a performance evaluation flops:

    - There is no face-to-face discussion.
    - There is no preparation by either party.
    - There is little identification of actual performance problems.
    - There has been little communication about performance during the period being appraised.
    - Supervisors have been concerned only with bad performance.
    - There has been no follow-up effort afterward.
    - Appraisal has just been a once-a-year event, not an ongoing process.

12. *Employee preparation.* An employee should be prepared to answer the following questions:

    - What do you feel was your biggest accomplishment or major contribution to the department?
    - In what areas do you feel you didn't perform well?
    - What prevented you from performing well in these areas?

- What can be done to make your performance better?
- What area would you like to develop over the next appraisal period?
- As your supervisor, how can I help?

13. *Self-appraisal.* As a supervisor, you should ask at least the following questions about your performance as a rater:

- How did I do overall?
- Did I set up good two-way communication?
- Did the employee truly understand the deficient areas?
- Was the employee really receptive to my suggestions for making changes?
- Did I concentrate on behaviors and avoid personality factors?
- Has the interview opened up new lines of communication?
- What must I do to follow up in the next week, month, and year?
- What will I do to motivate the employee to improve performance?

360-Degree Performance Evaluation

Most performance-rating systems make a mistake from the viewpoint of accountability. Police supervisors should be appraised by those to whom they are accountable. Leadership depends on accountability to a boss. Supervisors are supervised by managers.

The following questionnaire should be administered to your staff. Besides affording you an opportunity to learn about your supervisory practices, it will elevate trust, teamwork, empowerment, and a host of other positive workplace values.

STRUCTURED EXERCISE 12–3

HOW DOES MY PERFORMANCE RATE?

Ask the people who work with and for you—as well as your boss—to answer these questions about you. For each, have them circle their rating according to the following scale:

5 = to a very great extent	2 = to a little extent
4 = to a great extent	1 = not at all
3 = to some extent	NA = does not apply

The police supervisor . . .

1. Recognizes broad implications of polices

    5   4   3   2   1   NA

2. Understands complex concepts and relationships

    5   4   3   2   1   NA

3. Analyzes problems from different points of view

    5   4   3   2   1   NA

4. Makes decisions in the face of ambiguity

    5   4   3   2   1   NA

5. Makes sound decisions based on adequate information

    5   4   3   2   1   NA

6. Is quick to adapt to new situations

    5   4   3   2   1   NA

7. Translates departmental strategies into clear objectives and tactics

    5   4   3   2   1   NA

8. Provides clear direction and defines priorities for the team

    5   4   3   2   1   NA

9. Fosters the development of a common vision

    5   4   3   2   1   NA

10. Acts decisively

    5   4   3   2   1   NA

11. Is open and candid with others

    5   4   3   2   1   NA

12. Genuinely cares about the welfare of others

    5   4   3   2   1   NA

13. Empowers others to do their work

    5   4   3   2   1   NA

14. Champions new initiatives within and beyond the scope of the job

    5   4   3   2   1   NA

15. Involves others in the change process

    5   4   3   2   1   NA

16. Has the confidence and trust of others

    5   4   3   2   1   NA

17. Shows consistency between words and actions

    5   4   3   2   1   NA

18. Persists in the face of obstacles

    5   4   3   2   1   NA

19. Puts a top priority on getting results

    5   4   3   2   1   NA

How You Rate

If you score all 4s and 5s, you are viewed as competent. Focus on fine-tuning and making the most of your strengths.

If you score 3 on any item, determine how important the skill or behavior is to your job. If it's important, try to improve.

If you score below 3, it's fix-it time. Target those areas for development.

Organizational performance is derived from individual performance, and individual performance is heavily dependent on an accurate and valid personnel-evaluation process. Also, a well-designed evaluation process is only as effective as the boss who is responsible for administering it.

KEY POINTS

- High performance includes five prerequisites: (1) nonnegotiable high standards; (2) workplace opportunities; (3) one's character; (4) emotion intelligence; and (5) teamwork.
- Planning is a process for implementing goals and objectives.
- Police supervisors who plan their work typically outperform those who do not.
- In SBO, the objectives must be specific, set in collaboration with the employee, and used to measure performance.
- SBO comprises seven sequential steps:

  1. Identify the issue.
  2. Create a specific statement.
  3. Develop alternative strategies.
  4. Select a strategy.
  5. Implement the strategy.
  6. Evaluate the results.
  7. Provide feedback to the police employee.

- The three key reasons for assessing a person's performance are behavioral motivation, control, and feedback.
- Performance evaluation serves a large number of purposes, including making decisions about promotions and dealing with SBO contracts.
- For a performance-evaluation system to be reliable and valid, it must be job-related.
- Job-related performance-appraisal systems are based on a job analysis.
- An internally and externally sound performance-rating system must include

  - A job analysis
  - A rating method
  - More than one rater
  - Trained raters
  - Raters who are rated for their rating skills
  - A rating manual
  - The recording of significant incidents

- Feedback
- SBO
- Making mission statements happen

EXTENDED LEARNING

1. Is the phrase "to protect and serve" a goal or an objective? Why?
2. Convert the statement "We had best reduce our burglary rate" into an objective.
3. Besides the budget, can you identify one or more plans in your department or agency?
4. What do *reliability* and *validity* mean? How do they differ? What is the best tool for ensuring that they exist in a rating process?
5. It is underscored in this chapter that the raters must be trained to ensure the integrity of a performance-appraisal process. What are some of the ways to train police supervisors as raters?
6. How might individual feedback on performance enhance teamwork? How might it hinder it?

RESPONSIBILITY 13

Conflict

The police supervisor is responsible for anticipating, defining, and solving personal, interpersonal, and group conflicts with precision and compassion.

We live and work in an imperfect world. Mistakes are made. Most involve those of the mind, while some deal with the heart. Most often it is the supervisor who has the primary responsibility for resolving them.

The day soldiers stop bringing you their problems is the day you have stopped leading them. They have either lost confidence that you can help them or concluded that you do not care. Either case is a failure of leadership.

—Colin Powell

Most police officers are honest, hardworking, and helpful human beings. They project a positive mental attitude (PMA) and will make your job as a supervisor a rewarding one. Regretfully, the majority of police organizations also possess a few individuals who are seemingly dedicated to making things miserable. As their supervisor, however, you can master their fate.

Supervision is a people process. A select few people will command more of your thinking and attention than others. People problems can come at you on an individual or on a group basis (the whole crew is malingering). Solving people problems—individual or group—is a major job responsibility for the supervisor.

Problem police employees come in a variety of symptomatic packages. Basically, they can be categorized as either honest (making mistakes of the mind) or dishonest (making mistakes of the heart). Oddly, the honest problem employee—for example, the "whining, sniveling malcontent" (WSM)—is frequently more difficult to handle. The dishonest officer is detected, apprehended, discharged, and often prosecuted. The WSM requires considerably different treatment.

As a leader, you are destined to expend a large portion of your energy on the handling of problem employees. They will tax your patience, at times push your anger control, and test your ability to develop a creative response. However, you must not lose sight and contact with the productive and team-spirited employees. Concentrate on, reinforce, and reward the productive officers. The strength of your work team is centered here. Remember what I said in the introduction . . .

> Nobody said supervising was easy. If it were easy, everyone would be doing it.

The remainder of this chapter examines conflict as both a positive and a negative experience.

CONFLICT

Human conflict is to be expected; indeed, a certain amount of internal conflict is healthy. An analogy would be the necessity for tension on the mainspring of a watch. At the same time, however, too much tension will cause it to break. In an organizational setting, too much conflict is counterproductive to goal attainment. The police supervisor is in a unique position to control the degree of conflict in an agency.

When I use the term *conflict*, I am referring to perceived incompatible differences resulting in some form of interference or opposition. Whether the differences are real or not is irrelevant. If people perceive that the differences exist, then a conflict state exists. Additionally, this definition covers a range that includes the extremes, from subtle, indirect, and highly controlled forms of differences to overt acts, such as physical altercations, job terminations, and criminal acts.

Competition is different from conflict. Conflict is directed against another party, whereas competition is aimed at obtaining a goal without interference from another party. If misdirected, competition can lead to conflict.

Is Conflict a Plus or a Minus?

The answer is, "It all depends."

> Some conflicts support the goals of the organization; these are functional conflicts of a constructive form. Then there are conflicts that hinder an organization in achieving its goals; these are dysfunctional conflicts and are destructive forms.

It is one thing to argue that conflict can be valuable, but how do you tell if a conflict is functional or dysfunctional? Unfortunately, the demarcation is neither clear nor precise. No one level of conflict can be adopted as acceptable or unacceptable under all conditions. The type and level of conflict that create healthy and positive involvement in achieving one department's goals may, in another department—or in the same department at another time—be highly dysfunctional. Functionality or dysfunctionality, therefore, is a judgment call on your part. Hence it remains for you to make intelligent judgments concerning whether conflict levels in your unit are appropriate, too high, or too low.

The Value of Conflict

If harnessed and channeled, conflict does the following for you and your team members:

- Acts as a major stimulant for change
- Fosters creativity and innovation
- Clarifies issues and goals
- Encourages individuality
- Enhances communication
- Increases energy within a unit
- Promotes cohesiveness
- Is psychologically healthy

As a supervisor, it is imperative that you respect an officer's individuality and preferences as long as they do not detract from getting police work done in a professional and legally accepted manner. If you push for uniformity and ignore individual strengths and styles, you are promoting the negative aspects of conflict.

Sources of Conflict

Conflict can emanate from one of four sources: (1) existing conditions, especially novel ones, (2) our attitudes, (3) our thoughts, and (4) our behavior. Typically, all four combine to produce the conflict.

Fortunately, most conflicts are of minor importance. Few police officers are likely to be psychologically crippled by trying to decide between two patrol routes. Few of us encounter daily conflicts that we cannot respond to in a routine or "programmed" manner. The police officer, however, generally experiences the unusual. He or she is more often than not faced with highly diverse, nonprogrammable choices. Briefly stated, the police officer typically deals with novelty, rather than familiar and routine problems.

> There is a hidden conflict in our lives between the pressures of acceleration and those of novelty. One forces us to make faster decisions, while the other compels us to make the hardest, most time-consuming type of decision.

STRUCTURED EXERCISE 13–1

CONFLICT-MANAGEMENT CLIMATE INDEX

The purpose of this exercise is to permit you to assess your organization with regard to its conflict-management climate. On each of the following rating scales, indicate how you see your organization as it actually is right now, not how you think it should be or how you believe others would see it. Circle the number that indicates your sense of where the organization is on each dimension of the index.

1. Balance of Power

| 1 | 2 | 3 | 4 | 5 | 6 |

Power is massed either at the top or at the bottom of the organization.

Power is distributed evenly and appropriately throughout the organization.

2. Expression of Feelings

| 1 | 2 | 3 | 4 | 5 | 6 |

Expressing strong feelings is costly and not accepted.

Expressing strong feelings is valued and easy to do.

3. Conflict-Management Procedures

| 1 | 2 | 3 | 4 | 5 | 6 |

There are no clear conflict-resolution procedures that many people use.

Everyone knows about, and many people use, a conflict-resolution procedure.

4. Attitudes toward Open Disagreement

| 1 | 2 | 3 | 4 | 5 | 6 |

People here do not openly disagree very much. "Go along to get along" is the motto.

People feel free to disagree openly on important issues without fear of consequences.

5. Use of Third Parties

| 1 | 2 | 3 | 4 | 5 | 6 |

No one here uses third parties to help resolve conflicts.

Third parties are used frequently to help resolve conflicts.

6. Power of Third Parties

| 1 | 2 | 3 | 4 | 5 | 6 |

Third parties are usually superiors in the organization.

Third parties are always people of equal or lower rank.

7. Neutrality of Third Parties

| 1 | 2 | 3 | 4 | 5 | 6 |

Third parties are never neutral but serve as advocates for a certain outcome.

Third parties are always neutral as to substantive issues and conflict-resolution methods used.

(continued)

STRUCTURED EXERCISE 13–1 (*continued*)

8. Your Leader's Conflict-Resolution Style

| 1 | 2 | 3 | 4 | 5 | 6 |

The leader does not deal openly with conflict but works behind the scenes to resolve it.

The leader confronts conflicts directly and works openly with those involved to resolve it.

9. How Your Leader Receives Negative Feedback

| 1 | 2 | 3 | 4 | 5 | 6 |

The leader is defensive or closed and seeks vengeance on those who criticize him or her.

The leader receives criticism easily and even seeks it as an opportunity to grow and learn.

10. Follow-Up

| 1 | 2 | 3 | 4 | 5 | 6 |

Agreements always fall through the cracks; the same problems must be solved again and again.

Accountability is built into every conflict-resolution agreement.

11. Feedback Procedures

| 1 | 2 | 3 | 4 | 5 | 6 |

No effort is made to solicit and understand reactions to decisions.

Feedback channels for soliciting reactions to all major decisions are known and used.

12. Communication Skills

| 1 | 2 | 3 | 4 | 5 | 6 |

Few if any people possess or practice basic communication skills.

Everyone in the organization possesses and uses good communication skills.

13. Track Record

| 1 | 2 | 3 | 4 | 5 | 6 |

Very few if any successful conflict-resolution experiences have occurred in the recent past.

Many stories are available of successful conflict-resolution experiences in the recent past.

Scoring and Interpretation

To arrive at your overall Conflict-Management Climate Index score, total the ratings that you assigned to the thirteen separate scales. Then compare your score with the following index ranges:

Index Range	Indication
60–78	Ready to work on conflict with little or no work on climate
31–59	Possible with some commitment to work on climate
13–30	Very risky without unanimous commitment to work on climate issues

Assess your overall score. If possible, compare your bottom-line results to those of others in your group. Attempt to explain your lowest and highest scores per item. Use case examples when you can.

CONFLICT MANAGEMENT

Leaders who manage conflicts best are able to draw out all parties, understand the differing perspectives, and then find a common ideal that everyone can endorse. They surface the conflict, acknowledge the feelings and views of all sides, and then redirect the energy toward a shared ideal.

Handling relationships, however, is not as simple as it sounds. It's not just a matter of friendliness. Rather, conflict management is friendliness with a purpose: moving people in the right direction, whether that's agreement on a patrol strategy or enthusiasm about a new technology.

Socially skilled leaders tend to have resonance with a wide circle of people and have a knack for finding common ground and building rapport. That doesn't mean they socialize continually; it means they work under the assumption that nothing important gets done alone. Such leaders have a network in place when the time for action comes. And in an era when more and more work is done long-distance—by e-mail or by phone—face-to-face communication, paradoxically, becomes more crucial than ever.

> Being an adept negotiator is important to your success as a supervisor because you are destined to experience conflicting situations and groups and because you are in a front-line position to convert potentially negative conflict into positive problem solving.

SIX STEPS YOU CAN TAKE TO GET TO YES

Whether in police work, a personal business transaction, or our own family, we reach most decisions through negotiation. Even if we go to court, we almost always negotiate a settlement before trial. Although negotiation takes place every day, it is not easy to do successfully. Our natural approaches for negotiation often leave us and others dissatisfied, fatigued, and withdrawn.

We find ourselves in a catch-22. We envision two ways to negotiate: easy or tough. The easy negotiator wants to avoid personal conflict and so makes concessions readily in order to reach agreement. Easy negotiators want an amicable resolution, yet they often end up exploited and feeling bitter. The tough negotiator perceives any situation as a highly competitive contest of wills in which the side that takes the more extreme positions and perseveres wins. Tough negotiators need to win, yet they often end up creating an equally tough response, which exhausts them and their resources and harms their relationship with the other side. Other typical negotiating strategies fall between tough and easy, but each includes an attempted trade-off between getting what you want and getting along with people.

Principled Negotiations

There is a third and better way for you, as a leader, to negotiate. It is neither tough nor easy, but oddly both! It can be referred to as "principled negotiations." This approach strives to decide the issues on their merit, rather than who wins. It urges that you look for mutual gains wherever possible and that, where your interests conflict, you should agree that the result will be based on fair standards, independent of your will and that of your adversary. The method of principled negotiations is tough on the merits, easy on the people. It employs no tricks and no posturing.

> Principled negotiation shows you and your opponent how to obtain what you are entitled to and still be civil. It enables you to be equitable while protecting both of you against being taken advantage of. What follows is an all-purpose strategy. Unlike almost all other conflict-resolution strategies, if your adversaries learn this one, it does not become more difficult for you to use it; it becomes easier. If they read this chapter, all the better for the two of you.

Step 1: Don't Bargain over Positions.

When we bargain over our positions, we tend to lock ourselves into those positions. The more we clarify our position and defend it against attack, the more committed we become to it. As more attention is paid to positions, less attention is devoted to meeting our underlying concerns. Agreement becomes less likely. Any agreement reached may reflect a mechanical balance of the difference between final positions rather than a solution carefully forged to meet our legitimate interests.

- Arguing over positions creates, at best, unsatisfactory agreements.
- Arguing over positions is inefficient because the conflicting parties usually start at an extreme position and stubbornly hold to it, while at times making small concessions. This is highly time-consuming and thus inefficient.
- Arguing over positions endangers an ongoing relationship because each side tries to force the other to change its position.
- When there are many parties involved, all of these difficulties are compounded because coalitions are formed.

Step 2: Remember That Being Nice Is Not the Answer.

Many people understand the high costs of hard positional bargaining, particularly for the parties and their relationship. They hope to avoid them by following a more pleasant style of negotiation. Instead of seeing the other side as adversaries, they prefer to see them as "friends." Rather than emphasizing a goal of victory, they emphasize the necessity of reaching agreement. In a soft negotiation game, the standard moves are to make offers and concessions, to trust the other side, to be totally affable, and to yield as necessary to avoid confrontation. However, any negotiation focused on the relationship runs the risk of producing a weak agreement. More seriously, pursuing a soft and friendly form of positional bargaining makes you vulnerable to someone who plays a hard game of positional bargaining. In positional bargaining, a hard game dominates a soft one. The remedy for playing hardball is not pitching marshmallows.

The answer to the question of whether to use soft positional bargaining or hard is "neither." Change the game! The new game proposed to you, principled negotiation, is negotiation on the merits. It consists of four basic points. Each point deals with a basic element of negotiation and suggests what you should do about it:

- People: Separate the people from the conflict.
- Interests: Concentrate on interests, not positions.
- Options: Generate a variety of options before deciding what to do.
- Criteria: Insist that the solution be based on some objective standard.

Each point is examined further in the sections that follow.

Step 3: Separate the People from the Conflict.

This point acknowledges that you and I are creatures of strong emotions who often have radically different perceptions and have difficulty communicating clearly. Emotions typically become entangled with the objective merits of the problem. Taking positions just makes this worse because people's egos become identified with their positions. Hence before working on the substantive problem, the "people problem" should be disentangled from it and dealt with separately. We should see ourselves as working side by side, attacking the problem, not each other. Hence the first point: Separate the people from the conflict.

Step 4: Concentrate on Interests, Not Positions.

The second point was not intended to overcome the drawback of concentrating on people's stated positions when the object of a negotiation is to satisfy their underlying interests. A negotiating position often obscures what you really want in a conflicting set of situations. Compromising between positions is not likely to produce an agreement that will effectively take care of the human needs that led people to adopt these positions. So, concentrate on interests, not positions.

Step 5: Generate a Number of Options.

The third point responds to the difficulty of designing solutions while under pressure. Trying to decide in the presence of an adversary narrows your vision. Having a lot at stake inhibits creativity. So does searching for the right answers. Keep in mind that usually there is more than a single right solution or answer to the conflict. Set aside a designated time to think up a wide range of possible solutions that advance shared interests and creatively reconcile differing interests. Before trying to reach agreement, invent numerous options for mutual gain.

Step 6: Adopt Objective Criteria.

Where interests are directly opposed, an employee may be able to obtain a favorable result simply by being stubborn. That method tends to reward intransigence and produce arbitrary results. However, as a supervisor you can counter this tactic by insisting that the employee's single say-so is not enough and that the agreement must reflect some fair standard independent of the naked will of either side. This does not mean insisting that the terms be based on the standard you select, but only that some fair standard—such as custom, expert opinion, prior decisions, or law—determine the outcome.

By discussing a fair criterion, rather than what the parties are willing or unwilling to do, neither party need give in to the other; both can defer to a fair solution.

STRUCTURED EXERCISE 13-2

Tackle the following problems using the six steps for getting to yes. Have one member of your group serve as an observer and recorder of the deliberations. When finished with each case, critique your problem-solving process with respect to the six steps.

Problem 1

Ten workers, all over fifty years of age, from the department's Communications and Data-Processing Unit have submitted a letter of complaint to the chief about the status of the older workers in their unit. As they explain it, the nature of the communications and data-processing systems operation is such that college-trained, younger people are constantly being brought into the unit to work on a part-time basis. These youngsters, in their view, are more interested in short-term benefits and working procedures than are the older workers. When initially receiving the complaint, the chief told them that considerable savings are achieved by the employment of the younger workers. The older employees have hinted they may seek redress through the Fair Employment Practices Commission. What should the chief say and do at this point?

Problem 2

The captain in command of the Uniform Field Operations Bureau (patrol and traffic) has complained bitterly to the chief on two occasions that the department's Special Operations Bureau (SOB) has significantly reduced the quality of police-citizen relationships. He has asserted that the personnel in his unit are making every effort to provide just and effective law enforcement. The captain finds that the SOB, however, disrupts the development of a mutually supportive police-community relationship by its heavy-handed tactics. When questioned, the lieutenant in charge of the SOB indicated that his special enforcement staff was clearly successful in reducing major felonies. Furthermore, he implied that perhaps the captain was getting "soft" and could best be assigned elsewhere. The chief is convinced that both individuals are dedicated and professional individuals. Also, both have highly commendable performance records with the department. How should the chief resolve this situation?

Problem 3

Sixty percent of the detectives in the Investigations Unit filed a grievance regarding their performance evaluations. The percentage of grievances has been going steadily upward. The chief is beginning to think that the reason for this occurrence is that a grieving employee almost always gets some portion of his rating raised. Increasingly, it appears that the feeling among the detectives seems to be "Why not?" or "If the other guy does it, I had better also." How should the immediate situation be handled? What should be done in the long run?

PROBLEM EMPLOYEES

At times, I've been a problem employee. I confess to being overly critical, incessantly complaining, and miserably cantankerous. What about you?

Problem employees frequently are unaware of their misbehavior, usually lack social skills, and often do not have self-discipline. Basically, they have low emotional intelligence.

These people push and on occasion violate ethical standards of conduct. While fewer in number, others flagrantly violate ethical and professional norms and even the law.

Earlier I argued that there is no such thing as "business ethics" or "police ethics." Ethics are plainly and irrefutably ethics. Ditto for "work ethics." Your personal responsibility for being fair, truthful, courteous, helpful, loyal and so on does not change from your home to your work. It does not change from playing sports to financial investing. Ethics are ethics; they are not situational.

Problem employees are relatively few in number—perhaps up to 5 percent of a police agency—but they demand a lot of a supervisor's time and energy. There are many supervisors who expend more effort on conflicts created by problem employees than on supervising police work. Most supervisors discover that 80 percent of your time will be directed toward 20 percent of your staff.

For simplicity, I've categorized problem employees as (1) malcontented, (2) immoral, (3) unprofessional, and (4) criminal. Obviously, an unhappy or unethical employee may belong in more than one category.

Problem Employee 1: The Malcontent

The malcontent is the most common type of all the problem employees and often the most difficult to correct. Malcontents cause minor conflicts and then disappear, only to surface again to create more conflict. They're always happy to be a part of the problem, but they shun any responsibility for helping solve it. This employee is capable of being a daily doomsayer, a chronic malingerer, or a producer of low-quality police services. They grate on the supervisor, their coworkers, and most unfortunately the people they're paid to serve. They are internally miserable, depressed, and sour. Worse still, they want others to feel the same.

> The malcontent's bad attitudes and sloppy behavior are contagious. If unchecked, the malcontented employee will lower team morale as well as the quality of services.

Helping the Malcontent.   You can help problem police employees toward better behavior only after you have reassured them that you are trying to help—not looking for an excuse to get rid of them. No approach does more harm with a person of this nature than the "better get yourself straightened out or you will lose your job" attitude on the supervisor's part. You have to believe, and make the employee believe, that your intentions are good, that you want to help. Then you must give malcontents every opportunity to help themselves. This approach is called "counseling," and there are fifteen rules for you to follow:

1. Listen patiently to what the employee has to say before making any comment of your own. This act on your part may be sufficient to resolve the difficulties.
2. Refrain from criticizing or offering hasty advice about the employee's problem.
3. Never argue with a police employee while you are in the process of counseling.
4. Give your undivided attention to the employee.
5. Probe beyond the mere words of what the employee says; listen to see if the officer is trying to tell you something deeper than what appears on the surface.

6. Recognize what you are counseling an employee for. And don't look for immediate results. Never mix up the counseling interview with some other action you may want to take, such as discipline.

7. Find a quiet place where you won't be interrupted and won't be overheard. Try to put the employee at ease. Don't jump into a cross-examination.

8. Depending on the nature of the situation, multiple sessions may be necessary. They should last from fifteen to thirty minutes each.

9. If after two counseling sessions you are not making progress, you should consult with your manager about other options.

10. Counseling is a major job responsibility, and you must not avoid it.

11. Look at your task as a fact-finding one, just as in handling grievances.

12. Control your own emotions and opinions while dealing with the employee.

13. Be absolutely sold on the value of listening, rather than preaching.

14. Recognize your own limits in handling these situations. You're not a clinical psychologist. You're a person responsible for getting results out of your assigned officers.

15. If all else fails, then you still have your prerogative to use discipline.

Make no mistake: Handling a police employee who has become a malcontent can be frustrating. Sometimes it can become downright unpleasant. But the sooner you confront the person, the sooner the problems get solved.

> The belief that employees are basically good and therefore can be corrected is one of the most widely held beliefs in formal organizations. Yet it is both untrue and harmful. Those who believe in innate human goodness view the battle for a better employee as primarily a struggle between the individual and the department. The battle is within the individual and centers on one's character.

Earlier I stressed that problem employees represent a very small percentage of the department. I believe that many of them can and will correct their wrongful behavior. I also believe that, unfortunately, a few are losers, and there is nothing that you can do about it, no matter how hard you try. What you can and must do is assist them in exiting the department.

Problem Bosses.   Similar to problem employees, problem bosses are fortunately few in number. But because they direct the work of other people, their impact on the organization can be more drastic. They can make the workday of several people meaningless and miserable. They are avoided and rarely listen with any give-and-take.

Anyone who has ever worked in an organization for very long knows a problem boss. Problem bosses generate maximum anxiety over issues of minimum significance. This term refers to behavior that makes police work worse than it need be: petty harassment; open abuse of power and prestige; meanness disguised as discipline; and insistence on the letter rather than the spirit of regulations. This type of supervisor is clearly no leader. This person is small-minded and ignoble and takes the trivial seriously. This type can be recognized immediately because he or she never has anything to do with providing police services.

Drawing the Lines: Morally, Professionally, and Legally. It is impossible to construct an effective system of accountability without a strong and functional mechanism for maintaining behavioral control over police personnel (Figure 13–1). While the exclusionary rule, criminal and civil actions against police officers, and other external remedies serve as important constraints, you must accept primary responsibility for controlling the vast discretionary power of police officers.

Unfortunately, some police supervisors have not yet accepted this challenge, and this is the basic reason why there has been constant pressure for civilian review boards, ombudsmen, and other such external review agencies.

Your agency may be efficient and large enough to afford an "internal investigation" or "professional responsibilities" unit. However, the creation of an internal investigation unit does not relieve you of the need to maintain discipline. On the contrary, it strengthens it by providing assistance on request in the investigation of alleged misconduct of team members.

Although the community may disagree with or be uncertain about what constitutes police misconduct, the police cannot. Granted, without community consensus on this subject, the problem is a highly perplexing one for our police. Nonetheless, wrongdoing must be defined and policies must be set by the agency. Lines must be clearly drawn. Essentially, these lines should encompass three forms of misconduct: (1) legalistic, (2) professional, and (3) moralistic. The first involves criminal considerations; the second may or may not be criminal in nature but does entail professional considerations; and the third may or may not include professional canons but does embody personal ethics. Each form of errant behavior is examined further in the following paragraphs. There is a descending degree of clarity or precision with each type of wrongdoing.

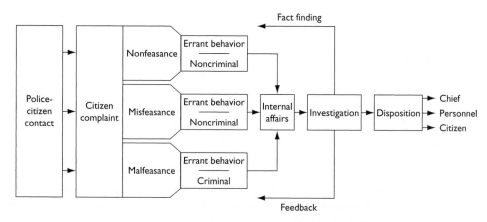

FIGURE 13–1   Internal discipline: A system of accountability. (*Paul Whisenand and Fred Ferguson,* The Managing of Police Organizations, *2nd ed., © 1978, p. 349. Reprinted by permission of Prentice Hall, Inc., Upper Saddle River, N.J.*)

Conversely, there is an ascending degree of administrative ambiguity on police and procedural violations. We start with the more vague type of misconduct: moralistic.

Problem Employee 2: Moral Misconduct

If an officer thinks certain citizens are deserving of aggressive police practices, the likelihood of his or her behaving aggressively is enhanced, perhaps to the point of overreaction or even physical abuse. If the officer thinks certain citizens are deserving of no police attention, the likelihood of his or her behaving passively is increased, perhaps to the extent of no reaction, and thus the possibility of corruption occurs. Moral misconduct it is at the very crux of other forms of misconduct.

Use-of-force abuses are one example of moral misconduct. The U.S. Constitution entrusts police officers with special powers not given to ordinary citizens. While engaged in their lawful duties, police officers have a legitimate right to use force to overcome resistance.

In situations involving use of force or injury sustained while in police custody, the agency should anticipate that the injured person will file a claim alleging negligence or excessive force. To reduce or eliminate liability arising from false or frivolous claims against a department or individual officers, it is critical that all uses of force and in-custody injuries be thoroughly investigated and documented.

An unbiased police investigation and accurate documentation immediately following a use-of-force or in-custody injury will help to protect a department and officers against liability and will identify unacceptable behavior, procedural concerns, and training needs. Additionally, the law enforcement services provided by the department will be viewed by the public as fair, impartial, and sensitive to the dignity and worth of each individual. See Figure 13–2 for excerpts from a use-of-force policy.

Problem Employee 3: Professional Misconduct

This form of misconduct can range from physical to verbal abuse of a citizen. On the one hand, a criminal or civil violation may have occurred; on the other, agency standards of professional conduct may be at issue. The possibilities for wrongdoing in this instance can fall within two rubrics: the law and professional conduct "unbecoming an officer." The distinction between this type of wrongdoing and corruption is that no personal gain for the officer or others is involved in professional misconduct. The key question is this: What conduct is permissible? Hence there is a need for established policies, procedures, rules, and sanctions that explicitly encompass the conduct of police employees.

Sexual harassment is one example of professional misconduct (and moral misconduct as well). Since 1977, police managers have had to deal with increased employee rights, civil litigation, and recruiting problems. But no issue is more complex than sexual harassment in the police environment. Currently, it is estimated that 15 percent of the sworn personnel are female, and this percentage will continue to increase. By the year 2010, an estimated one in five officers will be female. (The Equal Employment Opportunity Commission [EEOC] has targeted police agencies to have staff of which 50 percent will be women after the year 2000.)

POLICY

Officers shall use the lowest level of force necessary under the circumstances to properly perform their lawful duties. Officers should regard it as a matter of professional pride to be able to quietly, skillfully, and with a minimum of force arrest a suspect or bring order to a disorderly situation.

DEFINITIONS

Deadly Force. That force which when used might cause death or serious bodily injury or in the manner of its use or intended use is capable of causing a substantial risk of death or serious bodily injury.

Serious Physical Injury. Physical injury which creates a reasonable risk of death or which results in admission to a medical facility.

Deadly Weapon. Any instrument used for lethal purposes including a firearm or other instrumentality which in the manner of its use could cause death or serious bodily injury. This includes impact weapons.

Injury. Refers to any physical harm inflicted by police or sustained while in police custody and includes any wound, bruise, abrasion, or complaint of pain.

Force. Any action taken to control, restrain, overcome or stop a suspect's unlawful resistance. Police presence alone is a form of control; this control is frequently enough to bring about order to volatile situations. The following are the Levels of Force:

- Level 1. Verbal control techniques that rely on voice, tone, and voice inflection to gain a subject's compliance.
- Level 2. Hand-applied force to gain compliance, and includes defensive techniques, e.g., come-along holds, pressure point control, take-downs, and control techniques and chemical agents.
- Level 3. The use of personal weapon techniques (fist-, elbow-, knee- and kick-strikes), taser, K-9 and impact weapons (batons) that could temporarily incapacitate a subject (flashlights and radio pacsets are not designed as weapons, and their use as an impact weapon is not authorized unless clearly necessitated by circumstances).
- Level 4. The highest level of force which includes the use of firearms or deadly weapons to stop a subject.

SUPERVISORY RESPONSIBILITIES

- The assigned sergeant will assume command of the scene. The sergeant will identify all officers who have been involved in the use of force and who are witnesses to the incident. Statements will be obtained from all officers involved or identified as witnesses.
- The sergeant will also identify all civilian witnesses to the incident, obtain their statements and record their full name, address, and telephone numbers.
- The sergeant will thoroughly investigate the incident and take necessary action when required (provide medical care, approve arrests, make notifications, etc.).

FIGURE 13–2   Use-of-force police excerpts. *(Courtesy of Santa Ana Police Department, California.)*

Legal Definition of Sexual Harassment.   Let us review how the legal definition of the term has evolved:

1964: The Civil Rights Act of 1964 contained a provocatively novel amendment banning job discrimination on the basis of sex, which foes of the law had hoped would derail it.

1975: In the first reported sexual harassment decision under the new law, involving two women who claimed they suffered repeated verbal abuse and physical advances from a supervisor, an Arizona federal district court ruled that the act does not cover such a claim.

1977: A Washington federal appeals court ruled that sexual harassment is discrimination under the act. The case involved a woman who alleged that her job was abolished in retaliation for her refusing a supervisor's sexual advances.

1980: The EEOC issued landmark sexual harassment guidelines prohibiting unwelcome sexual advances, sexual requests that are made a condition of employment, and conduct that creates a hostile work environment.

1986: The U.S. Supreme Court upheld the validity of the EEOC guidelines and ruled that sexual harassment that creates a hostile or abusive work environment is a violation of the act.

1991: A Florida federal district court ruled that nude pinups in the workplace can create an atmosphere that constitutes sexual harassment; a California federal appeals court ruled that a hostile environment should be evaluated from the standpoint not of a "reasonable person" but of a "reasonable woman."

1993: The U.S. Supreme Court ruled that a hostile work environment need not be psychologically injurious, but only reasonably perceived as abusive.

Compliance.   The U.S. Supreme Court (*Meritor Savings Bank* v. *Vinson,* 447 U.S. 57, 1986) decided that a policy stating that there were to be "no unwanted sexual advances between employees and that employees must report this type of unwanted conduct to management" does not comply with all the mandates cited by the *Vinson* ruling.

What can police agencies do to comply? Establishing preventive policies and training will lessen the likelihood of liability if a complaint is filed.

Sexual harassment is more than supervisory employees making demands for sex on the threat of adverse employment decisions. Employers may also be liable for physical and verbal conduct of a sexual nature that has the purpose or effect of creating a hostile work environment. It is behavior that is indicative of a "hostile atmosphere," such as sexually stereotyped insults and jokes, demeaning propositions and remarks, indecent or vulgar comments, staring or ogling that causes discomfort or humiliation, demands for dates that are viewed as offensive, and physical harassment.

Protection.   How can a department protect itself from this liability?

- Have an explicit antiharassment policy.
- Publicize and enforce the policy.
- Make it clear that harassment that creates a hostile environment is prohibited.
- Regularly and repeatedly publish the policy.

277.10 POLICY STATEMENT

It is the policy of the county of San Bernardino Sheriff's Department to provide a work environment free from unwelcome sexual overtures, advances, and coercion. Employees are expected to adhere to a standard of conduct that is respectful to all persons within the work environment. The Sheriff's Department will not tolerate any form of sexual harassment, nor will it tolerate any act of retaliation against any person filing a complaint of sexual harassment.

277.20 DEFINITION

Sexual harassment is defined as unsolicited or unwelcome sexual advances, requests for sexual favors, and other verbal, physical, or visual conduct of a sexual nature when:

- Submission to such conduct is made either explicitly or implicitly as a term or condition of an individual's employment.
- Submission to or rejection of such conduct by an individual is used as the basis for employment decisions affecting such individual.
- Such conduct has the purpose or effect of unreasonably interfering with an individual's work performance or creating an intimidating, hostile, or offensive working environment.

277.30 SHERIFF'S DEPARTMENT RESPONSIBILITIES AND PROCEDURES

The Sheriff's Department recognizes its obligation to take immediate and appropriate action if an incident of sexual harassment occurs and to avoid or minimize the impact of any incident of sexual harassment. The Sheriff's Department will pursue all reasonable preventive measures to ensure employees are not subjected to sexual harassment. Pursuant to these obligations, the Sheriff's Department will do the following:

- Investigate any complaint of sexual harassment. The investigation will be immediate, thorough, objective, and complete. The investigation will be conducted in as confidential a manner as is compatible with a thorough investigation of the complaint and is consistent with the rights of employees under the Personal Rules and state law.
- Fully inform any complainant of his rights and any obligations to secure those rights.
- If a complaint of sexual harassment is proven by an impartial investigation, prompt and appropriate remedial action will be taken. An employee found to have harassed another employee or applicant will be subject to disciplinary action, up to and including dismissal. In addition, appropriate steps will be taken to prevent any further harassment or retaliation, and action will be taken to remedy the loss, if any.
- The Sheriff's Department will disseminate this policy to all employees and will include this policy in all orientation packages for new employees.

FIGURE 13–3   Policy statement on sexual harassment. (*Courtesy of the San Bernardino Sheriff's Department, California.*)

- Establish a grievance system that allows employees to report all incidents of sexual harassment.
- Administratively and promptly investigate all allegations. If the allegations are sustained and warrant disciplining the offending employee, you should consider entering into a compromise with the offended employee to reduce the chance that he or she will seek further remedy outside the department.

- Communicate the facts and the resulting discipline to employees. (Don't use names.) Reinforce that this type of behavior will not be tolerated and that discipline can result.

See Figure 13–3 for an example of a policy statement on sexual harassment.

Problem Employee 4: Criminal Misconduct

Criminal misconduct is also commonly referred to as "corruption." Police corruption is an extremely complex and demoralizing crime problem, and it is not new to our generation of police personnel. Police corruption includes (1) the misuse of police authority for the police employee's personal gain; (2) activity of the police employee that compromises, or has the potential to compromise, his or her ability to enforce the law or to provide other police service impartially; (3) the protection of illicit activities from police enforcement, whether or not the police employee receives something of value in return; and (4) the police employee's involvement in promoting the business of one person while discouraging that of another person. In other words, police corruption consists of acts involving the misuse of authority by a police officer in a manner designed to produce personal gain for the officer or for others. And this is illegal!

CITIZEN COMPLAINTS

Frequently, you will be the first to hear a citizen's complaint. "I want to see your supervisor" is the request of citizens who feel they have been mistreated. A complaint starts with its receipt, then proceeds to an investigation, and concludes with adjudication.

Phase 1: Receipt of Complaint

- A viable complaint reception provides you with a useful tool for officer performance evaluation.
- It is imperative that all complaints (via letters, telephone calls, or in person) be investigated.
- A form should be designed and used for complaint processing (see Figure 13–4).
- The complaining citizen should be given a completed copy of the form as a receipt.

Phase 2: Investigation

- All supervisors should be given specific training in investigating internal discipline complaints and should be provided with written investigative procedures.
- Every police agency should establish formal procedures for investigating internal misconduct allegations.
- Every supervisor should conduct internal investigations in a manner that best reveals the facts, while preserving the dignity of all persons and maintaining the confidential nature of the investigation.

CITY OF ANAHEIM, CALIFORNIA
Police Department

MESSAGE FROM THE CHIEF OF POLICE

The Police Officer of today works in an extremely complex society. A goal of the Anaheim Police Department is to ensure that the public is served in a most efficient and effective manner by highly trained Police Officers.

To assist us in achieving this goal, you, as an individual, can help by letting us know if you have a complaint. Rest assured that your complaint will be quickly, professionally, and objectively investigated in order to arrive at all the facts which will clear the Officer's name or substantiate the individual's complaint, whichever is appropriate.

Roger Baker
Roger Baker
Chief of Police

POLICE COMPLAINT PROCEDURE

HOW DO I FILE A COMPLAINT? If you wish to file a formal complaint, it will be necessary for you to complete a Personnel Complaint form. You may obtain this form at the front counter of the Police Department, the City Clerk's Office, any Anaheim Public Library, the Community Services Office, or by calling or writing the Anaheim Police Department and requesting that a form be sent to you. When the Personnel Complaint form is filled out, it should be delivered to the Anaheim Police Department, 425 South Harbor Boulevard, or mailed to P.O. Box 3369, Anaheim, CA 92803-3369.

WHAT WILL HAPPEN TO THE OFFICER? It will depend on what the Officer did. If the Officer's actions were criminal, he/she could be dealt with in the same way as any other citizen. If the Officer's actions were improper but not criminal, he/she may be disciplined by the Chief of Police. If the Officer is falsely accused, the complainant may face civil and/or criminal action.

WILL I BE TOLD OF THE RESULTS OF THE INVESTIGATION? Yes. You will receive a letter from the Chief of Police advising you of the disposition of your complaint.

MESCHIEF.RWG

JR:RWG:hml

P. O. Box 3369, Anaheim, California 92803-3369

FIGURE 13–4   Complaint form. *(Courtesy of the Anaheim Police Department, California.)*

CITY OF ANAHEIM, CALIFORNIA

Police Department

UN MENSAJE DEL JEFE DE POLICIA

El policia de hoy en dia trabaja en una sociedad compleja. Una de las metas del Departamento de Policia de Anaheim, es la de asegurar que al publico se le sirva de manera eficiente y efectiva por un Cuerpo de Policia lo mas altamente entrenado posible.

Usted, como una persona particular, puede ayudarnos a lograr esta meta, haciendonos saber si tiene alguna queja, la cual se investigara rapidamente, profesionalmente y objectivamente, para asi poder descubrir los hechos que absolveran de toda culpa el nombre del agente de la Policia, o justificaran la queja de la persona particular, cualquiera de las dos que sea la apropiada.

Roger Baker

Roger Baker

Jefe de Policia

PROCEDIMIENTO PARA PRESENTAR UNA QUEJA

¿COMO REGISTRO UNA QUEJA? Si usted desea registrar una queja formal, sera necesario que complete una forma que usted puede obtener en la oficina de la policia de la ciudad de Anaheim, la oficina del escribano de la ciudad (office of the City Clerk), cualquier sucursal de la biblioteca, la oficina de servicios de la comunidad, o puede llamar o escribir al departamento de policia de Anaheim para solicitar una forma por correo. Cuando complete la forma, devuelva al departamento de policia de Anaheim, 425 South Harbor Boulevard, o mandela por correo al P.O. Box 3369, Anaheim, CA 92803-3369.

¿QUE LE PASARA AL AGENTE DE LA POLICIA? Esto depende en lo que haya hecho. Si cometio una accion criminal, se le tratara igualmente como cualquier otra persona que haya cometido una accion similar. Si fue una accion impropia, el Jefe de la Policia se encargara de disciplinarlo. Si por el contrario, se determina que usted hizo una queja falsa a sabiendas, se le puede someter a un proceso civil o criminal.

¿ME DIRAN EL RESULTADO DE LA INVESTIGACION? Si. Usted recibira una carta del Jefe de la Policia, donde la comunicaran la accion que tomo tocante su queja.

MESCHIEF.RWG

JR:RWG:lml

P. O. Box 3369, Anaheim, California 92803-3369

FIGURE 13–4 *(continued)*

ANAHEIM POLICE DEPARTMENT
PERSONNEL COMPLAINT/QUEJA DEL PERSONAL   File Number: _____

Print your NAME, ADDRESS and PHONE NUMBERS, BUSINESS & HOME / En Letra de Molde Escriba su Nombre, Domicilio, y Numeros de Telefono, Trabajo Y Casa

Print the DATE, TIME and LOCATION OF THE INCIDENT / Fecha, hora y Sitio del incidente

Print the NAMES, ADDRESSES and PHONE NUMBER OF any Witnesses / Nombres, Domicilios y Numeros de Telefonos de Testigos

DESCRIBE the incident in detail. Begin in the space below and if more space / is needed, continue on a second sheet. Sign all pages.   Describa en detalle el incidente, Empiece en el espacio de abajo, y si necesita mas espacio, continue en una segunda hoja. Firme todas las paginas.

YOU HAVE THE RIGHT TO MAKE A COMPLAINT AGAINST A POLICE OFFICER FOR ANY IMPROPER POLICE CONDUCT. CALIFORNIA LAW REQUIRES THIS AGENCY TO HAVE A PROCEDURE TO INVESTIGATE CITIZENS' COMPLAINTS. YOU HAVE THE RIGHT TO A WRITTEN DESCRIPTION OF THIS PROCEDURE. THIS AGENCY MAY FIND, AFTER INVESTIGATION, THAT THERE IS NOT ENOUGH EVIDENCE TO WARRANT ACTION ON YOUR COMPLAINT. EVEN IF THAT IS THE CASE, YOU HAVE THE RIGHT TO MAKE THE COMPLAINT AND HAVE IT INVESTIGATED IF YOU BELIEVE AN OFFICER BEHAVED IMPROPERLY. CITIZEN COMPLAINTS AND ANY REPORTS OR FINDINGS RELATING TO COMPLAINTS MUST BE RETAINED BY THIS AGENCY FOR AT LEAST FIVE YEARS. IT IS AGAINST THE LAW TO MAKE A COMPLAINT THAT YOU KNOW TO BE FALSE. IF YOU MAKE A COMPLAINT AGAINST AN OFFICER KNOWING THAT IT IS FALSE, YOU CAN BE PROSECUTED ON A MISDEMEANOR CHARGE.
I have read and understood the above statements, and have presented true and accurate facts. I understand that if I knowingly make a false accusation, I may be subject to criminal or civil action.

USTED TIENE EL DERECHO DE HACER UNA DEMANDA EN CONTRA DE UN OFICIAL DE POLICIA POR CUALQUIER CONDUCTO INAPROPIADO. LA LEY DE EL ESTADO DE CALIFORNIA REQUIERE QUE ESTA AGENCIA TENGA UN PROCESO PARA INVESTIGAR DEMANDAS DE CIUDADANOS. USTED TIENE EL DERECHO A UNA DESCRIPCION ESCRITA DE ESTE PROCESO. ESTA AGENCIA PUEDE ENCONTRAR, DESPUES DE INVESTIGAR, QUE NO HAY DEMASIADA EVIDENCIA PARA TOMAR ACCION EN SU DEMANDA. AUNQUE ESO SEA EL CASO, USTED TIENE EL DERECHO PARA HACER LA DEMANDA Y TENERLA INVESTIGADA, SI USTED CREE QUE UN OFICIAL DE POLICIA SE COMPORTO INAPROPIADO. DEMANDAS DE CIUDADANOS Y CULQUIER REPORTES O ENCUENTROS RELACIONADOS A DEMANDAS TIENEN QUE SER MANTENIDAS POR ESTA AGENCIA POR LO MENOS DE SINCO AÑOS. ES ENCONTRA DE LA LEY HACER UNA DEMANDA QUE USTED SEPA QUE ES FALSA. SI USTED HACE UNA DEMANDA EN CONTRA DE UN OFICIAL DE POLICIA, SABIENDO QUE ES FALSA, USTED PUEDE SER PROCESADO(A) POR UN CARGO DE LEY.
Yo e leido y entiendo los datos de harriba, y e presentado datos eficientes y verdaderos. Yo entiendo que si ago una acusasion falsa sabida, yo estoy subjeto a accion criminal o civil.

Signature/Firma _____   Date / Fecha _____

FORM ISSUED BY: _____   DATE: _____   DATE: _____

FORM RECEIVED BY: _____   DATE: _____   TIME: _____

ASSIGNED TO: _____   **DISTRIBUTION**: WHITE - Special Investigations, GREEN - Chief, CANARY - Division Commander, PINK - Watch/Bureau Commander, GOLDENROD - Complainant

APD-296 Rev. 1/96

FIGURE 13–4   *(continued)*

- Every police agency should provide all its employees at the time of employment and, again, prior to the specific investigation with a written statement of the employees' duties and rights when they are the subject of an internal discipline investigation.
- Every police chief should have legal authority during an internal discipline investigation to relieve police employees from their duties when it is in the interests of the public and the police agency.
- All internal discipline investigations should be concluded within thirty days of the date the complaint is made unless an extension is granted by the chief executive of the agency.
- Results of the investigation should be submitted to the complaining party.

Phase 3: Adjudication

The role of the supervisor during phase 3 is normally that of an adviser to the police manager. More than anyone else, the immediate supervisor should be able to evaluate the overall conduct and performance level of his or her staff and, if a penalty is indicated, to determine how severe it should be. Or, conversely, the supervisor may argue that (1) the officer should be exonerated, (2) the complaint is unfounded (the act did not occur), or (3) the complaint is not sustained (insufficient facts to make a determination). If the charge against the officer is sustained, then the supervisor can recommend one of the following penalties:

- Oral reprimand
- Written reprimand
- Remedial training
- Loss of time or of annual leave in lieu of suspension
- Suspension of up to thirty days (but no longer)
- Removal from service

The third phase involves the following:

1. A complaint disposition should be classified as sustained, not sustained, exonerated, unfounded, or misconduct not based on the original complaint.
2. Adjudication and, if warranted, disciplinary action should be based partially on recommendations of the involved employee's immediate supervisor.
3. An administrative fact-finding trial board should be available to all police agencies to assist in the adjudication phase. It should be activated when necessary in the interests of the police agency, the public, or the accused employee and should be available at the direction of the police chief or upon the request of any employee who is being penalized in any manner that exceeds verbal or written reprimand. The recommendations should be advisory to the chief.
4. The accused employee should be entitled to representation and logistical support equal to that afforded the person representing the agency in a trial board proceeding.
5. Police employees should be allowed to appeal the chief's decision. The police agency should not provide the resources or funds for appeal, however.
6. The chief should establish written policy on the retention of internal discipline complaint investigation reports. Only the reports of sustained and, if appealed, upheld investigations should become a part of the accused employee's personnel folder. All disciplinary investigations should be kept confidential.
7. Administrative adjudication of internal discipline complaints involving violations of law should neither depend on nor curtail criminal prosecution. Regardless of the administrative adjudication, every police agency should refer all complaints that involve violations of law to the prosecuting agency for the decision to prosecute criminally. Police employees should not be treated differently from other members of the community in cases involving violations of the law.
8. If the citizen complaint is found to be intentionally malicious, then the officer has legal redress available.

MEDIA RELATIONS

During the past few years there has been tremendous change in the telecommunications industry. Expansion of television news coverage, increased professional competition, and instantaneous breaking news segments and Internet news capabilities have changed the industry. Technology has allowed the media to get the message out farther, faster, and in more ways than ever thought possible. Twenty-four-hour news stations, wireless Internet, and Internet news agencies are just some of the different ways the media now cover events. Events that were at one time highly localized have now become national news. Images and stories can be broadcast into our living rooms and homes within a matter of minutes of the event's occurring. Chat rooms and blogs buzz with activity after every major breaking news story.

> The immediacy of news coverage permits little time for police agencies to react and communicate their message.

Consequences of Poor Media Relations

There are significant negative consequences associated with the poor handling of media relations. These include

- Loss of professional reputation and community support
- Civil liability
- Poor morale
- Political oversight
- Changes in political status quo
- Change in working conditions

In many instances, the negative consequences of "crisis" incidents could have been negated or significantly curtailed if department personnel were prepared to respond to the media. How a police department handles crisis media communications in the first few minutes after the event sets the tone for how the community will later perceive the department. Pre-planning and training can produce favorable media relations.

Crisis Communication Strategies

The following are key considerations when communicating with the media during a crisis:

- *Take responsibility.* People want you to accept responsibility whether you're actually to blame or not. It is important to recognize that taking responsibility is not the same as taking the blame. Later investigation may reveal extenuating circumstances, but in the end it will still be your employees who fired the gun, made the arrest, or drove code-3. Your name will still be associated with the incident regardless of the outcome.

- *Recognize a crisis.* A crisis is best described as an event that has potentially negative media coverage for the agency. Yet in every agency there is a tendency to respond with a knee-jerk reaction to every news story that generates bad publicity. Meetings will be called, and management will want "heads on a platter," but in truth, many of the situations we see as media crises are in fact short-lived bad publicity. In strategy sessions it is important to ask, "Who really cares?" Is there widespread outrage, or is negative reaction very localized within the department itself? Police agencies are often hypersensitive to criticism and will often assume immediate defensive postures. What does the average person think about the "crisis"? Elevating bad publicity to crisis levels can lower morale and cause undue stress throughout the organization. Ironically, high-profile investigations—while media-intensive and a lot of work—do not often attain the level of a crisis.

- *Have people trained to deal with crisis communications.* A great deal of time and effort is spent training officers to prepare for just about every conceivable scenario they will face in their career. Police supervisors must be trained to have an understanding of media relations and crisis communications strategies. Law enforcement is accountable to the public, and the media take their role as a community watchdog very seriously. Like it or not, sometimes the best and only means departments have for communicating with the public is through the media. Your organization is best served by having someone who has regular and frequent contact with the media, plus supervisors who can (if necessary) interact with the media.

- *Recognize the value of third-party support.* In crisis situations, departments should have an understanding of where support will come from in the community. The media and public will often perceive "third-party" support favorably. This support could come from citizens' groups, clergy, professional organizations, internal organizations (labor associations, fraternal organizations), or even other police agencies. Many departments will use established clergy associations for support in minority communities. If the media have questions about tactics used during an operation, they could refer to recognized scholars or teaching institutions that will support the action taken. The public wants to trust law enforcement, and if uninvolved third parties lend their support, it makes law enforcement more credible. Third-party referrals should not be made unless the third party has been contacted and thoroughly briefed on the facts surrounding the incident.

- *Treat the media as a conduit.* The media are a major conduit by which your organization communicates with the public. A month's worth of community meetings will not reach as many people as one article in the newspaper. A ninety-second clip on the evening news reaches an even wider audience. These opportunities to communicate must not be overlooked or avoided. Too often organizations take the stance of pulling up the drawbridge and hiding behind the walls. This "siege mentality" does more harm than good. Siege mentalities are the result of personal and institutional prejudice toward the media, lack of preparedness, and oftentimes well-meaning but bad advice. The public will view "no comment" or lack thereof as "guilty as charged." There are creative ways to say "no comment" without digging yourself deeper. Staying within the siege walls will also allow your critics to have free reign with their own point of view. You may not like the information conveyed, but the game goes on whether you participate or not; it's better to learn the rules of the game and then play to win.

- *Do not let attorneys dictate your public relations.* You must accept the fact that you might be sued. This is America, the most litigious society in the world. Once you accept that litigation is inevitable, you can work to minimize your exposure. Many law firms in the country now work in concert with public relations firms in formulating media strategies. Attorneys, while well intentioned, are not trained to deal with or handle the media.

- *Monitor the media.* Once your message is delivered, it must be monitored. This is how you measure the effectiveness of your strategy. Newspapers, television, and radio are some of the primary media that should be monitored. Are those who are transmitting your message to the public understanding what you said? If there are errors (contextual or factual), or if the message is not being delivered clearly, it must be dealt with proactively. If necessary, your position may have to be reevaluated and modified. In most crisis situations, there will be discussion on the Internet. This is an opportunity to see what the average person on the street thinks about what is happening. Someone should monitor newsgroups and chat rooms to see how the news coverage is being received. You may find that what you thought was a crisis has generated little public interest.

- *Speak from the heart, not from the head.* During a crisis, the public may not think rationally. People are looking for pictures and statements that communicate on the emotional level. Trying to give people facts, figures, policy, and procedure during a crisis will have little impact. The public wants to know how you and your agency feel about the incident. If in the initial stages you throw mud, you will get dirty. Attacking detractors during the initial stages of any crisis will make you look defensive and less credible. Presenting a defensive or confrontational attitude sends its own negative messages. The public wants to see sincerity, caring, and empathy.

- *The first twenty-four hours are the most critical.* The first images and impressions the public sees will set the tone for future coverage. If your agency is inaccessible for comment, the message is that you have something to hide. If your first comments are defensive and terse, you set the stage for confrontation. Formulate your position early, and remember that you have to view the crisis from an external perspective. Establishing a departmental position should be done in concert with the highest levels of management, taking into account the wide range of consequences. The bottom line is, what is the public's perception of what is occurring? It is okay to be nonjudgmental, but acknowledge it.

- *Plan.* You can plan and prepare for crisis communications. You can establish response plans and matrices specific to your organization that will give you a roadmap. Law enforcement agencies can run through the "what ifs" just as they do with any other significant event. Regrettably, most agencies do not recognize crisis communications as a priority. Many operate under the assumption, "We have a good organization; that kind of stuff only happens to the other guy." Every time a crisis in another agency is covered in the media, they should convene and ask themselves, "If this happened here today, how would we have dealt with it?"

See Figure 13–5, a model guide for interacting with the media about police operations.

What Information Can Be Made Public

ARRESTEE INFORMATION

1. The full name and city of residence of the arrestee; the arrestee's physical description, including age, color of eyes and hair, sex, height, and weight
2. Date and time of arrest
3. Date and location of booking
4. Factual circumstances surrounding arrest
5. Amount of bail set
6. Time and manner of release or location where the suspect is being held
7. All charges on which subject is being held, including outstanding warrants and probation/parole holds

INCIDENT INFORMATION

1. Time, substance, and location of all complaints or requests for assistance
2. Time and nature of response, including (to the extent that such information is recorded)
    a. Time, date, and location of occurrence
    b. Time and date of the report
    c. The factual circumstances surrounding the crime or incident
    d. General description of
        (1) Injuries (usually nonspecific)
        (2) Weapons involved (nonspecific)
        (3) Property involved
3. Victim name, age, and city of residence except as prohibited or if it would jeopardize the victim's safety or progress of investigation

WHAT CANNOT BE RELEASED

- Prior criminal record, reputation, or character of arrestee
- The identity of a juvenile suspect or arrestee
- The existence or contents of any confession or statement given by a suspect or his or her refusal to make a statement
- Information regarding physical evidence that corroborates or impeaches a confession, admission, or other statement
- Performance level on any examinations or tests or a suspect's refusal to submit to an examination or test
- The identity or reliability of prospective witnesses and sex-crime victims
- Personal opinions as to a suspect's guilt or innocence or merits in the case
- The name of a specific gang involved in an incident
- Details that could create an inflamed public reaction

SCHOOLS

The media are generally allowed access to schools as long as it is not disruptive to school activities. If action is requested, it should be at the request of school authorities.

FIGURE 13–5   Model media resource guide.

CRIME AND DISASTER SCENES

A supervisor should be notified immediately when media are present at a scene. The media representative should be notified of the crime scene boundaries and any areas of potential risk. Disaster scenes may be closed to the general public, but news media representatives are exempt from this restriction. This does not apply to crime scenes. Airplane crashes should be treated as crime scenes.

Crime scenes should be restricted to both public and media access. It is permissible to allow the press greater access than that afforded to the general public. Reporters and photographers shall be kept sufficiently distant from a crime scene being searched or preserved to protect it from being disturbed or evidence from being destroyed or contaminated.

In any major incident the Public Information Officer can be contacted for response or as a resource.

FIGURE 13–5 (*continued*)

KEY POINTS

- Human conflict is a natural and therefore a normal phenomenon.
- It is up to the supervisor to convert dysfunctional conflict into productive energy.
- Conflict can have both positive and negative consequences for a police agency.
- Conflicts emanate from (1) existing conditions, (2) our attitudes, (3) our thoughts, and (4) our behavior.
- In negotiating ("getting to yes"), do not bargain over positions or believe that being nice will resolve the conflict.
- Furthermore, in negotiating, separate the people from the conflict; concentrate on interests, not positions; generate a number of options; and adopt objective criteria.
- Problem employees represent a small percentage of workers.
- Problem employees can engage in one of four types of behavior: (1) malcontented, (2) immoral, (3) unprofessional, and (4) illegal.
- The creation of an internal investigations unit does not relieve the supervisor of disciplinary duties.
- A citizen complaint starts with the receipt of the complaint. Next comes an investigation and finally an adjudication.
- Poor media relations have an explosive potentiality for far-reaching negative consequences. The first step in the proper handling of the media is taking responsibility (not blame) for tackling the problem.

EXTENDED LEARNING

1. Have you witnessed conflict being a plus for an organization? If so, describe how it occurred and what the results were.
2. How have you dealt with a problem employee (coworker, boss, subordinate)? Were you successful? Explain.

3. How can conflict be a positive force? Give examples.

4. Why not bargain over positions? Give examples.

5. Develop an actual or a hypothetical conflict. Now apply the key steps in principled negotiations to it. Critique the results.

6. Incidents of sexual harassment and use of force were presented as key supervisory issues. Name three others.

7. Peruse the newspaper for one week. How many articles were devoted to police work? How many had positive coverage? How many were negative?

14

Community-Oriented and Problem-Oriented Policing

Community-oriented policing is a strategy for forging a partnership between the police department and its customers. Problem-oriented policing is a set of tactics for making it work.

Community-oriented policing (COP) and problem-oriented policing (POP) are both an ending and a starting point. All of the previous responsibilities serve as a springboard for COP and POP. At this point, it is up to the supervisor to step forward and make them a reality.

Community partnerships and problem solving—the two core components of community policing—can be accomplished in a variety of ways.

—National Institute of Justice

Community-oriented policing (COP) depends on police supervisors who lead their lives and manage their relationships around values and ethics. They see and believe in a mission that is devoted to serving and helping their customers. They exercise self-discipline and are not afraid of hard work. They know how and where to allocate their time. They also know that individual effectiveness precedes organizational effectiveness.

Problem-oriented policing (POP) depends on police leaders who can translate COP into operational reality. They take the goals of a mission statement and cast them into very specific and attainable objectives and projects. POP is a logical and practical component of COP.

COP gives us a destination, while POP provides answers on how to get there.

COMMUNITY-ORIENTED POLICING

Although the acronyms *COP* and *POP* are relatively new to many, some basic elements—such as citizen participation, officers knowledgeable of the community values of the area they serve, police officer-citizen communication, and the like—are not. They were present to one extent or another in earlier policing in the United States, whether by design or as a result of individual style, especially in the late nineteenth and early twentieth centuries and especially in large cities with dense populations.

Police-Community Relations

During the late 1960s and 1970s, following recommendations from the President's Commission on Law Enforcement and Administration of Justice, a proliferation of federally funded police-community relations models sprang up throughout the country. The purpose was to bring police officers closer to the community, to promote mutual support, to encourage communication, and so on.

Some programs experienced relative success; others did not. Most were relegated to test areas and specific officer assignments, as opposed to total departmental understanding, involvement, and support. Even those programs held up as positive examples were, in almost every case, gradually phased out or modified in such a way as to become isolated from the mainstream of their respective agencies. The programs did little to strengthen relationships between the community and response-oriented police officers, or even between police officers assigned to "community relations" and other officers.

Team Policing

The 1970s also gave birth to team policing. Early team-policing programs were burdened by lack of documented successes and failures. Agencies that experimented with team policing were not aware that elements of team policing would prove to be incompatible with preventive patrol and rapid response to calls for service. In the early 1970s, the Holyoke, Massachusetts. Police Department instituted a program considered by many to be the showcase of federally funded team-policing programs. At first it was unbelievably successful. The team consisted of fifteen highly motivated, people-conscious officers—one captain, two sergeants, and twelve patrolmen, all of whom volunteered to be on the team. In addition to routine police functions, the focus was on human relations, language, and traditional cultures of those residing in the ward. These officers were in for the duration (no transfers), and they got to know the people and to be known by the people. And they became effective. However, after a time with a substantial infusion of more federal dollars, the program was expanded, ward by ward, and ward by ward it began to fail. Officers assigned to the new teams were not all volunteers.

Transfers were routine. Many were "old-timers" who simply would not or could not change, and they were not motivated or motivative. Some were said to be simply insensitive. A "we-they" attitude prevailed.

Why Adopt Community-Oriented Policing?

If conditions in the past indicated the need for community-oriented policing, consider the greater need today, with the burgeoning immigration of different races and cultures, clustering together in crowded, often substandard housing areas, where the police and citizens do not share common beliefs, know or trust one another, or even speak a common language, and where it is not understood that the success of each in his or her personal role is predicated, at least in part, on mutual respect and assistance from the other.

There are at least twenty-two solid reasons for adopting COP:

- Continued reliance on random, preventive patrol should be minimized. Random, preventive patrol should be used as a strategy only when police visibility is an issue.
- Citizens will accept a range of response times for different types of calls.
- Differential police response strategies should be implemented to improve the leadership of dispatch/communication.
- Effective leadership of the patrol function is dependent on effective dispatch/communication.
- Effective leadership of criminal investigations is indirectly dependent on dispatch/communication and directly related to the patrol function.
- Case management systems must be developed and implemented to fit the needs of various investigative functions.
- Work demands and resource allocation studies are necessary to ensure equitable deployment of personnel.
- The development of crime and operational analysis procedures is vital in managing patrol and investigative operations.
- The use of directed and self-directed patrol activities for officers should increase when and where appropriate.
- Officers assigned to the patrol function must be actively involved in criminal investigations (e.g., conducting follow-up investigations, recommending early case closures).
- Patrol officers need enhanced status and enriched job responsibilities.
- Attention must be devoted to reassessing the purpose and function of existing beat configurations.
- Initiatives must be taken by the police to identify citizen service expectations and to work with citizens in addressing and resolving neighborhood crime and disorder problems.
- To facilitate the development of stronger ties with the community, policies requiring frequent rotation of officers across shifts must be carefully evaluated.
- Regular public forums should be established so frequent exchanges of information can occur between the police and the public, preferably between patrol officers and neighborhood residents.

- Performance measurement systems should serve as a management tool that guides personnel development and facilitates organizational change.
- More meaningful performance evaluation criteria must be developed to reflect the change in officer roles and responsibilities.
- Training curricula must be redesigned so they are more relevant to and supportive of patrol and investigative operations.
- Disciplinary processes must become part of a behavioral system that incorporates education, training, and counseling as strategies designed to assist officers experiencing behavioral problems.
- Leadership styles must be more adaptive to varying situations and personalities.
- Leaders (and especially supervisors) must begin directing their attention toward the qualitative aspects of service delivery processes and outcomes.
- Police agencies must cultivate leaders who are comfortable and effective working in an environment characterized by constant demands for change.

CRIME CONTROL

> The central mission of the police is to control crime. Crime fighting enjoys public support as the basic strategy of policing precisely because it embodies a deep commitment to this objective. In contrast, other proposed strategies, such as problem solving and community policing, appear to ignore this focus.

Crime fighting today mainly relies on three tactics: (1) motorized patrol, (2) rapid response to calls for service, and (3) follow-up investigation of crimes. The police focus on serious crime has also been sharpened by screening calls for service, targeting patrol, and developing forensic technology (e.g., automated fingerprint systems, computerized criminal record files). Although these tactics have scored their successes, they have been criticized within and outside policing for being reactive, rather than proactive.

Reactive tactics have some merits, of course. The police go where crimes have occurred and when citizens have summoned them. They keep their distance from the community and thereby retain their impartiality. They do not develop the sorts of relationships with citizens that could bias their responses to crime incidents.

Many police forces have developed proactive tactics to deal with crime problems that could not be handled through traditional reactive methods. In drug dealing, organized crime, and vice enforcement, for example, where no immediate victims exist to alert the police, the police have developed special units that rely on informants, covert surveillance, and undercover investigations rather than responses to calls for service. In the area of juvenile offenses, the police have created athletic leagues and formed partnerships with schools to deal with drug abuse, gang activity, truancy, and so on. It is not accurate, then, to define policing as entirely reactive.

The greatest potential for improved crime control does not lie in the continued enhancement of response times, patrol tactics, and investigative techniques. Rather, improved crime control can be achieved by (1) diagnosing and managing problems in the community that produce crimes, (2) fostering closer relations with the community to facilitate crime solving, and (3) building self-defense capabilities within the community itself.

A DECISION FOR QUALITY

In the 1980s, police agencies began to explore the crime-fighting effectiveness of tactics that built on previous approaches. At the same time, they sought to extend them by looking behind offenses to the precipitating causes of crimes. They endeavored to build closer relations with the community and to enhance the self-defense capacities of the communities themselves.

Their guiding theory was that the effectiveness of existing tactics can be enhanced if the police increase the quantity and quality of their contacts with citizens (both individuals and neighborhood groups) and conditionally include in their responses to crime problems thoughtful analyses of the root causes of the offenses. The expectation is that this will both improve the direct effectiveness of the police and enable them to leverage the resources of citizen groups and other public agencies to control crime.

The 1980s saw, therefore, many police agencies attempting to "work smarter and not harder" and to "do more with less." What still remains unanswered is the consequence of shifting a whole department to a different style of policing. For example, if officers are taken from patrol and detective units to do problem-oriented or community-oriented policing, it is fairly certain that response times will lengthen—at least until the problem-solving efforts decrease the demands for service by removing the problem that is producing the calls for service. And even though longer response times do not necessarily indicate a loss in crime-fighting effectiveness, they will be perceived as indicating this because the public and the police value rapid response to crime calls.

What is tempting, of course, is to avoid deciding between these strategies and to adopt the strengths of these various approaches while avoiding their weaknesses. This could be seen in decisions to create special units to do COP within existing organizations whose traditions and main forces remained committed to traditional patrol and investigation tactics. But this means more resources, which means more money, and more money is difficult to acquire.

Community-oriented policing is not merely a matter of budget dollars, however. It is primarily a matter of philosophy, administrative style, and structure. COP requires a greater degree of decentralization than does the current policing strategy. It depends more on the initiative of the officers. And they reach out for a close rather than a distant relationship with the community. It is very different from the kind of current administrative posture that stresses centralization, control, and professional separation from the community, and it has a very different mission statement. Mission statements are revised to reflect the transition to community policing. The protection of life and of property is still important, but the emphasis is changed from the police's enforcing laws and making arrests to forming proactive partnerships with the community to solve problems (Table 14–1).

TABLE 14-1 *Stages of Community-Policing Implementation.*

	WORK ENVIRONMENT		
	Communication	Leadership	Employee Development
Awareness	Awareness of need to improve communication present at all levels of organization.	Senior management has developed a plan to begin implementing community policing and problem solving.	Introduction of community-policing program to employees.
Understanding	Employees and managers learn methods of better communication among themselves and with the public.	Senior management outwardly demonstrates commitment by initiating and participating in team training and understanding organizational alignment.	Senior management demonstrates commitment to program; all employees involved in training.
Utilization	Improved communication increases flow of information and encourages employee and community input; improves morale and community satisfaction.	Managers and employees routinely apply problem-solving techniques. Agency management sets parameters and uses appropriate level of participation in decision making.	Employees make a conscious effort to apply tools and techniques in daily operations.
Normalization	Open communication is practiced and encouraged.	Managers, supervisors, and lead personnel serve as models of leadership by constantly reinforcing quality philosopy, decision making, and use of problem-solving techniques.	Employees consider improving processes through natural work groups and multidepartmental teams as an integral part of their daily operations.
Excellence	Organizational and community issues are openly discussed.	Community-policing and problem-solving implementation plan absorbed into ongoing strategic plan; leadership demonstrated by employees at all levels of the organization through accomplishing city goals and achieving vision.	Employees willingly hold themselves accountable for continuous process improvement.

CONTINUOUS IMPROVEMENT

	Process Improvement	Community	Strategic Planning
Awareness	Employees and management are introduced to process and measurement and philosophy of COP/POP.	Internal and external stakeholders are identified; feedback methods primarily focus on complaints.	Linkages needed for budget planning, goals, objectives, and performance.
Understanding	Critical processes and key measures are identified; process improvement begins.	Requirements are determined, and feedback methods are improved.	Vision, purpose, and goals are established; a process is developed to incorporate strategic planning into annual budget/plan.
Utilization	Routine application of process improvement and monitoring in daily operations begins; data collection and measurement are widely utilized.	Requirements are continually met; service delivery is driven through quality indicators and service standards.	Senior management implements the strategic plan, which supports vision purpose and goals; employees are given feedback on attainment of objectives as part of performance evaluation.
Normalization	Data collection and measurement are applied to planning and decision making.	Community requirements are exceeded; improvement ideas are solicited from community.	Vision, purpose, goals, and objectives drive the annual budget/planning process.
Excellence	Process/system improvement is imbedded in operations and planning.	Partnering with community is routine; community feedback is used for planning.	Community participates in the planning process; strategic planning involves all levels of organization.

> COP does not hinge on a need for more money but rather a need for administrative change, with organizational and community support, with the understanding and belief that crime is everyone's business—that the cops really cannot do it alone.

RESPONSIBILITY AND IMPLEMENTATION

If we believe that the police department is the first line of defense against disorder and crime, and the source of strength for maintaining the quality of life, what should its strategy be? The traditional view is that the police are a community's professional defense against crime and disorder: Citizens should leave control of crime and maintenance of order to the police. The COP strategy is for the police to promote and buttress the community's ability to create safe neighborhoods.

Oddly enough, when the police move in to attack dangerous street crime aggressively, the very neighborhoods plagued by disorder reject their approach. The citizens are not ready to surrender control of their neighborhoods to remote police officers who show them little respect. Are police the first line of defense in a neighborhood? No—citizens are! And if they are, law enforcement must first provide communities with sufficient information—in a manner they will accept—to understand and develop interest in the "new" relationship with community protection and the police. And then law enforcement must provide proper training and continuing education to ensure that communities are prepared to assume their new responsible role and to work within specified parameters.

Changing from one style of policing to another takes time, and it is not easy. In terms of time, COP requires three to five years before significant results can be measured. Figure 14–1 shows the stages of implementation. This figure contains an enormous amount of baseline summary information on COP. Study it carefully.

WHO BENEFITS FROM COMMUNITY-ORIENTED POLICING?

COP will benefit both the community and the police.

Community Benefits

- *A commitment to crime prevention.* Unlike traditional policing, which focuses on the efficient means of reacting to incidents, COP strives to confirm that the basic mission of the police is to prevent crime and disorder.
- *Public scrutiny of police operations.* Because citizens will be involved with the police, they will be exposed to the what, why, and how of police work. This is almost certain to prompt critical discussions about the responsiveness of police operations.
- *Accountability to the public.* Until the advent of COP, officers were accountable for their actions only to police management. Now officers also will be accountable to the public with whom they have formed a partnership.

- *Customized police service.* Because police services will be localized, officers will be required to increase their responsiveness to neighborhood problems. As police-citizen partnerships are formed and nurtured, the two groups will be better equipped to work together to identify and address specific problems that affect the quality of neighborhood life.
- *Community organization.* The degree to which the community is involved in police efforts to evaluate neighborhood problems has a significant bearing on the effectiveness of those efforts. The success of any crime-prevention effort depends on the police and citizens working in concert—not on one or the other carrying the entire load alone.

Police Benefits

- *Greater citizen support.* As people spend more time working with the police, they learn more about the police function. Experience has shown that as people's knowledge of the police function increases, their respect for the police increases as well. This increased respect in turn leads to greater support for the police.
- *Shared responsibility.* Historically, the police have accepted the responsibility for resolving the problem of crime in the community. Under community policing, however, citizens develop a sense of shared responsibility.
- *Greater job satisfaction.* Because officers are able to resolve issues and problems within a reasonable amount of time, they see the results of their efforts more quickly.
- *Better internal relationships.* Communication problems among units and shifts have been a chronic problem in police agencies. Because COP focuses on problem-solving and accountability, it also increases cooperation among the various segments of the department.
- *Support for organizational change.* COP requires a vast restructuring of the department to ensure the integration of various functions, such as patrol and investigations. The needed changes are new management systems, new training curriculums and delivery mechanisms, a new performance evaluation system, a new disciplinary process, a new reward system, and new ways of managing calls for service.

Citizen police academies (CPAs) are now frequently seen in law enforcement agencies throughout America. Nearly one-half of the police departments offer some form of CPA. Participation in an academy gives people insight into police work that the general public rarely obtains. These programs provide police agencies with an opportunity to involve citizens in law enforcement efforts. This opportunity offers three benefits.

First, CPAs give citizens a working knowledge of a police department's mission, operation, policies, personnel, and challenges. As a result, citizens become more familiar with the day-to-day operations of their police department and the actual role of the police. Second, CPAs give people a means to interact positively with police, compared with the way many people experience police contact. Typically, the only contact most people have with police officers is during a traffic stop, which usually results in a traffic citation. Third, CPAs may help to develop a relationship of trust and cooperation between the police and citizens. Police managers believe that CPAs help to dispel suspicions and misconceptions that people have about the police. They are designed to humanize citizens' impression of officers and to help the public realize how tough it really is to police a locality.

STRUCTURED EXERCISE 14–1

Examine the problem assigned to your group. Determine a plan of action based on COP/POP philosophy that you will direct your patrol team (sergeant and officers) to employ. Using a flip chart, list at least ten approaches that might be used to effectively mitigate or eliminate the community problem. Be creative, considering all resources. (Andrew Borrello of the Sam Gabriel Police Department, California, is responsible for producing the excellent cases that follow.)

Case 1: Let It Rock

A local restaurant/bar in your area has started featuring live amateur rock bands on weekends, and the bands draw large crowds of young people. Over the past two months, noise complaints have tripled in the area, and citizens have complained about excessive trash, drunken bar patrons urinating in their yards, drug use in the area, fights in the street, speeding vehicles, and an increase in property damage in the immediate area. Drunken driving arrests have increased and have been linked to the bar. Also, two of the bands' staff members were arrested for possession of firearms. The restaurant owner has ample security/bouncers and has done all he can do to mitigate problems, but he is making a lot of money and is in compliance with all the city's requirements in terms of zoning, permits, business license, etc. As a police supervisor, what steps can you take using COP/POP philosophy to solve this problem?

Case 2: Home Sweet Home

Several large shelters for the homeless in neighboring cities have closed down due to funding problems. With the warm summer weather, there has been a sharp increase in your city's transient population. The city's many parks with twenty-four-hour bathrooms have become a refuge for a variety of homeless and emotionally disturbed people. Wide-scale complaints are being made regarding drunks asleep or passed out in the parks, human feces in public areas, fights, thefts, and several stabbings. In addition, there are reports that the public restrooms are being used for bathing and lewd activity. An article in the local newspaper about the problem was titled, "Hobo Park Needs Help." As a police supervisor, what steps can you take using COP/POP philosophy to solve this problem?

Case 3: Fast and Furious

Your beat areas of responsibility consist of primarily industrial areas with wide multilane roadways. During nights and weekends, there is virtually no activity other than through traffic and nightshift personnel working inside the buildings. Complaints are starting to become regular regarding high-speed vehicles in the area. Business owners report finding heavy acceleration burnout tire marks, long skid marks, and doughnut-type skid marks in their parking lots and on the streets. They have also been finding numerous beer bottles, trash, and condoms in the area. Graffiti and broken windows are now common calls for service. Gas-and-runs have increased during the weekends, and car part thefts and window smash thefts of auto part stores are starting to occur. One of your agency's explorers turned in a flyer that advertised a race on Saturday (unknown location) that called for "street racers to take the challenge." The flyer was one of hundreds circulating through the high school. Finally, one of your officers went in pursuit of two custom high-performance vehicles in the industrial area but quickly lost them after they reached speeds of 120 mph. As a police supervisor, what steps would you take using COP/POP philosophy to solve this problem?

Case 4: Two-Wheel Terror

In one of your residential areas, there is a disabled veteran who has an assortment of medical problems. He is an alcoholic, becomes angry when he is intoxicated, and often defecates in his own clothing. He is bound to a wheelchair as he only has one leg. He has hepatitis, reoccurring skin diseases and sores, substantial body lice, and a serious asthma condition that requires frequent medication. The subject sporadically lives in a house where an elderly nurse cares for him and manages his state income checks. However, the nurse cannot control him. The subject has no family and is in the streets most of the time panhandling in order to purchase alcohol. Several small groceries have restraining orders against him, and he is the source of continuing complaints. When he drinks, he yells profanity at anyone in the area, disrupts traffic, trespasses onto other people's property, and often falls out of his wheelchair. Most citizens will not press charges against him, and officers do anything to avoid arresting him, including ignoring minor warrants for his arrest. Twice while in custody, the subject required medical treatment that resulted in a substantial medical bill for the city. Finally, the fire department is all too familiar with the subject and except for a medical emergency will have nothing to do with him. As a police supervisor, what steps can you take using COP/POP philosophy to solve this problem?

Case 5: Build It and They Will Come

A methadone and addiction treatment clinic has opened in your area, and numerous heroin addicts and chemically dependent drug users visit the clinic daily. Many of the center's clients are parolees and gang members. The local business owners have launched continuous complaints, stating that shoplifting is rampant, that drugs are being used in parking lots and alleys, and that their sales are suffering because their customers are too scared to come to the area. Several fights have occurred in and around the clinic between competing gang members. Many of the subjects obtaining treatment or who are on the methadone program tend to hang out in the area after their treatment. One of the local business owners, a member of your city council, was horrified when his eight-year-old grandson picked up an uncapped syringe in the rear parking lot of his business. As a police supervisor, what steps can you take using COP/POP philosophy to solve this problem?

PROBLEM-ORIENTED POLICING

One should view COP as an overall departmental strategy for improving police work. Similarly, POP should be treated as a tactical method for making COP work.

Problem-oriented policing emphasizes the value of being able to diagnose the continuing problems that lie behind the repeated incidents that are reported to police employees and to design and implement solutions to those problems. Herman Goldstein, one of the foremost thinkers in the police field, defines a police department as practicing POP when it

- Identifies substantive community problems
- Inquires systematically into their nature
- Analyzes community interest and special interest in each problem
- Assesses current responses
- Conducts an uninhibited search for tailor-made solutions

- Takes initiative in implementing solutions
- Evaluates the effectiveness of solutions

Many police departments concentrate on one incident at a time as they respond to calls for service. They neglect to assemble into a single picture the separate symptoms they treat. A neighborhood may be experiencing a flood of troubles—street fights, insults to passersby, solicitation by prostitutes, pickpocketing, and drunken driving—but the department does not recognize their sources in a sports bar.

> When the sole police response to a community problem is to arrest the current troublemakers, that department is not engaging in POP.

INCIDENT- AND PROBLEM-DRIVEN AGENCIES

Incident-Driven

Most police agencies are incident-driven. That is, most police activities are aimed at resolving individual incidents rather than groups of incidents or problems. The incident-driven police department has four characteristics.

First, it is reactive. Most of the workload of patrol officers and detectives consists of handling crimes that have been committed: disturbances in progress, traffic violations, and the like. The exceptions—crime prevention and narcotics investigations, for example—make up but a small portion of police work.

Incident-driven police work relies on limited information, gathered mostly from victims, witnesses, and suspects. Only limited information is needed because the police objectives are limited: Patrol officers and detectives are trying only to resolve the incident at hand.

The primary means of resolving incidents is to invoke the criminal justice process. Even when an officer manages to resolve an incident without arresting or citing anyone, it is often the threat of enforcing the law that is the key to resolution. Alternative means of resolution are seldom invoked.

Finally, incident-driven police departments use aggregate statistics to measure performance. The department is doing a good job when the citywide crime rate is low or the citywide arrest rate is high. The best officers are those who make many arrests or service many calls.

Remember, a police agency is not constrained to one strategy for accomplishing its mission. However, if two or more strategies are adopted, it is important that they be compatible and not confrontational. See Figures 14–2 and 14–3 for a comparison of incident-driven and problem-oriented policing.

Problem-Driven

The practice of POP seeks to improve on other professional crime-fighting models by adding proactivity and thoughtfulness. It differs from COP by the emphasis on specific analysis. It assumes that the police can anticipate offenses and resolve them.

Problem-oriented policing takes a different paradigm about crime. In POP, it is not automatically accepted that crimes are caused by predatory offenders. True, in all crimes there will be an offender. But POP makes the assumption that crimes could be caused by

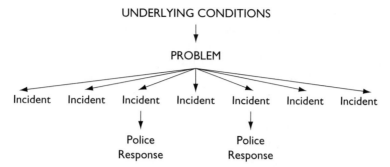

FIGURE 14–2   Incident-driven policing. *(From Timothy N. Oettmeier and Mary Ann Wycoff, "Personnel Performance Evaluations in the Community Policing Context," in* Community Policing: Contemporary Reading, *2nd ed., ed. Geoffrey P. Alpert and Alex R. Piguero [Prospect Heights, IL: Waveland Press, Inc., 2000], pp. 399–400. Used with permission.)*

particular continuing problems in a community, such as drug dealing. Hence crimes might be controlled, or even prevented, by actions other than the arrest of particular individuals. For example, the police might be able to resolve a chronic dispute or restore order to a disorderly street. Arrest and prosecution remain crucially important tools of policing, but ideas about the causes of crime and the methods for controlling it are expanded substantially.

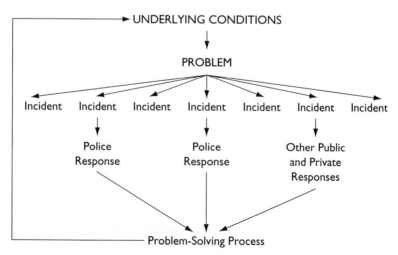

FIGURE 14–3   Problem-oriented policing. *(From Timothy N. Oettmeier and Mary Ann Wycoff, "Personnel Performance Evaluations in the Community Policing Context," in* Community Policing: Contemporary Reading, *2nd ed., ed. Geoffrey P. Alpert and Alex R. Piguero [Prospect Heights, IL: Waveland Press, Inc., 2000], pp. 399–400. Used with permission.)*

> In POP, the applied imagination of police employees, sworn and civilian alike, is galvanized as a crime-fighting tool. Problem identification and problem definition are essential steps in POP. The superficial symptoms of crime are avoided, while the root causes are fervently sought. The common linkage of POP, COP, and the professional crime-fighting incident-driven model, however, remains the same—crime control!

The subtle but fundamental switch in perspective requires law enforcement agencies to broaden their methods for responding to crime beyond patrol, investigation, and arrest. For example, the police can use negotiating and conflict-resolving skills to mediate disputes before they become crime problems. Why wait for crime to occur? Moreover, the police can take corrective action the second time they are called to the scene, rather than the sixth or seventh time, thus making timely savings in the use of police resources.

The police can use civil licensing authority and other municipal ordinances to enhance neighborhood security. Bars can be cautioned on excessive noise and children cautioned on curfew violations, and loitering ordinances can be expanded to reduce situations that require police involvement. The fire department can be asked to inspect "crack houses" for fire safety regulations. The public works department can be asked to inspect buildings and property for code violations. To the extent that problem solving depends on the initiative and skills of officers and civilians in defining problems and devising solutions, the administrative style of the organization must change. Since POP depends on individual initiative, the agency must decentralize.

POP: REASONS, METHODS, PRINCIPLES, AND SARA

POP may appear to be another label for crime prevention. Or it may look like several clever tactics for "cracking down" on a specific police problem. POP is much, much more than this. It involves an organization-wide and in-depth shift in policies, practices, and thinking. POP places effectiveness first and efficiency second.

Reasons

There are eight reasons for POP:

Lack of success. There is an old adage that "nothing succeeds so much as a successful failure." The professional crime-fighting strategy, although not a disaster, has not proved itself effective in crime control. Herman Goldstein and a few others pointed this out and in 1979 started their quest to refine an alternative policing approach.

Efficiency has been inefficient. Police management has been preoccupied with internal operations and "doing things right": "right" statistics, "right" training, "right" procedures, and looking "right." POP addresses the highly value-laden question of "Why?" Or, rather than simply doing things right, "Are we doing the right things?"

Scarce resources. Whatever the budget, there is never enough to do the entire job. Hence some demands for service may go begging. POP seeks to establish police priorities. If drug trafficking is the most significant problem, then the first allocation of resources goes to that, and so on. POP means priorities!

Reaction. It seems that everyone today is talking about, and doing little about, proactivity. POP requires self-initiative on the part of the police to prevent or reduce community problems.

Community partnership. POP encompasses COP or vice versa. The past has seen this partnership attempted in a random or haphazard way. POP is based on a systematic and continuing working relationship between the police and its public.

Brainpower. POP depends on the thinking of everyone in the department (sworn, civilian, part-time, etc.). Once more, we return to the need for empowerment. Unfortunately, many police agencies function as if the only "good ideas" come from the top. POP operates on the premise that good ideas can come from anyone and must be encouraged and rewarded.

Culture. POP requires that the old ways of doing things be carefully replaced with a different organizational structure and management ethic. This is difficult because most new ideas or systems are suspected of being grossly inefficient or plainly stupid. Usually, the first reaction to POP is, "Big deal! We've been doing this for years." The POP culture is keyed to effectiveness and not efficiency.

Expanded mission. POP envisions an altered and much better articulated police mission. Earlier, I discussed the police mission and mission statements. It is vital to POP and to the department that everyone is "reading off the same page." In other words, the police employee, the department, the policy makers, and the community must understand and, it is hoped, appreciate what the police are accountable for doing.

Four Problem-Solving Methods

There are four methods by which problems can be solved, and the best one depends on the characteristics of the problem:

- Eliminating it totally
- Decreasing . . .
- Designing . . .
- Removing . . .

Application Principles

Five principles serve as a guideline for the application of a successful POP program:

- It must involve all department members—all ranks and units, all sworn officers and civilian volunteers—in the identification, study, and resolution of problems.
- It must foster the use of a wide variety of data sources—from internal records and officers' knowledge to other government agencies and private individuals and organizations—to understand the causes and consequences of problems.

- It must encourage police department members to work with members of other public and private agencies to devise effective, long-lasting solutions to problems.
- It must be capable of becoming an integral part of police decision making, without creating special units or requiring additional resources.
- It must be capable of being applied to other law enforcement agencies.

Problem Analysis Guide: SARA

In the late 1980s, the Police Executive Research Forum and the Newport News, Virginia, Police Department designed and tested a problem-solving process called SARA. SARA stands for

Scanning: identifying the problem

Analysis: learning the problem's causes, scope, and effects

Response: acting to alleviate the problem

Assessment: determining whether the response worked

In addition, a problem-analysis guide was formulated, which suggested potential information sources (see Figure 14–4). The guide plus a problem-analysis report (Figure 14–5) should be helpful when completing Structured Exercise 14–2. The problem-analysis report is based on a hypothetical situation. Insert your facts as presented in the structured exercise.

IMPLEMENTATION

Eleven interrelated steps comprise POP. The steps fall into one of three phases:

- Identification of problems
- Analysis of problems
- Options

Phase 1: Problem Identification

The identification and definition of police problems encompass Steps 1, 2, and 3. Problem identification is two-thirds of the effort in getting a solution.

Who Identifies Problems?   Police problems may be surfaced by the community, police leadership, and line employees.

Community.   Community involvement in problem identification has benefits and downsides. On the one hand, community members will express their needs and frustrations. On the other, their problems may not involve situations that the police are equipped or obligated to handle. Actually, it may be someone else's problem. For example, a needed traffic signal near a senior citizen home is not likely to be something the police can resolve. They may help, but some other agency is actually responsible for installing the signal. This is where candor and openness must occur.

ACTORS

Victims
- Lifestyle
- Security measures taken
- Victimization history

Offenders
- Identity and physical description
- Lifestyle, education, employment history
- Criminal history

Third parties
- Personal data
- Connection to victimization

INCIDENTS

Sequence of events
- Events preceding criminal act
- Event itself
- Events following criminal act

Physical context
- Time
- Location
- Access control and surveillance

Social context
- Likelihood and probable actions of witnesses
- Apparent attitude of residents toward neighborhood

Immediate results of incidents
- Harm done to victim
- Gain to offender
- Legal issues

RESPONSES

Community
- Neighborhood affected by problem
- City as a whole
- People outside the city

Institutional
- Criminal justice system
- Other public agencies
- Mass media
- Business sector

Seriousness
- Public perceptions
- Perceptions of others

FIGURE 14–4   List of topic headings in a problem-analysis guide.

OXNARD POLICE DEPARTMENT
PROBLEM-ANALYSIS REPORT

1. SUBMITTED BY:__B. Kelley_____   ID#__3399_____
2. Date Submitted:__07-03-07_____

A. PROBLEM IDENTIFICATION (SCANNING):

3. Describe the Problem: (Who, what, when, where, how, and why)
    Drug usage and dealing from a location historically known as "The Fence".
    Actual address is 232 Avenida Gaviota.

4. Problem Reported by _____Officers on patrol_____
5. Location of Problem (circle) BEAT 1 ② 3 4 5 6 7
6. Date(s) and Time(s) Problem(s) Occurring _Problem has existed in_____

    _various degrees for 30 years._____

B. PROBLEM EXAMINATION (ANALYSIS):

7. Shifts affected: (Circle)   I   II   ⓘⓘⓘ   IV
8. Division affected: ___Patrol_____Investigations_____

9. Information Sources: (This list does not include all possible information sources.
    There may be other places where you can get information.) Please indicate <u>all</u>
    sources.

[xx] Crime Analysis Unit	[xx] Parole Office
[xx] Vice	[xx] Investigations
[xx] Crime Watch	[xx] Neighborhood Canvass
[ ] Literature Search	[xx] Citizen Complaints
[xx] Personal Observations	[ ] Surveys
[xx] Police Informants	[ ] Churches
[ ] Schools	[ ] Media
[ ] Central Records	[xx] Community Leaders
[xx] Local Businesses	[ ] DMV
[ ] Other Law Enforcement Agencies	
[ ] Government Agencies, list _____	

10. Findings: (Based on the information you have collected, describe the problem.)
    Historically a location that is a gathering point for those persons
    involved in narcotic usage, dealing and other illegal activities.
    Suspects gather on private property behind a wooden picket-type fence
    for purposes primarily to illegally use and deal controlled substances.
    These persons gather with the consent of the resident. Assaults, muggings,
    etc. have occurred to passersby at the location. Numerous arrests and
    selective enforcement has not eliminated the problem.

FIGURE 14-5 Problem-analysis report.

C. STRATEGIES (Responses):

11. Goals and Objectives: (What do you expect to accomplish?)
    Eliminate the gathering of persons for illegal activities at the
    location.

12. Recommended strategies: (How do you expect to obtain the above result?)
    The non-resident owner of the rental property has been located and has
    agreed to abate the problem. Officer Kelley, the property owner, and
    the resident have met and the resident has agreed not to allow loiterers,
                                                   place a lock on the gate and to
13. Date and time for implementation: ___08-15-07_____
14. Expected date and time for termination: _____continual_____   (con't)
15. Expected number of officers needed: _routine patrol to monitor_____
16. Expected number of vehicles needed: ___same_____ Types: _____

D. SUPERVISORY REVIEW OF STRATEGIES:

    [ ] Approved   [ ] Disapproved

    Recommendations:

    Date: ___08-17-02_____ Supervisor: _____RKelly LT_____

E. EVALUATION (Assessment):

17. Did you get the results you expected?

    [✓] Yes   [ ] No   [ ] Partially   [ ] Temporarily

18. Actual number of Officers Used: Routine patrol
19. Actual number of Vehicles Used: _____
20. Actual Number of Hours Used: _____
21. Describe the results of what happened.

22. Is any further action required? If yes, explain.
    Continued monitoring of activities at the location.

23. Additional comments:

    (12) con't.

    sign complaints against trespassers.

FIGURE 14–5 *(continued)*

STRUCTURED EXERCISE 14–2

To: PAAC
From: Lieutenant Donald Garvey
Subject: Rugby Time Disco

Details

In the last four years, the Rugby Time Disco, 1132 Hollywood Boulevard, has had a greater increase in calls for service and reported offense violations than any other liquor-serving establishment in the area.

On September 29, 2006, Officer N. Traub submitted a problem analysis report to the Problem Advisory Analysis Committee (PAAC). The majority of the complaints occurred on Wednesday nights between the hours of 2100 and 0230. On Wednesdays, the Rugby Time featured "ladies night" with $1 draft beer special. The complaints included overcrowding, disorderly persons, fights, drinking in public, drunk persons, loitering, and firearms violations.

A statistical analysis of the Rugby Time and eight other liquor establishments in the area was conducted by Officers Traub and J. Baker. During the period of January 1 through June 30, 2006, in comparison to the eight liquor establishments located in the north end of the city, the Rugby Time had 42 percent of the calls for service. From March 2005 to March 2006, the Rugby Time had 102 calls for service, with 51 calls occurring on a Wednesday night. Of the 51 calls, the majority were for fights, disorderly and intoxicated persons, and firearms violations.

The problem analysis form was approved by Sergeant R. Tiberio on September 30, 2006, after supervising the investigative work and analysis done by Officer Traub. (Officer Traub had enlisted the help of Officers Baker and S. Swanson.)

On September 21, 2006, Officer N. Traub with Officers R. Fulmer and D. Fucci observed at the establishment in plainclothes to review the inside problems. On the exterior, videotaping was conducted of violations in the area.

Using SARA

At this point, scanning and analysis have occurred. Your job is to consider the R (response) of SARA, and the second A (assessment). Each participant should list a number of possible responses, including violations, other perspectives that should be considered, who should be involved (other agencies, etc.), and strategies.

Appoint someone to list each participant's responses, one participant at a time, on a chalkboard or flip chart. For each repeat, add one mark.

Your group is now the PAAC. Review all inputs, and delete those that the committee does not support. Remember, the number must be manageable, and the response must be logical.

For our purpose, assessment will be PAAC's perception of the desirable and probable outcomes. At the conclusion, each participant should score his or her responses against the final PAAC selection.

Police leadership.   Police leaders and supervisors are positioned to see the so-called big picture. I covered the importance of vision earlier.

Line employees.   Of the three, the line employees are in the best position to identify problems. I spoke of empowerment earlier. Employees should be not only encouraged but also rewarded for their observations and ideas. (The term *employees* includes everyone working—paid workers and volunteers, sworn servants and civilians—for the agency.)

Problems Are Limitless   Typically, more problems will crop up than time or resources can address. Once a list has been created, then the problems must be prioritized. Some of the criteria for achieving this are as follows:

- Is it really a police problem?
- What is its impact (size and cost) on the community?
- How much support can be anticipated from the community in tackling the problem?
- Does it in any way threaten our civil rights?
- How much enthusiasm do the police employees possess in combating it?
- Is it indeed something that can be solved with existing resources?

Step 1: Grouping Incidents as Problems.   Police incidents are usually dealt with as stand-alone, unique events. Hence the first component of POP is to move beyond just incident handling. It requires that incidents be looked on as symptoms of a problem. The police have to probe for relationships (how the incidents connect with one another) and conditions (the real cause of the problem).

Step 2: Focus on Substantive Problems.   Recurring problems are substantive problems—or what we think of as police work. Police are prone to identify substantive problems in terms of internal management (e.g., not enough staff, poor training, malingering officers, low pay). Simply, but importantly, substantive problems are those very problems that justify establishing a police agency in the first place. The "internal management" habit is tough to break. It takes time and practice. As a leader, you're responsible for making the transition.

Step 3: Effectiveness First.   Some would attempt to define effectiveness in terms of solving a problem—making something stop or go away. To conceive of doing this in police work is ridiculous and even counterproductive. After all, zero crime is impossible. Some agencies point with pride to statistics that reveal a reduced increase in crime rates over last year. *Effectiveness is defining for a specific agency, in a particular community, what ought to be tackled and in what order of priority.*

Phase 2: Problem Analysis

This phase includes Steps 4 through 7. The analysis of problems includes types of information, sources of information, and scientific rules.

Types of Information.   Those who identified the problem in the first place are likely to be the best resource for deciding what kinds of information are needed to solve it. Brainstorming is an excellent technique for arriving at what's required.

Sources of Information.   Some of the sources are

- Existing literature (research reports, current journals, and the like)
- Police files
- Knowledge of line employees
- Victims
- Community
- Perpetrators
- Other agencies (general government, criminal justice, and businesses)

Scientific Rules.   By their very nature, our police are "applied social scientists." They are constantly being challenged to think, act logically, and be objective. Long and detailed reports are turnoffs to many people. POP doesn't demand time-consuming and profound reports. A page or two is sufficient—if it adheres to the facts and is objective and logical.

Step 4: Setting Up a System.   Once the seemingly random incidents have been categorized into groups, a system for the collection of pertinent facts and their analysis must be designed. Crime and service statistics are helpful, but much too limited. Systematic analysis includes (1) telephone questionnaire and individual surveys of those who might know something about the problem (e.g., citizens, victims, offenders, officers, other governmental personnel) and (2) literature searches of government and private-sector repositories.

Step 5: Redefining Problems.   What at first blush is a traffic problem on further analysis might be categorized as a drug problem. Problem definition can make or break a POP program. Is there any doubt that attempting to solve a traffic problem involves different methods and training than attempting to solve a drug problem? Additionally, there is an enormous difference between thinking tactically about dealing with burglars from a legal viewpoint and coping with burglary as it exists in the community. *How we perceive and label a problem ultimately determines how we go after it.*

Step 6: Who's Interested (or Should Be)?   Simply viewing conduct as illegal is not efficient in constructing a response to a problem. To determine who is or ought to be interested in criminal activity, ask, why is the community concerned? What are the social costs? Who is being harmed and to what degree? There are obviously many more questions of a similar bent. For the police to develop a successful plan to deal with gangs (or any other problem), they must find out who is interested in it. From this set of multiple interests will emerge a plan of attack.

Step 7: What's Working Now?   I have witnessed police agencies discarding successful operational practices. They tend to leap from one fad or technique to another. Frequently, the officers have the answer, but management fails to ask them. It is here that

POP surfaces one of its major strengths: "If it's not broke, don't fix it." If the agency's approach to spousal abuse is successful, then don't fuss with it unless some other tactic can guarantee an improvement.

Phase 3: Options

The development of choices includes Steps 8 through 11. After we've found and analyzed the problem, what are the options for hammering it? Obviously, the choices are infinite. To gain some focus here, I've placed them into nine groups:

Frequent offenders. These are the few who create many incidents. They should be targeted.

Interagency cooperation. The problem can be handed to another agency or jointly handled.

Conflict management. This means "getting to yes" via mediation and negotiation.

Process of making "public" public information. This is an underused but potentially highly potent problem-solving tool. Here are some of the uses: (1) to reduce fear, (2) to help people solve their own problems, (3) to educate people about their rights and responsibilities as citizens, (4) to warn possible victims, (5) to develop cooperation and support, and (6) to indicate what the police can and cannot do.

Galvanizing of citizens. POP depends on it! It goes beyond informing them to include organizing their support.

Existing controls. Here authority figures deploy their influence. Examples are teacher-student; apartment manager-renter; parent-child; employer-employee.

Defensible space. This denotes attempts to fortify our physical environment in some fashion, thus making crime and undesirable behavior more difficult, if not impossible. Alarm systems, antitampering packaging, lighting, and locking systems are a few examples.

Increased or expanded regulations. This option requires a lot of imagination and risk taking. Some police agencies have used city building codes and land-use regulations to combat drug and prostitution problems.

Legal intervention. This also requires experimentation and a willingness to take a chance. For example, some police agencies are placing public inebriates and the mentally ill under "temporary detention." Some are using decoys and sting operations. Some may target or saturate a crime problem, such as gang violence. Some may intervene without making an arrest (traffic violations) or make an arrest without intending to prosecute (civil disturbance violations—e.g., "right to life").
More and more police agencies are aggressively confiscating property that aids in, or is the result of, a crime ("asset forfeiture").

Step 8: Customized or Canned?   In the 1970s, the criminal justice system was filled with talk of "technology transfer." If a piece of equipment or a program functioned well in one organization, then it could be easily lifted and inserted into another. Many departments borrowed or purchased "turn-key" computers, helicopters, modified workweeks (4–10, 3–12, 5–9, and so on), and a variety of operational programs (e.g., team policing, neighborhood watch, Drug Abuse Resistance and Education). Most found that canned approaches, when incorporated into an agency, had to be retrofitted, redesigned, and restudied.

> POP relies on tailor-made responses. Problems are specific to an agency, and any method of resolving them must be specific.

POP is not implying, however, that agencies should shun the innovations of others. On the contrary, agencies should avidly seek them out and rigorously examine them for potential use.

Step 9: Take the Offensive.   Taking the offensive is accomplished in three ways. First, the initial identification of problems must be constant and systematic. Second, the police must be active in educating members of the public and placing choices before them. Third, the police should be advocates for the community (reporting if garbage is uncollected, potholes are unfilled, or vehicles are abandoned).

Step 10: Decision Visibility.   More and more I'm seeing the officer educating the public on why certain things are or are not done. Decisions are explained. It assists members of the public in understanding that the police do not have as much authority as they think and that the police will take risks and sometimes fail.

Step 11: Evaluation and Feedback.   Evaluation and feedback are not a concluding POP step. They are designed to support all of the other components in making incremental adjustments and improvements. For example, a reliable evaluation should be able to inform the department if its original grouping of problems was valid. **Without Step 11, POP is likely to fail**.

> If POP is approached as a method for improving the police, it will fail. If, however, it is looked on as a way to solve community problems, it has a chance of working. Quality and effectiveness are being redefined, thanks to POP, from "response times" and "crime rates" to getting solutions.

KEY POINTS

- Although not identical, POP and COP are highly complementary of one another.
- A strategy encompasses the community-oriented policing programs and leadership style for achieving the department's mission.
- A police agency can adopt more than one crime-control strategy—but they must be compatible.
- POP improves on professional crime-fighting tactics by adding proactiveness and thoughtfulness.

STRUCTURED EXERCISE 14–3

COP/POP APPROACHES TO POLICING IMPROVEMENT WORKSHEET

This exercise is best handled in groups of four to eight people. Look over the multiple approaches that can be taken toward COP/POP efforts in policing. Note that the listed approaches are illustrative, not conclusive. Fill in the empty boxes in the diagram below with any approaches that your organization uses toward COP/POP or any unique agency-specific COP/POP strategies that have

been highly successful. After filling in the blank boxes, work with your group to complete the COP/POP Approaches to Policing Improvement Worksheet.

With your group, select one of the COP/POP approaches identified in the diagram or added to the blank boxes. As a group, select a scribe, complete this worksheet, and select a spokesperson to present your findings. *Note:* Your methodology should be from a management perspective. Think big, with creativity and positive change as your goal, and use whatever resources you think might be available.

(continued)

STRUCTURED EXERCISE 14–3 *(continued)*

The COP/POP approach your team selected:

_____

How could this existing approach could be expanded or improved?

_____
_____
_____
_____
_____
_____
_____

What resources or key players in the community could assist with this effort?

_____
_____
_____
_____

What obstacles or constraints might occur with this improvement effort?

_____
_____
_____

How could external funding or equipment be obtained to assist this effort?

_____
_____
_____

- The common linkage among POP, COP, and the professional crime-fighting model is crime control.
- Patrol work has to be given enhanced status and rewards for POP to be successful.
- POP emphasizes effectiveness over efficiency.
- POP comprises eleven steps that commence with the grouping of incidents together.
- Problems are best identified and defined by line employees.
- Those who identified the problem are probably in the best position to decide what kinds of information are needed to solve it.
- There are at least nine options for handling a problem.

EXTENDED LEARNING

1. What are the similarities and differences between POP and COP?

2. The professional crime-fighting strategy contains two significant flaws. What are they? How does POP avoid them?

3. How does POP differ from the professional crime-fighting model?

4. What type of structural changes must be made in an organization as it moves toward POP?

5. What can be done to make patrol work more appealing and prestigious?

6. Which one of the several ingredients of POP is the most important?

7. Eight reasons for POP were listed in the chapter. Rank them in terms of their influence on police work today.

8. What are "substantive problems"? Cite some examples.

9. What are the benefits and disadvantages to having the community involved in problem identification?

RESPONSIBILITY 15

Anticipation

The police supervisor is responsible for sensing, clarifying, and adapting to evolving trends in his or her work environment and career field.

Responsibilities 1 through 14 are relatively enduring. They have a proven staying power. On occasion, though, the winds of change will add to or modify the steps a leader should consider taking when fulfilling a responsibility. Anticipating trends that signal the need for change is by far superior to reacting to them.

> *Only two things are infinite—the universe and human stupidity, and*
> *I'm not so sure about the universe.*
>
> —Albert Einstein

A sports commentator remarked about a highly rated team that suffered a dismal loss, "Once is an accident. Twice is a trend."

The celebrated futurist John Naisbett cautions us that we must endeavor to distinguish fads from trends. He explained that fads are explosive and accompanied by a lot of hype and gimmicks. Fads are short-lived and frequently emanate from Washington, D.C. Conversely, trends emerge quietly without much fanfare. You have to concentrate on the horizon to spot them. Trends are conceptualized and take root where we live and work. The advice of the sports commentator can be relied on here. Once may be a quirk, but if you see it twice or more, then you may be looking at a trend.

WHY ANTICIPATE?

> *Not everything that is faced can be changed, but nothing can be changed*
> *until it is faced.*
>
> —James Baldwin

Being highly alert to developing trends and incoming demands for change and adaptation is the prerequisite for anticipation. Once you spot a trend on the move, you are able to anticipate its consequences for you as a leader and for those in your work unit. In essence, you are able to get ahead of it, perhaps harness it, and respond to it after thoughtful consideration. Trend spotting guarantees the time and opportunity to initiate action that is likely to succeed. Hence one reason for enhancing your anticipatory capacity is to make early and better decisions on what to do in light of an identified trend.

Another reason for a police supervisor to be mentally anticipative is to predict trends. Predicting trends is different from spotting them after they have surfaced. It is also much more esoteric, and the error factor is higher. There is less risk in discovering a trend and then anticipating the consequences of your choices about how to cope with it. When you anticipate that which is unseen, you are entering the arena of future-gazing. Anticipating future trends is a blend of some luck and a lot of labor.

Community-oriented policing (COP) is not a fad; it is a trend. Thus you can anticipate its consequences for you and your department. More demanding is trying to anticipate what is next. What type of a police services model can you anticipate eventually supplanting COP? Similarly, what might we anticipate as the next major thorn in the side of our police system? (Did you anticipate the terrorist attacks of September 11, 2001?)

WAYS TO ANTICIPATE

Many of the preceding responsibilities contain ideas or ways to enhance your ability to anticipate incoming events and trends. See in particular the section on problem-oriented policing (POP) and the SARA method.

Anticipation begins with a heightened perception of the way our lives move forward. We suspend our doubts and distractions in order to glimpse events starting to unfold. Typically, it is accompanied by a profound sense of restlessness.

Anticipation occurs when we become conscious of the coincidences in our lives. When we organize them and correctly interpret them, trends can be detected. Being acutely aware of who you are, where you are, and what you are doing is critical. Where we are today is not just the evaluation of technology; it is the evaluation of thought.

Watch for coincidences, ask why, and your capacity to anticipate will be measurably enhanced.

TREND 1: CAREER PATH CIVILIANS

The question is not "Will we employ civilians?" but "Where and how many civilians will we employ?"

In the 1950s, some police agencies discovered that civilian employees were beneficial. They freed sworn officers to do "real" police work. Their numbers gradually grew to the point that police departments now average one civilian for every three police officers.

This trend applies not only to their number but to their power. Civilians in police agencies are paving career paths; they are being promoted. This trend will result in major divisions of a police agency being commanded by civilian employees. Civilians will supervise sworn personnel.

There is a supplemental nuance to civilianization: volunteerism. Many agencies are building a cadre of volunteers that complement current operations (reserves, cadets, seniors on patrol, etc.) or add new expertise (clergy, pilots, accounting, etc.). They are providing much needed services and saving agencies a lot of money.

TREND 2: TECHNOLOGY AND TOUCH

The use and influence of technology in police work will accelerate. Electronic files, laptop (palmtop) data processing, miniaturization of hardware, increased microprocessing speeds, portable digital communication devices, and more will proliferate. The information superhighway is taking shape. The majority of our mail will be e-mail or faxes. We'll be defined by our Web site. We'll be a cold fact, a set of impersonal numbers. Incidentally, those who believe data-processing technology will create a "paperless" society are going to be surprised. There will be more, not less, paper.

The police supervisor will be asked to counter our loss of "self." Overriding all of the virtual reality and touchless technology will be a human being. The police leader will be expected to forge a human linkage between the officer and his or her department. The leader will be asked more than ever before to instill a feeling of appreciation and care into a cold and technology-driven working environment.

TREND 3: WORKFORCE DIVERSITY

Workforce diversity is a well-recognized trend. The vast majority of police organizations comprise both genders, more than one race, two to three generations, and much more. In some parts of our country, there is no majority; everyone represents one or more minorities. One should expect that this trend will expand and accelerate. A few years ago there were a few civilians or a few female officers in our departments. Now there are many. Many police agencies report that one in three employees in supervisory and management jobs is civilian and female.

What can and should be done to understand diversity? To begin with, do not limit your thinking or approach to the notion of "cultural diversity." Workplace diversity is much more encompassing. Being a successful supervisor in a work environment that consists of diverse employees demands that you first know yourself, and then those who work for you, very well.

TREND 4: ETHICAL DILEMMAS

A person I know often comments, "I can resist everything except temptation." By our very nature, all of us experience temptation. Temptations can range from ordering a second piece of pie to stealing evidence from the property room. With all of the temptations bombarding us daily, our judgment is constantly being tested.

Our ability to rationalize or shift accountability exacerbates our problem in dealing with ethical dilemmas. A police agency can and should anticipate that more employees will succumb to temptations that are unethical or unlawful. Fortunately, this trend can be countered and even eliminated. Better recruitment and selection is one approach. Of equal importance is training! I am quick to acknowledge that integrity and ethics can't be taught. On the other hand, we know that integrity and ethics can be learned! We learn our integrity and ethics by example and constant training and retraining on doing what is right when confronted by an ethical dilemma. As mentioned earlier, character counts in all aspects of life, and it *really* counts in police work.

TREND 5: FEWER QUALIFIED JOB SEEKERS MEANS MORE OLD GEEZERS

Studies of U.S. demographics predict that there will be fewer people available to work. Following the "baby boomers" is a generation that does not contain as many folks. When you consider this in light of the large number of police employees who will retire within the next five years, you see that there is going to be a scramble for available talent. Police agencies can and should anticipate a serious challenge in recruiting and selecting police officers and civilian employees.

Not only will there be a shortfall in the sheer numbers of employable people, but the number of those qualified to do police work is likely to diminish. Drug abuse and an absence of "life experience" are two culprits that reduce the talent pool. (Life experience is an amalgam of emotional intelligence, maturity, self-reliance, and a solid work ethic.)

Police agencies can expect to commit an enormous amount of time and energy to attracting and then ensuring that they are hiring honest and responsible employees who can be trained to do good police work. One response to this shortfall of needed talent will be to reenlist the retirees. Some will work part-time, others full-time. Some will telecommute, rather than work on-site. They're likely to work on a contract basis, thus preserving their retirement income. The old geezers will bring valued technical expertise and a proven work ethic to the agency.

TREND 6: TERRORISM

International and domestic acts of terrorism will not abate. There are a few very angry and mentally ill people in our global community who want to be heard, and they do so by attempting to hurt us and scare us. A few years ago the federal government said, "Hey, we'll take care of the terrorists." That has changed to "We need your support, cooperation, and understanding. We need you—state and local police." Our antiterrorism strategy has forged a more open and powerful partnership among the various levels and types of criminal justice agencies.

I think I see the federal police concentrating on international terrorism while the state and local police collar domestic terrorists. I also see our local police agencies developing direct working relationships with their foreign counterparts (for example, the New York Police Department collaborating with the London Metropolitan Police or the Los Angeles Sheriff's Department working in concert with the Cape Town Police, in South Africa).

TREND 7: COMMUNITY-ORIENTED POLICING— GENERATION 2

Community-oriented policing and problem-oriented policing are not fads but trends. Granted, some COP and POP programs are paper tigers. Nonetheless, many agencies are exerting enormous energy to make them operable and thus a reality. (Responsibility 14 covered this subject.)

The police supervisor can and should anticipate that COP and POP will change. In other words, how might they be made better? Are there any new programs or tactics that would make them more effective? Such thinking confutes the adage "If it ain't broke, don't fix it." As soon as anything proves workable, start anticipating how you can improve it.

I am having difficulty envisioning what "COP: Generation 2" will consist of. It is safe to speculate that there will be more of the same—more volunteer programs, citizen academics, in-service training, permanent beat assignments, school resource officers, and the like. Perhaps Generation 2 will emphasize physical and mental fitness programs for all employees, sabbatical leaves of three months every seven years, performance appraisal systems that are based on departmental mission and values statements, and a specialized unit of senior officers to handle the needs of our aging America.

TREND 8: SERVICE EVALUATION

It's small, but I believe I see a trend toward service evaluation. Some police agencies, like their business counterparts, are systematically asking community members, "How are we doing?"

Police supervisors can and should anticipate designing and implementing a method for reaching out to those whom they serve and asking questions like (rate the following from 1 through 7; 7 is high):

1. My sense of security in our community
        1   2   3   4   5   6   7

2. The quality of our police services
        1   2   3   4   5   6   7

3. My chance of being the victim of a major crime
        1   2   3   4   5   6   7

4. Overall I would rate my police agency
        1   2   3   4   5   6   7

There are three major ways to elicit feedback on a service evaluation questionnaire: telephone, mail, and a direct handout to those contacted. Agencies that have employed such a feedback instrument have found the results reinforcing, rewarding, and helpful in anticipating evolving community needs.

TREND 9: CATCH AND RELEASE

Those who enjoy fishing are familiar with the term "catch and release." Basically, it means hooking a much sought after fish and then releasing it alive back into the water. Technology, improved training, proven tactical practices, POP, and more have measurably increased the quantity of police-criminal contacts.

Now, here is the paradox: While the contacts have increased, the "rules of engagement" are shifting. Lethal weapons are being supplemented by less-than-lethal weapons such as taser guns. Pursuit policies are undergoing revision and being made more restrictive. For example, some police agencies restrict the speed of vehicular pursuits; others limit the time or distance that an officer can chase a fleeing suspect. A few agencies have acquired portable optical scanners in their vehicles that link to a database containing the license plates of "wanted" vehicles. Officers are recording "hits." However, if an officer pursues a vehicle that exceeds a given speed, the pursuit must be terminated.

Are we viewing a trend that increases the number of "catches" but simultaneously mandates more "releases"? It seems that as technology helps us detect more criminal suspects, we are adopting policies that limit the followthrough necessary to make detection meaningful.

TREND 10: YOUR TURN

I have identified nine trends and briefly anticipated their impact on police supervisors and police agencies. Now it's your turn to envision a trend and then anticipate its consequences for the supervisor and the agency.

> The daily privilege and effort to fulfill all fifteen responsibilities are up to you. I have no doubt that you and other police leaders will do so and thus make police work all the more professional, rewarding, and successful.

Index